27

AN INQUIRY INTO THE
POVERTY OF ECONOMICS

An Inquiry into the Poverty of Economics

CHARLES K. WILBER

and

KENNETH P. JAMESON

UNIVERSITY OF NOTRE DAME PRESS
NOTRE DAME & LONDON

Library of Congress Cataloging in Publication Data

Wilber, Charles K.
   An Inquiry into the Poverty of Economics.

   Includes index.
   1. United States — Economic policy — 1981-
2. Economics — History.   I. Jameson, Kenneth P.
II. Title.
HC106.8.W54   1983   338.973   83-3659
ISBN 0-268-00742-X
ISBN 0-268-00743-8 (pbk.)

For

Kenny, Terry, Matt, Alice, Mary,
Angela, and Louie Wilber

Rex and Matthew Jameson

Contents

Preface   ix

1. Introduction: Symptoms of Failure   1

PART ONE: THE REIGNING ORTHODOXIES

2. Free Enterprise and Laissez Faire Economics   23

3. The Triumph of Keynesianism: Forty Years of
   Placid Progress?   36

4. The Assault on the Keynesians: Free Enterprise
   Once Again   62

PART TWO: TWO CHALLENGING CRITIQUES

5. Cycle Theories: Watch and Hope   95

6. Marxism: Inherent Cycles and Inevitable Crises   111

PART THREE: THE ALTERNATIVE:
POST-KEYNESIAN INSTITUTIONALISM

7. Toward a New Political Economy: Methodological
   and Historical Considerations   145

8. Structure and Operation of the U.S. Economy:
   The PKI View   167

9. Stagflation and Economic Crisis   205

10. Toward a New Social Contract   230

Notes   265

Index   283

Preface

This book has had a long gestation period that we hope has led to a more complete and mature product. Initial work was begun in 1976 and a rough first draft was done by 1978. The final version began to take shape during the summer of 1981, and the final manuscript was completed during the summer of 1982.

There is much more that could be done, but the time has come for the book to see the light of day. The basic starting point of the book has become even more important than when we started: the contemporary problems of the U.S. economy can only be understood against the backdrop of the history of the institutional development of the U.S. economy and the history of economists' efforts to understand and explain the economy. Had such a lesson been heeded, the headlong rush to reform the economy into some image from the past would have been seen for what it was — futile and destructive.

We have tried to learn from history and think that we have developed an analysis and a policy program that is consistent with the lessons of the past.

While we hope that the work presented here is objective, there is no artificial stance of neutrality. We are committed to certain values that undoubtedly influence the choice of questions asked and the variables considered for investigation. We are committed to the view that the economy should be the servant, not the master, of peoples' goals. Further, we believe that these goals include the provision of life-sustenance, esteem and fellowship, and freedom. Finally, the economy should be evaluated on the extent to which it aids in the fulfillment of these goals. With these values in mind the reader can judge the degree of objectivity attained in this study.

Over the years, a number of people have contributed in many different ways, all of which have improved the final version. James Weaver has read each version as it appeared, and his comments have always been useful. Before we undertook the final, and extensive, reworking, we asked the help of a number of others, and their insightful and encouraging comments greatly affected the final direction. For this we thank, and the reader should thank, Frank Bonello and Jim Rakowski of Notre Dame, Bob Keller of Colorado State University, and Howard Richards of Earlham College. We thank Tom Swartz for earlier joint work which we have incorporated into chapter 10.

A number of our students contributed, both by going through the text in their courses and by taking an active part in the work on specific chapters. Special mention should be made of Mary Beckman and Roland Hoksbergen, who worked on the full manuscript; to Mark McCarthy, who had an important role in the writing of chapter 5; Peter Sullivan, who helped draft chapter 6, and Bob Harrison, who contributed to chapters 7 and 8.

Someone had to get all of these inputs together into the final draft, and that burdensome task fell on Teri Chapleski, whose virtuosity with the word processor sped the work along and whose good humor lessened some of the chagrin at the form in which the rough drafts were delivered to her. We thank her immensely.

Finally, it is always a pleasure to work with a professional press such as Notre Dame's, and with its director, Jim Langford. We appreciate his support and interest in the project and thank him for the suggestions made in the process.

1. Introduction: Symptoms of Failure

The now-famous "Economic Dunkirk" memorandum of David Stockman and Jack Kemp, predicting an economic cataclysm in the absence of new policies, is far from the only alarmist manifesto of the day. Judging from the many books and articles on the subject, "economic crisis" must sell books nearly as well as sex and violence.

As one result of this perception of crisis, the American electorate has opted to embrace the old-time religion of unfettered private enterprise under the guise of supply-side economics. This was in preference to Carter's slightly more liberal version, masquerading as the descendent of the New Deal-Keynesian consensus that has been the dominant political force in America. But in both the political sphere and in the selling of the crisis, very little attention has been given to the historical context. It is as if our economic difficulties recently and magically appeared and as if there were no precedent for dealing with such difficulties. Let us provide some historical perspective.

Political democracy in the United States was founded on the assumption that contending political parties shared a minimum agreement on the core economic and social structure of the nation. They might argue about high or low tariffs, gold or silver backing for the money supply, or the appropriateness of child labor laws, but these could all be fought out as an intramural battle because the economic and social structure resulting from a commitment to a private enterprise economy would not be affected by the outcome.

During the 1930s, however, this minimum agreement was threatened by the collapse of the economy into a prolonged depression. Glaring inequalities of income and wealth, widespread mortgage foreclosures, bankruptcies, the absurdity of idle men and idle machines in the face of obvious need, and the failure of the state to take responsibility for alleviating this massive suffering came near to tearing the very fabric of society. But New Deal politics and Keynesian economics rescued capitalist democracy by providing a new mainstream consen-

1

sus. Potentially disruptive conflicts such as massive income and wealth redistribution programs or major changes in the private ownership of productive property were sidetracked by policies designed to provide minimum economic security through old-age benefits, unemployment insurance, minimum wage laws, and guarantees of the right of workers to organize. World War II provided the fiscal stimulus to restore full employment, and the Employment Act of 1946 gave the Federal government the right and responsibility to utilize macro-stabilization policies.

In the wake of the recessions of the 1950s, in addition to economic security and full-employment policies, emphasis was given to rapid economic growth as a means to maintain full employment and to avoid conflicts over allocation decisions. More guns and more butter was the answer, and the determination of the particular composition of national output — after expenditures for Vietnam — would be left to the free market.

The emphasis on economic growth required that the post-World War II economy be built upon an ever expanding per capita consumption level. Thus was born the "high mass-consumption" society.[1] This type of society has profound implications far beyond the economy itself. Producers have to entice consumers to spend at least at the same rate from an ever expanding personal income. Thus advertising, product differentiation, and physical and stylistic obsolescence were developed to new heights to convince consumers that they needed the new products and had to discard the old. To accomplish this, consumption had to be turned into a virtue; and thrift — which had been one of the cardinal American virtues and part of the Puritan ethic — had to be demoted to at best a minor virtue for consumers. At the same time the absence of thrift remained as the favored explanation (along with laziness) for individual poverty. The continuous expansion of new products resulted in a sharp increase in natural resource use and a concomitant increase in environmental pollution. Potential resource shortages were dismissed with the argument that science and technology would provide timely substitutes, and pollution was dismissed as the price of progress.

In this consumer society, government was called upon to play an ever more active role. To aid this ever-expanding consumption and to attempt to ensure that the poor participated, at least marginally, in the American Cornucopia, both the macromanagement functions of government and its economic security efforts had to expand dramatically.

To fuel this consumer economy, the United States had to tap the world's resources — oil, coffee, nickel, to name but a few. As a result, foreign investments by United States corporations increased fourfold between 1945 and 1965. To protect these investments and to prevent socialism from closing off areas of the world market to our resource needs and exports, Communism, first in its Soviet then in its Chinese versions, had to be opposed at all costs.* Thus the United States had to maintain a worldwide military network with all its attendant budgetary and foreign exchange costs. This system was built after World War II at a time when the other capitalist countries were economically prostrate and thus were no competitive threat. The U.S. export surplus allowed financing of this overseas military burden without undue stress. The cost of a growing domestic military class was submerged in the pork barrel of military public works.

The "golden age" of American capitalist democracy was 1961-67. Per capita income and consumption expanded dramatically. Keynesian economics seemed to meet its test, for full employment and stable prices were achieved. In the euphoria of the moment, "fine-tuning" was expected to banish forever the twin evils of inflation and unemployment. In addition to successful macromanagement the period saw the launching of the Peace Corps and the War on Poverty. It was the era of the New Frontier and the Great Society. The Achilles heel of democratic capitalism — unemployment — was finally conquered, and few were concerned with the first rumblings of inflation.

But cracks in the facade began to appear in 1965, spreading through 1968, changing directions in 1969-70, resulting in 1973-75 in the longest and deepest recession/depression since the 1930s and culminating in seemingly endless stagflation. First came the war in Vietnam, then the revolt of the young, inflation, pollution, food and oil shortages, recession, and stagflation. Economists began to talk about a wide variety of new institutional developments that somehow seemed to have an ominous role in all these crises — the rise of multinational corporations with their transfer pricing and cross-subsidization; the development of foreign multinational firms as competitors; the coincidence of the business cycles of the United States, Japan, and the Western European capitalist countries; OPEC, the oil cartel; and the apparent impotence of government. And as if this weren't enough, the whole Keynesian consensus was shattered by the simultaneous appearance of massive unemployment and double-digit inflation — stagflation.

And this is where we find our economy today. In some years somewhat less inflation, but at a large cost in unemployment, and as unem-

---

*This does not deny that the United States opposed Communism for higher reasons — i.e., liberty — but the existence of the lower reasons strengthened its resolve.

ployment falls, prices increase at an accelerated pace. Having briefly situated our economy historically, let us examine what we might expect from an economic system. Then specific comparisons can be made with this ideal, allowing us a better empirical feel for the present economic situation.

THE GOALS OF AN ECONOMY

There is a wide variety of "economies" in the world today, ranging from that of the Tasaday in the Philippines to the sophisticated and integrated Swedish or Swiss economies. If we can escape the bounds of our enthnocentrism, it may come as a surprise that a clear ranking in terms of success or desirability may not be possible when we compare economies. A Tasaday given the opportunity to live in New York might die rather than benefit from the opportunity.

How can we evaluate the operation of different economies and of our own United States economy? The first step is to realize that there is no single criterion, that success can only be assessed in reference to the needs of the human beings who constitute the economy. Thus we often hear that "efficiency" is the highest goal of the economy and that certain steps must be taken to encourage it. This may be true, but it can only be judged so if efficiency leads to the attainment of people's needs. Otherwise efficiency becomes an incantation whose magic may be misleading.

But what can be said about an economy and indicators of successful performance? One approach would be to identify the natural laws of the economy and then to assess its performance in conformity to these laws. This would be a return to an Aristotelian conception of society that might convince some by its sheer logic. We feel that there would be little agreement on the identity of these laws and thus reject this perspective.

Another approach would survey persons and their views on what the economy should do. In this we would find some surprising results. For example, Richard Easterlin carried out the exercise and discovered that a crucial component of the evaluation was the perception of one's relative situation.[2] Thus it would seem to be exceptionally difficult for an economy to improve its performance, for every relative gain would imply a relative loss, or no net gain!

But we think that we can go further than this by looking at broader psychological studies and information gathered across different societies.

A popular and useful approach is to speak of human needs. Following Abraham Maslow, a hierarchy of six needs can be developed: physiological needs, safety, love and belonging, esteem, self-actualization, and finally transcendence.[3] His claim is that we require satisfaction at each level before we can move to work toward satisfying higher order needs. Adoption of the framework would allow us to develop correlates with these needs as expressed in the economy and to assess the degree to which the economy is satisfying the needs. This would provide our criterion for assessing economic performance, i.e., for defining the crisis in the economy.

From our perspective, the one problem with the framework is exactly in the area of developing the correlates with the economy. How can we measure the degree to which the society facilitates loving, and what could we suggest as the role of the economy in satisfying this need?

So some modification is in order. We draw upon work which comes from a somewhat different tradition—cross-cultural studies which have attempted to find absolute needs or needs that are expressed in a variety of societies. Following the work of Denis Goulet,[4] three goals can be specified for an economy.

The first is "life-sustenance," which corresponds generally to Maslow's physiological needs. Thus every society strives to provide its citizens with the basic goods that are necessary for life—adequate food, water, housing, clothing, education, and health care, and a successful economy will be one which can provide these. The satisfaction of this goal is quite directly linked with overall economic performance. Unemployment will affect the ability of those without jobs to satisfy their need for life-sustenance, inflation can erode the purchasing power of portions of the population, and growth may be necessary to provide life-sustaining jobs. Instability in the economy, the economic cycle, can also affect life-sustenance.

But we must also ask how we can specify life-sustenance. One manner is to differentiate among three types of goods. The first are necessities such as food and water. And within some limits the needs of people in this realm can be specified. The second type of goods are "enhancement goods," those which make life more vital, more interesting, more worth living. Examples might be music, religious institutions, various forms of entertainment, some household goods, and so on. The third level of goods involves what are commonly known as luxury goods. Driving a Cadillac instead of a Chevrolet, buying a marble-topped table instead of a wooden one, and walking on a llama rug instead of one of polyester are all instances of consuming luxury goods. So what level of goods are we referring to when we talk of life-sustenance?

That is a difficult question. We can all agree that basic needs must be met. Most believe that enhancement goods are worthy of pursuit. But there is less accord on luxury goods. Traditional economics in the U.S. has claimed that individual wants are unlimited and that luxury goods satisfy wants, as do basic goods. If individuals want Cadillacs and llama rugs, and if the economy can produce such luxuries, it ought to. There are voices which dispute this view. Scitovsky has suggested that we think about consumption not of goods but of certain characteristics, and in this way we might be able to satisfy more of our needs. He finds that the simple increase in the amount of consumption in the U.S. has not increased people's happiness.[5]

A second component of societal goals found in most societies is esteem and fellowship. The system should provide a sense of worth, of dignity to its citizens. One's goods can be a measure of societal esteem. But there is more. The institutions in which citizens work should support them physically *and* give them a sense of belonging and of contributing to an important undertaking. Society should have clubs, churches, or other entities which support the individual. If the family is the basic social and economic unit, as is the case in the U.S., the economy should support it and lend to families a sense of self-esteem that can sustain them. Another term for this is fellowship, that the economy should promote right relations among its participants, that to the extent it can it should keep life from being "nasty and brutish," while providing life-sustenance to lengthen it.

For no society can function smoothly, without disruptive tensions, if there is no fellowship among its members. If people are alienated from one another and if society is fractured into myriad self-interested and self-centered individuals or groups, society will not long survive. If there exists no genuine concern for one's neighbors and if empathy for others disappears, then each small self-sufficing entity (whether this be family, occupational group, or individual) will eventually withdraw into itself and live at odds with others. No social system can prevail which endorses or engenders such self-centeredness. If material economic well-being is at the heart of social success, then surely fellowship is the lifeblood that sustains the community. Fellowship is the cohesion in a society that makes one individual feel a closeness and a unity of purpose with all others in that society, whether known personally or not. Consequently, we insist that besides providing for the material needs of its members, one goal of an economic system is also to encourage the growth of widely shared esteem that yields a life-giving and life-sustaining fellowship.

This implies an element of equity among the citizens. No society could provide esteem or fellowship which gave minimal income to most of the population, but fabulous wealth to one or a few families. Equity, of course, does not necessarily mean equality, but it does mean that there be some consensus regarding the justness of the distribution of wealth and income.

The third goal of the economy is freedom. It has played a major role in our own history as an important component of the drive for independence from England. And yet it is still a difficult goal to specify clearly. It obviously does not mean that every individual must have complete freedom to do whatever that person wishes, for that would be anarchy and the death of society. At its weakest, an increase in freedom means that the range of options open to the individual or the group has increased, that there are more choices available. This has its physical side in choice of goods, but it can also operate in other spheres such as the political or religious.

There are three component parts to the goal of freedom. The first, and the one which is usually at the center of much economic theorizing in the United States, is the provision of consumer sovereignty. As noted above, this means that individuals should be able to choose the goods that they wish to consume. The second part is worker sovereignty. People must have a choice of jobs, jobs that they find meaningful and that enhance their human capacities. There must be some mechanism for finding people's preferences on work, adding them up, and generating the types of jobs required. A variety of mechanisms could satisfy this need: labor mobility among jobs of widely different characters, control by workers over their job situations, or provision of capital resources to laborers to allow them to establish their own undertakings. Whatever the mechanism, this characteristic is important because work is an important activity which plays a part in human development.

Third, a society must provide citizen sovereignty, a mechanism to aggregate people's preferences for community. What will be the community with which an individual interacts? What kind of community do people want? What kind of environment do they want? The concept of citizen sovereignty implies that a way to express preferences and to control communities is provided to the citizen. A number of mechanisms may be found which satisfy this requirement, and they may be quite different from our usual image of democracy based on voting procedures in the U.S. One way of enhancing citizen sovereignty could be through the formation of local groups for citizen participation in decision-making, e.g., block committees in urban areas and communal farms and cooperatives in rural areas. Or perhaps local residents might participate in the operation of local industries in their areas so as to minimize the negative aspects of industrial production such as noise and pollution.

As we set out to examine the U.S. economy and its performance, we have as criteria three goals which seem to characterize all societies: life-sustenance, esteem and fellowship, and freedom. They are broad goals, and rich ones. They will aid us in evaluating economic performance. The existence and acceptance of such goals is central to our examination of various approaches to the economy and the possible policy options for dealing with our current economic crisis.

Let us now turn to the actual performance of the U.S. economy. We will see that the economy is not fulfilling the goals set out above.

GOAL VS. REALITY: HOW THE U.S. HAS MEASURED UP

In some ways the U.S. economy and economic policy are a bit like the government bureaucrat described in *The Peter Principle*: years of striving, increasing attainments and successes accompanied by accolades and fanfare, with promotion to ever more prominent positions, only to be ultimately undone when the bureaucrat is finally promoted to the position beyond his or her capabilities, a position where obvious incompetence clouds memory of the previous successful performance.[6]

The parallel pattern of the U.S. economy is easily seen. Imagine that the economy assumed its first position on the promotion ladder in the late 1930s, during the recovery from the Great Depression. The dismal performance of the economy during the early thirties led to the adoption of the activist economic policies of John Maynard Keynes. The program of the Keynesians began to perform well and by the late thirties the economy was undergoing a gradual recovery. Then came World War II and the recovery was greatly accelerated by huge and unprecedented government demand for war goods. By 1943 the economy was once again moving along at a bustling pace. All productive resources were in use.

At the end of the war some economists feared that the economy would sink back into depression, for now government demand for armaments would drop precipitously. But the expected slide did not come to pass, since the savings accumulated by consumers during the war were now unleashed and business could not retool fast enough to satisfy the wants of the newly optimistic American consumer. People began to free themselves from the psychological effects of the Depression. No longer did a defeatist and pessimistic attitude rule their lives. They began to feel good about themselves again, about their nation, and about their economic prospects. Expectations rose and confidence in the economy soared to new heights.

And the economy did not let them down. Even though the 1950s were marred by three recessionary periods, with unemployment and low economic growth, the new optimism could not be quelled. These slowdowns were nothing compared to the crash and standstill of the early thirties. And to ease further the discomfort of recession the proliferation in the fifties of new types of consumer goods appeased consumers sufficiently to outweigh any ill effects brought by the declines. The high mass-consumption society was underway. Also, American businesses were prosperous because of the demand for their products generated by the European aid of the Marshall Plan.

Perhaps the final "promotion" of economic policy as the solution to our economic problems came in 1964 when it was applied in a grand tax cut scheme. Economic growth took off and unemployment dropped below 4 percent. So confident of the economy's ability to overcome scarcity were the national leaders that they set out on an ambitious program to end poverty for then and forever. Inflation also seemed to be under control. Finally, an integrated world capitalist economy developed and was knit together by flows of goods, services, and capital which were facilitated by international tariff reduction agreements. Economic policy was now at the height of its success.

In the midst of all this glittering success economists, especially the macroeconomists dealing with inflation and unemployment, were in their glory. By the 1960s economic theory had developed to the point that sanguine predictions about the ability to fine-tune the U.S. economy were common, i.e., it was felt that policy could adjust the economy carefully to reach whatever goals were set. Cyclical instability was no longer a preoccupation. Government policymakers, utilizing the tools of fiscal and monetary policy and listening attentively to their "knowledgeable" economic advisors, could easily ensure a stable and successful economy in which all participated — or so it was thought.

In terms of the goals of the economy, success in life-sustenance seemed more attainable than ever before as the economy grew at a rapid rate. Throughout the 1950s and into the 1960s, freedom was also unquestioned, especially in the consumer area. In the 1960s "The Great Society" envisioned by President Johnson expanded life-sustenance to more people in the society and attempted to increase self-esteem as we moved toward a society which responded to the needs of all the population. Freedom was to be retained and defended as it always had been in our capitalist democracy, but government involvement through taxes and public programs did impinge more on consumer sovereignty. This was counterbalanced to some degree by improvements in citizen sovereignty, particularly for the poor and disadvantaged. Worker sovereignty was not an important concern.

With the major economic questions now satisfactorily answered, expectations of further unprecedented achievements were commonplace. But such was not to be. The Peter Principle came into operation and the 1970s signalled that the level of incompetence in economic policy had finally been reached. Growth slowed and became increasingly unstable with three recessions by 1977, a fourth in 1980, and perhaps the worst of all commencing in 1981. Unemployment rose to levels unseen since the recovery from the Great Depression, and inflation, generally presumed to diminish in recessionary times, remained stubbornly resistant to policy influence. The period is probably best described as one of prolonged stagflation with cycles of unemployment, inflation, and economic growth. Economic policy is immobilized. Any proposal to alleviate unemployment is decried as inflationary, and any effort to fight inflation is berated as recession-inducing. For example, the Comprehensive Employment and Training Act (CETA) was organized in the sixties to help provide training and employment for the jobless. Now, in the drive to reduce the budget deficit, which is believed to be a direct cause of inflation, CETA funding is being cut back. Unemployment thus goes up whether inflation comes down or not. In this example we can see both sides of the apparent dilemma. Raise CETA funding, reduce unemployment, and fan the fires of inflation; or decrease CETA funding, watch unemployment rise, and hope inflation declines. In addition, the seventies experienced a renewed rise in poverty, a phenomenon that in the 1960s had been expected to disappear within a few decades. Life-sustenance is now under attack.

As if that were not enough, the sense of self-esteem is also under attack from patterns such as the accelerating decay of the cities and of public services in general. Despite being richer than ever before in history, suddenly we cannot afford to maintain our schools, public transit systems are going bankrupt, cities have fired large numbers of policemen in the face of rising crime rates, and the troubles seem endless.

Furthermore, our major industries — autos, steel, among others — are being outmatched in the competition of the world marketplace by foreign firms, particularly the Japanese and Germans. This had led to alarm over the productivity of our workers and of industry generally.

For a crowning blow, as if to destroy our self-esteem after all else has already been taken away, the U.S. is in danger of losing its dominant position in the international economic order. The dollar, so long the unquestioned and highly respected international currency, was depreciated in 1970 and 1973 and then took a precipitous fall in 1978.

Although there were later periods of recovery in the value of the dollar, the glib assurance that the dollar is "as good as gold" began to ring hollow. We became aware that our performance is closely linked with that of the rest of the world, and have been treated to a series of "economic summits" in search for some agreement on policy.

Finally, questions of freedom, which in the 1960s had been subdued by economic success and by movement toward the "Great Society," resurfaced with a vengeance. As the government tried harder and harder to control the system that seemed to be slipping away, it taxed more, spent more, regulated more, and soon had people demanding a return to the freedom they believe early Americans enjoyed. Recent attacks on the regulations of OSHA (Occupational Safety and Health Administration) and the rise of citizen movements in favor of tax cuts such as California's Proposition 13 evidence a feeling that government has begun to undermine personal freedom. On the other side, those caught firmly in the grip of debilitating poverty, now losing the hope promised by the policies of the past, wait and wonder in bewilderment mixed with resignation and anger.

What is the result of all this? The euphoria and sense of well-being and success are gone. Many term this a state of "crisis": a state in which seemingly enormous problems of all shades and dimensions invade and take over national life, and a state which reveals our society as pitifully weak and incapable of overcoming these social problems with any weapons used previously or currently imaginable. We are in the midst of social turmoil and on the brink of economic and social disaster, and we do not know how to extract ourselves from its clutches. Reagan administration insiders called this our "Economic Dunkirk."

The situation is unquestionably serious, and we will look to history to guide our thinking and understanding. However, before we undertake this, it is important to be more specific on the actual performance of the economy so that we can be realistic about both previous success and present problems. In doing so we can examine the four traditional measures of macroeconomic performance, realizing that they relate in a very direct way to the three economic goals we specified.

Growth

Although some are now suggesting that growth has, for all practical purposes, come to an end, the 1970s nevertheless saw a rise in real GNP of 36 percent. This was better than the 35 percent of the 1950s, though less than the 47 percent during the 1960s. However, from 1970 to 1979 there were three different periods punctuated by negative growth, with stagnation in 1980-81 and decline in 1982. Previous to

1970 there had been eleven straight years of continuous growth.[7] Are such times of unabated expansion now coming to an end? Looking once again at the seventies, we see that growth in some years of the decade was respectable by historical standards, and of course the total for the decade was positive, but how did this affect people?

The 36 percent growth of real GNP over the decade is deceptive, since this was achieved at the same time average weekly earnings of workers in non-agricultural employment *declined* by 3 ½ percent. That is, families kept their real incomes from falling by having the regular bread-winners take on a second job or having another member of the family, usually the wife, become an additional wage earner. Thus, it is not surprising that people perceived the 1970s as a period of falling living standards. In fact, families were altering their traditional life styles to keep from falling back.

Unemployment

In 1975 and 1976 the groping arms of unemployment lines reached further and encircled a larger percentage (over 8 percent) of the work force than they had since before World War II. The recession of 1981-82 pushed those rates even higher, to 10.8 percent. Since WWII there has been a trend toward higher unemployment with each successive business cycle. In the late 1970s the lowest unemployment dropped was to 5.8 percent, and that was at the peak of business activity between two recessions. In the fifties and sixties a 5.8 percent unemployment rate would have been a sure signal of a serious recession. But now, even in the best of economic times, unemployment remains stubbornly high. Based on analysis of this trend it would not be surprising if the unemployment rate in the 1980s remains above 7 percent even in boom times.

But what do such statistics mean? Are people actually hurt by unemployment? Indeed some people, like Milton Friedman, writing in his biweekly *Newsweek* column, suggest that unemployment is not all that painful anymore given the unemployment insurance benefits now available.[8] In fact, there are claims that it is a mildly pleasant occurrence to be thrown out of work for short periods. But anyone who really has experienced joblessness knows that this is not true. In fact, income is often significantly reduced to an average of around 60 percent of normal working income even for those with unemployment benefits.[9] For those with jobs not covered by unemployment insurance to be laid off from their jobs means even less income. Sometimes welfare is the only alternative to starvation: life-sustenance itself is threatened.

But beyond the mere loss of income there are even deeper effects. In his book *Mental Illness and the Economy,* Dr. M. Harvey Brenner demonstrates a clear statistical relationship between high unemployment rates and increases in admissions to mental hospitals. Brenner says that "virtually no major factor other than economic instability appears to influence variations in the mental hospital admission rates."[10] Andrew Levinson notes further that "in congressional testimony, Brenner extended these findings to include cardio-vascular disease, infant mortality, and suicide."[11] Thus in self-esteem and in worker sovereignty, unemployment is a categorical failure.

Allen Smith, in *Understanding Inflation and Unemployment,* elaborates on this. He says, "unemployment is a social catastrophe as well as an economic one. The social costs cannot always be measured in dollar terms. But they involve an intolerable amount of human suffering. Unemployment means idleness, loss of self-respect, poverty, and fear to those individuals who are jobless. . . . Furthermore, millions of workers who do not lose their jobs live in constant fear that they will soon join the ranks of the unemployed."[12]

Who are those most likely to be unemployed? In 1982 when unemployment was 9.8 percent, the nonwhite community experienced an 18.8 percent unemployment rate, while 8.6 percent of whites were out of work. Teenage unemployment at 24.0 percent was much higher than the overall average. Beyond the categorical differences, it tends to be the people with the lower overall wages and income that are most likely to lose jobs in a downturn, not surprisingly the very ones who can least afford it. Nor is one surprised, therefore, that the reduction in the decline in poverty is accompanied by higher rates of unemployment than in the sixties, for the very group of people who obtained jobs in the sixties lost them in the seventies.

Inflation

Argentina is the world champion in inflation in recent years, with the rates rarely falling below 100 percent per year. We should be thankful we are doing so well!

Nonetheless, the promise of policy to deliver stable prices was less fulfilled during the 1970s than the 1960s. In the former period, prices increased at an average annual rate of 2.4 percent, slightly higher than the 2.2 percent rate of the 1950s. However, the next decade saw an acceleration in this pace to a 7.4 percent rate, with the highest annual average being 1979's 13.3 percent rate.

Inflation rates were unstable, falling as low as 3.4 percent in 1971 and 1972. But the pattern reaching back into the late 1960s was one of higher average rates.

Is inflation a serious problem? To many this may seem a silly and almost flippant question. But let us propose a simple illustration. If inflation is 8 percent, wages must also increase 8 percent in order for a worker not to be hurt. In past periods of inflation such occurrences have not been uncommon, for often inflation is more a perceived problem than a real one. When our wages increase 10 percent, we are possessed with the belief that we therefore deserve to consume 10 percent more goods. But when inflation also rises 8 percent, we can only consume 2 percent more than before, and we don't like it. The simple truth of the matter is that our wages probably would never have risen 10 percent if inflation had not been present; they might have increased only the 2 percent that we ended up with anyway. So why do people get so upset with inflation? Why should inflation be labeled "public enemy #1"? Perhaps the effects of inflation are more insidious than this simple illustration suggests.

Is it really possible that hardly anyone is affected adversely, even though inflation is high? Under certain circumstances, argues Robert Gordon, inflation may have virtually no harmful effects on anybody.[13] These circumstances are that everyone receive proportionate increases in his or her income and that the inflation rate be known in advance. Harmful effects arise, however, when the inflation is unexpected, or when it has differential impacts. Suppose, for example, there is a contractor who bids on a four-year project at one million dollars, and expects inflation to be 5 percent, building that into the bid. But then the price level begins to surge at a rate of 10 percent. Workers now demand higher wages, material costs push upward, overhead in general increases, and the contractor's profit outlook grows dimmer and dimmer because of the initial bid. Another example is the home mortgage obtained at a constant interest rate of, say 6 percent, as was the case for many home buyers in the 1960s. Now, with a much higher inflation the debtors are benefitting while the creditors are hurting badly. In general, when there is an unexpected inflation, creditors are hurt and debtors are helped, income is redistributed toward those who owe money and away from those who lend it. One may ask, however, if this is so then why not just live with the inflation rate whatever it may be? Why should we fight inflation? One response to this would be to attempt to provide assurances about inflation rates and to protect all from the effect of inflation by "indexing" wages and contracts, i.e., adjusting the contractual values to take into account inflation's effects.

But while the above analysis might seem convincing to many of us, other economists insist that even an anticipated inflation hurts certain groups disproportionately. For instance, Joseph Minarik argues that inflation hurts those who have enough money to buy a significant number of bonds because the rate of return on the investment does not keep up with inflation as well as do hourly wages.[14] On the other side of the COIN (an acronym which stands for Consumers Opposed to Inflation in the Necessities) are those who argue that inflation is much more pronounced in the basic necessities of life (food, housing, energy, health) than in other consumer products.[15] As a consequence the poor are hurt more than others since the poor must spend a higher proportion of their income on basic necessities than those with higher incomes. The poor will always lose, because inflation leads to a struggle over income shares, and the poor do not have political power to protect themselves in the struggle.

The problem here is that the evidence on neither side is strong enough to convince wary listeners. But the fact remains, if people feel inflation is a serious economic ill, it must be dealt with. In addition, the impact of inflation on the social cohesion that binds us together as a people is a real danger.

> The corrosive effects of inflation eat away at the ties that bind us together as a people. One of the major tasks of a democratic government is to maintain conditions in which its citizens have a sense of command over their own destiny. During an inflation individuals watch in frustration as the value of last week's pay increase or last month's larger social security check is steadily eroded over the remainder of the year by a process that is beyond their individual control. All of us have to plan for the future when we lend or borrow, save for a child's education, change a job, buy a home, or choose a career. The future is uncertain enough in any event, and the outcome of our plans is never fully within our own control. When the value of the measuring rod with which we do our planning — the purchasing power of the dollar — is subject to large and unpredictable shrinkage, one more element of command over our own future slips away. It is small wonder that trust in government and in social institutions is simultaneously eroded.[16]

The *need* to fight inflation is probably inflation's most serious consequence. Unfortunately the way usually chosen is with a recession or with massive cuts in the federal budget, particularly social expenditures. This situation is far removed from the economic theory of the 1960s which had all believing that we could enjoy both full employment and no inflation.

The International Sphere

At least since WWII the United States has been the premier world economic power. The U.S. has dominated the international economy and the economic decisions of the non-Communist countries. Our dollar has been the world currency and practically everyone has looked to the U.S. for answers to economic troubles. But the reign of the U.S. is ending, and perhaps the throne has already become vacant.

The clearest signal that the U.S. hold on world economic affairs was weakening came in 1971 when Richard Nixon announced his New Economic Policy. On the international front he put an end to the convertibility of the dollar into gold, and on the domestic front, in an effort both to end inflation and reduce our burgeoning trade deficits, he imposed a program of wage and price controls.[17]

Whether or not this program could have worked is open to discussion. What we do know is that the program itself was less than assiduously applied, inflation was not conquered, and the concern over U.S. trade balance deficits was not allayed.

In 1973 two dramatic international events occurred. One was the success of OPEC in raising oil prices, and the other was the shattering destruction of the 1944 Bretton Woods Agreement for regulating international exchange. With OPEC came the quadrupling of oil prices, which resulted immediately in higher balance-of-trade deficits, not only for the U.S., but also for many other oil-consuming nations. Combined with President Nixon's announcement that the value of the dollar would no longer be defended, this sounded the death knell for the international economy as it had once been known. U.S. influence was diminishing in a changing world and America was becoming merely one of the players of the international economic game instead of its director. A new era was being ushered in: one characterized by flexible exchange rates; one in which many other industrialized countries would have considerable power; and one into which the newly rich OPEC countries would have to be integrated. The transition is not yet complete and the final consequences of the changes are not yet known. What is known is that there are many problems yet to be worked out.

As one example, the high oil prices have pressured international credit markets to create mechanisms to soak up the new wealth of the OPEC nations. This has largely been done through the Eurodollar market, but in the process a large quantity of the debt created by these institutions has taken on a dubious value because it has little backing. The current Brazilian or Mexican dilemma is a case in point. These countries have borrowed heavily to finance their development, but now find themselves in difficulty in paying the loans back. As a result the banks find themselves lending them more money just to pay off what they previously owed. Can this go on forever? One surmises that it cannot, but the final outcome to these problems remains to be found in the future. Poland was the initial test of this structure, and only fears of major economic dislocation kept the U.S. administration from allowing a declaration of default.

In terms of the immediate economic problems in the U.S., perhaps the most significant new development of the changing international arena is its effect on the viability of U.S. policy. In an open economy, where foreigners can invest freely and purchase goods and services freely, the ability of monetary policy to stimulate or contract the level of economic activity is weakened. Suppose, for example, that the monetary authorities decided to stimulate the economy by raising the rate of the growth of the money supply. This in most circumstances would lower interest rates. Borrowing for spending or investment becomes more inviting, and jobs are created as the economy is stimulated. But in an open economy, when the interest rate begins to fall, foreign depositors withdraw their money from U.S. banks and put it in other foreign banks where the interest rate remains higher. This tends to offset pressures toward lower interest rates, and the effects of the initial stimulus are weakened. Monetary policy can eventually have its way, but only with greater difficulty and with a series of added effects. This policy limitation was previously not so pronounced because the American economy was by far the largest capitalist economy and outside influences were not so great nor disruptive as they are now. Thus, another result of losing the status of director of the international economic game is that the U.S. is no longer quite so independent in directing its own economy.

The working of the international economy is a complex and involved issue. For our purposes it suffices to say that the world economy of the seventies was a far cry from that of the earlier decades. Whether or not the new international picture will increase or decrease our national economic fortunes is unclear. But since the U.S. has become more dependent on the world economy than ever before, the vulnerability of the U.S. to international instability is heightened. This can only complicate the task of economic policy and make the Peter Principle appear even more correct.

HOW CAN WE REACT?

Based upon the experience of the 1970s (and the 1980s to this point appear to be more of the same), the goals of the economy which seemed to be attainable during the 1960s appear to be slipping away. The simple optimism which seemed to carry us so far after the Second World War is no longer adequate. The world is obviously much more complex, and our understanding will have to match that reality. So what are our options?

One possible reaction is a sort of bemused indifference. Paul Samuelson, writing his column in *Newsweek,* suggests that the West has reached its autumn.[18] There will be a time of continued high unemployment and unstable growth (at least through the 1980s). But Samuelson sees this as a natural outgrowth of industrial maturity, of affluence which leads to devoting less effort to production of material things. It is a sensible reaction. But as Samuelson turns on for us the glow of autumn, he is casting into the shadows the entire set of goals which have characterized the U.S. economy in the post-war era—full employment, growth in output, low inflation, reduced poverty, and international stability. A cynic might paraphrase this view: "Yes, the U.S. economy is in crisis, but for those of us who have become well-situated, the autumn can be warm and pleasant."

Another and more hopeful reaction comes from a study prepared for the Organization of Economic Cooperation and Development—the club of the industrialized countries. The authors of that study claim to be "cautiously hopeful." Even so, a reading of the study reveals precious few reasons for hopefulness, for inflation is felt to be built into all the economies, and it is seen as a major drag on growth. The international sphere is viewed as being in disarray. The only indicator of the origin of the hope comes from a dismissal of the entire experience of the 1970s. As the authors write: "our reading of recent history is that the most important feature was an unusual bunching of unfortunate disturbances unlikely to be repeated on the same scale, the impact of which was compounded by some avoidable errors in economic policy."[19] Thus the hope is that the catalogue of maladies will simply disappear.

Our approach is different from these. In the first place, we see no reason to jettison the goals that have characterized our economy. Perhaps economic performance will never match that of the 1960s, and that may have its beneficial aspects, but there is no reason simply to give up the creative effort to understand the economy and to develop policies which can promote our desired goals.

Similarly, we disagree with the OECD study. We cannot simply dismiss the 1970s. Yes, poor grain harvests and the disappearance of the anchovies were unfortunately contemporaneous, but our view is that the performance of the economy reflected underlying structural developments, and those will not disappear. Thus unless new thinking and new suggestions are developed, we will be in essence accepting the "autumn" economy of Samuelson.

In what follows, we will provide the basis for such new thinking and the needed new orientation to the economy. The first section of the book will provide the historical context for how one can think about the economy, and will look for the roots of the present malaise in economic thinking in the pre-existing traditions of economic analysis. Chapters 2 through 4 concentrate on the two major views of the economy, the views that dominate public debate. These are the free enterprise-laissez faire theory and the Keynesian theory. Chapter 5 delineates a theory which has little role in the contemporary debate in the U.S., the cycle theories. This is done because there are a number of useful insights from the framework, but also because it has substantial influence outside of the U.S. and Western Europe. The same is true of Marxian analysis in chapter 6.

The second section of the book builds upon this context and distills from these assorted and sundry explanations the portions that most accurately depict the American economic reality. We incorporate these into our own view, which is called "Post-Keynesian Institutionalist." We suggest a policy direction in which to move that will be more fruitful than present attempts either to go back to earlier approaches or to quit the battle. We feel it is useful as a guide to the changes that have to be made. It is not as neat and clean as the traditional approaches, which have quite specific and limited policy steps to be taken. But then, our claim is that reality is not so neat and clean, and our analysis will be more successful if it mirrors that reality.

PART ONE

The Reigning Orthodoxies

2. Free Enterprise and Laissez Faire Economics

The sense of crisis in the American economy is pervasive. Of that there is little doubt. We must ask why the science of economics has been unable to counter this view and to present convincing solutions. Surely economists have had enough time to study, reflect on, and understand the intricacies of the economy, so why can't economists tell us what to do to escape the critical circumstances of the seventies and eighties? The short answer to these questions is that the vast majority of economists at one time believed that most of these problems had been solved. The longer answer is presented in this and the next two chapters.

Until the mid-1930s, most economists believed a "free market" economy would solve whatever problems arose. If goods and services and inputs into production were bought and sold in markets, the economy would function as well as possible. Thus they called for a laissez faire policy of "hands-off" of markets by public authorities. With the breakdown of the economy in the 1930s, laissez faire economics seemed discredited and the activist policies of Keynesian economics became the dominant force until the doldrums of the 1970s. Today a renewed version of laissez faire economics is again ascendant. This chapter will examine the original laissez faire economics and its breakdown. Chapter 3 will focus on Keynesian economics and chapter 4 will chart the revival of laissez faire in its new form of "conservative economic individualism."

THE ORIGINS OF LAISSEZ FAIRE ECONOMICS

Modern economics is usually dated from the 1776 publication of Adam Smith's *The Wealth of Nations*.[1] This book initiated a tradition in economic thinking which continued through John Stuart Mill in the mid-nineteenth century and which has become known as the classical school in the history of economic thought. The core of classical

23

economic analysis is the model of competitive market capitalism. It was believed that an uncoerced person could be depended upon to act rationally to maximize his or her individual self-interest; and more importantly, it was thought that an automatic, self-regulating mechanism to manage economic affairs was possible if it were built on basic human nature. Free individual choices were expected to overcome scarcity and result in the common good through the automatic adjustments of free exchange in markets. The forces of competition ensured that the economy produced those goods which people desired and that maximum output was produced at a given cost or cost was minimized for a given output. This was the result of the "invisible hand" of competition.

Thus, from Adam Smith to this day, mainstream economists have argued that the best way to ensure life-sustenance and to maximize personal freedom, especially consumer sovereignty, is to rely on the individual's pursuit of self-interest in a private property system regulated by the force of market competition, where the government simply acts as the neutral umpire of the rules of the economic game. In order to maximize his or her income each person would have to produce something (product, service or labor) which others wanted and were willing to pay for and this would maximize overall production.

But what prevents a system of private property based on self-interest from degenerating into a jungle, where the powerful oppress the weak? According to classical economists, competition is the great regulator of economic life. The forces of competition ensure that the economy produces those goods which people desire in the quantities that are desired. Although they were not blind to the faults and machinations of business people, they argued that little harm could be done in a society dominated by freely competitive enterprise. If producers tried to sell products at a higher price than the market price, customers would buy from others. No one would buy at a price above the market price. On the other hand, if one attempted to pay workers less than the going wage, they would leave to take higher-wage employment. Therefore, the force of competition insures that workers are paid the going wage and that consumers get their products at the lowest possible price.

As each individual attempts to maximize income and become wealthy, society, made up of the individuals living in it, benefits. Thus, private profit and public welfare become reconciled through the automatic and impersonal forces of competition.

The fact that all economies were characterized by widespread poverty, unemployment, and low wages posed a problem to the classical economists. The claim to ensure life-sustenance seemed to ring hollow. They explained it in two ways. First, there were those countries which restricted the free operation of markets. If they would remove the restrictions to the free play of self-interest, much of the poverty would be eliminated by the resulting economic growth. Second, in those countries that had free market systems, continuing poverty was explained as the result of the niggardliness of physical nature and the improvidence of human nature. The first was enshrined as the law of diminishing returns and the second as the law of population.

Adam Smith, Thomas Malthus, David Ricardo, and John Stuart Mill all explained poverty as the result of the interaction of physical scarcity and population growth. In each version of classical economic theory, economic growth ultimately culminates in a stationary state where growth in per capita GNP is zero and wages have settled at the subsistence level. The tendency of the wage level to subsistence is brought about by the behavior of population, or the supply of labor, in the long run: an increase in wages brings forth a proportionate increase in population which drives wages back down through the force of competition. Higher wages increase population through lower mortality because families can afford better nutrition and health care.

The origin of this dismal view of life's prospects is often attributed to Malthus. However, the notion that improved living conditions would be swamped by a resultant increase in population had been a familiar one in England for some time. The Reverend Robert Wallace, famous minister of Greyfriars' church in Edinburgh and good friend of Adam Smith, published in 1761 *Various Prospects of Mankind, Nature, and Providence.* In it he argued that people were always inclined to marry and multiply their numbers until the food supply was barely enough to sustain all of them. This was such a well-known book that Richard Godwin spent considerable space in his *Political Justice* refuting the population argument. It was Godwin's book in turn that Malthus's *Essay on Population* was directly aimed at countering.

Adam Smith's views were not quite so pessimistic as Wallace's. He did believe that economic growth eventually led to a stationary state where wages would return to subsistence. Smith softened this picture, however, by arguing that people do not breed to their physiological capacity, but are regulated by customary living standards. Thus the subsistence level in England is much higher than in China. In addition, as long as economic growth is maintained wages will stay above subsistence. Since the threat of the stationary state is off in the distant future, the basic tenor of Smith's work is one of optimism. Wages will remain high if investment continues at a rapid rate; investment will be maintained if the free market economy is not restricted domestically or internationally.

But Smith's optimism was not shared by Malthus, who was to have a much greater influence over classical economists. The success of Malthus's *An Essay on the Principle of Population, as It Affects the Future Improvement of Society, With Remarks on the Speculations of Mr. Godwin, M. Condorcet, and Other Writers* (1798) must be understood in terms of a latent pessimism in the whole body of economic liberalism epitomized by Adam Smith.[2] The problem of the scarcity of resources lay at the core of Hobbes's *Leviathan* (1651), where it was because of the scarcity of nature that one man's gain was another's loss. But in general from the time of the supremacy of Parliament in 1688 to the French Revolution in 1798 the battle of wits between man and nature was regarded with optimism, as English thought was dominated by the theory of progress. Smith's optimism can be seen in the complete title of his work, *An Inquiry into the Nature and Causes of the Wealth of Nations*. It was Malthus who transformed the contest between man and nature from a lighthearted sparring match into a struggle to the death. His essay on population could have been entitled *An Inquiry into the Nature and Causes of the Poverty of Nations*. To the Hobbesian scarcity of physical nature, Malthus added the improvidence and perversity of human nature. So whereas Smith had focused upon the way a free economy would channel the acquisitive aspect of human nature to overcome scarcity, Malthus found in that same human nature the roots of poverty.

The classical economists and their later laissez faire followers have continued to use arguments about the perversity of human nature to explain the inability to provide life-sustenance to everyone in free market economies. These same arguments have been used to demonstrate that major changes are impossible in the social and economic institutions of a free market society. In a very real way the arguments being presented in the 1980s are the direct descendents of those used by the classical economists. Thus, it is worth spending time to review the classical arguments.

An important goal of Malthus's theory was an attack on the English Poor Laws. The Poor Laws had originated in an Act of 1536 in the reign of Henry VIII and had been extended many times since. They provided for relief of the poor by local government units with the cost covered by taxes levied on landed property. In 1795 the Speenhamland Act amended the laws to provide supplementary assistance to employed workers whose wages were below a minimum subsistence calculated by the Poor Law commissioners. By Malthus's time increased relief rolls had greatly raised the burden of the tax rates. Malthus argued that the Poor Laws damaged not only the rich but the poor as well, and he argued his case with such eloquence and effectiveness that Pitt dropped his plan for family allowances and Whitbread his plan for public housing.[3] The new Poor Law of 1834 embodied the Spirit of Malthus.[4] It is worthwhile to quote Malthus at some length:

> The poor-laws of England tend to depress the general condition of the poor in these two ways. Their first obvious tendency is to increase population without increasing the food for its support. A poor man may marry with little or no prospect of being able to support a family in independence. They may be said therefore in some measure to create the poor which they maintain. . . .
>
> Secondly, the quantity of provisions consumed in workhouses upon a part of the society that cannot in general be considered as the most valuable part diminishes the shares that would otherwise belong to more industrious and more worthy members. . . .
>
> Hard as it may appear in individual instances, dependent poverty ought to be held disgraceful. Such a stimulus seems to be absolutely necessary to promote the happiness of the great mass of mankind, and every general attempt to weaken this stimulus, however benevolent its apparent intention, will always defeat its own purpose.[5]

The implication of these comments is central to understanding the laissez faire treatment of poverty. While there may be some hope for the poor, they will derive no benefit from policies which tamper with the institutions of a free market society. Any radical change in the institutions would be even worse. An important influence on their thinking was the French Revolution which first attracted, then repelled, Malthus and most middle and upper class Englishmen. It was not only the Terror that worried Malthus but also the ideas about the perfectibility of man spawned by the Revolution. His essay's title even refers to Godwin and Condorcet, two of the best known French "Perfectibilians." His distaste for the French Revolution and all its works is stated with force and passion in the essay.

> To see the human mind in one of the most enlightened nations of the world, and after a lapse of some thousand years, debased by such a fermentation of disgusting passions, of fear, cruelty, malice, revenge, ambition, madness and folly, as would have disgraced the most savage nation in the most barbarous age must have been such a tremendous shock to [Godwin's] ideas of the necessary and inevitable progress of the human mind that nothing but the firmest conviction of the truth of his principles, in spite of all appearances, could have withstood.[6]

Godwin had posited that man was infinitely perfectible and all present-day evils could be traced to the corrupting influence of bad social institutions. He envisioned a future communitarian society where love was the guiding principle of human behavior. Malthus found these ideas particularly unacceptable because they contradicted Adam Smith's position that self-interest led to the common good and because they were based on the abolition of private property, which he considered the very basis of civilization. His population theory was the weapon Malthus used to prove that Godwin's vision was unworkable and undesirable. His position was simple and clear:

> Population, when unchecked, increases in a geometrical ratio. Subsistence increases only in an arithmetical ratio.
>
> . . . This natural inequality of the two powers of population and of production in the earth and that great law of our nature which must constantly keep their effects equal form the great difficulty that to me appears insurmountable in the way to the perfectibility of society.[7]

His belief in private property derived from his view that it is only the necessity of supporting one's self and family that drives people to work and makes them limit their family size. Malthus argued "there can be no well-founded hope of obtaining a large produce from the soil but under a system of private property." It is visionary to believe that "any stimulus short of that which is excited in man by the desire of providing for himself and family and of bettering his condition of life" can overcome the "natural indolence of mankind."[8] In a communal society, "the corn is plucked before it is ripe, or secreted in unfair proportions . . . . Provisions no longer flow in for the support of the mother with the large family. . . . At length self-love resumes his wonted empire and lords it triumphant over the world." Thus, the most perfect society imaginable would necessarily degenerate into "a society divided into a class of proprietors, and a class of labourers, and with self-love the mainspring of the great machine."[9]

Thus, according to Malthus there is very little hope indeed, and perfectibility is an illusion. In the first edition of the *Essay* he sees only vice and misery as restraints on population growth. He concludes one discussion by saying: "It has appeared that from the inevitable laws of our nature, some human beings must suffer from want. These are the unhappy persons who, in the great lottery of life, have drawn a blank."[10] In the second edition (1803) he introduces moral restraint as a possible, but not probable, limitation on population growth and therefore on poverty. The only hope, therefore, was in moral education of the poor by the middle and upper classes:

> Among the poor themselves, its effects would be still more important. That the principal and most permanent cause of poverty has little or

no direct relation to forms of government, or the unequal division of property; and that, as the rich do not in reality possess the power of finding employment and maintenance for the poor, the poor cannot, in the nature of things, possess the right to demand them; are important truths flowing from the principle of population, which, when properly explained, would by no means be above the most ordinary comprehensions. And it is evident that every man in the lower class of society who became acquainted with these truths, would be disposed to bear the distresses in which he might be involved with more patience; would feel less discontent and irritation at the government and the higher classes of society, on account of his poverty; would be on all occasions less disposed to insubordination and turbulence; and if he received assistance, either from any public institution or from the hand of private charity, he would receive it with more thankfulness, and more justly appreciate its value. . . .

The mere knowledge of these truths, even if they did not operate sufficiently to produce any marked change in the prudential habits of the poor with regard to marriage, would still have a most beneficial effect on their conduct in a political light.[11]

Both of the other major classical economists, David Ricardo and John Stuart Mill, incorporated Malthus's population principle into their economic theories. In Ricardo's case it was an aid in his attack upon the Poor Laws and an important pillar of his income distribution theory. Mill was an ardent social reformer who believed that education of the poor and technological development in contraception would allow the poor to restrict their numbers and thus overcome poverty.

Writing in the classical tradition ended with Mill, and "neoclassical" economics, beginning in the 1870s, turned away from the concern with growth and poverty and concentrated instead on the problem of efficient resource allocation. In the static neoclassical world, input supplies, including labor, are taken as given and, thus, ideas about population receded into an ad hoc explanation that was trotted out whenever the free market was blamed for continuing poverty. For example, W. Stanley Jevons commented on the continued existence of "pauperism" in England 100 years after the beginning of the industrial revolution:

Such a melancholy fact . . . is a verification of the [economists'] unheeded warnings; it is precisely what Malthus would have predicted of a population supplied with easily earned wealth . . . and bribed by mistaken benevolence of the richer classes into neglect of the future. . . . The wise precautions of the present poor law are to a great extent counteracted by the mistaken humanity of charitable people. . . . Nothing so surely as indiscriminate charity tends to create and perpetuate a class living in hopeless poverty. It is well known that those towns where charitable institutions and charitable people most abound are precisely those where the helpless poor are most numerous.[12]

It did not seem to occur to Jevons that the causation might run in the reverse direction: an abundance of poor people might call forth a large number of charitable institutions and good works.

Alfred Marshall held that Malthus's "position with regard to the supply of population . . . remains substantially valid."[13] However, he believed that in England technological change in agriculture, education of the working classes, and improved birth control techniques had combined to raise living standards.[14]

So population was available as an explanation of the anomalous continuation of poverty, but the major concern of the neoclassicals was very different. It was the development and articulation of the technical characteristics of the market economy. This effort required a number of choices in how the economy could be viewed, and those choices which were made partly for their simplicity, partly for their descriptive realism, and partly because of the kinds of analysis they facilitated, have affected greatly the development of neoclassical economics.

Perhaps the central idea was that of equilibrium. The market economy was treated as a system which was stable and if there were impulses to move it out of its given state, there would be a tendency to move back to stability or equilibrium. Equilibrium is an "end-state," and its use in analysis focused thinking on that end-state, making the problems of disequilibrium or movement toward that equilibrium less central.

A second technical category is "marginal analysis," the analysis of the effect of small, incremental changes. On the one hand, marginal analysis using the calculus allows a rigorous analysis of the conditions for the individual to maximize personal satisfaction (or "utility" as economists call it) or the firm to maximize profit. On the other hand, and in a fashion very parallel to the effect of Malthus's views on structural changes in the economy, it removes from the concerns of economics the entire idea of structural change. The focus for these economists was literally on marginal adjustments to the economy. The motto inscribed on the title page of Marshall's *Principles* was *Natura Non Facit Saltum* (Nature makes no leaps).

The neoclassical economists also analyzed the conditions of the supply of goods to a market, and the demand for goods on that same market, using again the equilibrium and marginal constructs to frame the analysis. By analogy with the market for wheat or for pencils, the macro economy was held to be guided by supply and demand. In particular, in what came to be called "Say's Law" after J. B. Say, supply was seen to create its own demand in the national economy. That is, it was assumed that a seller sold in the market to get the funds necessary to buy other goods or services. Thus every seller was a buyer. And given free markets, the operation of Say's Law would lead economies to equilibrium at full employment of resources, for any unused resource such as labor would see its price drop until enough of it was used in production to provide full employment.

In using the equilibrium and marginal analysis concepts to analyze the behavior of firms in markets, Marshall distinguished between a short period equilibrium and a long period equilibrium. Because he was concerned with influencing businessmen Marshall concentrated on problems of short period equilibrium. He said little about long period equilibrium because he considered it of purely theoretical interest with no practical use. However, Leon Walras, the inventor of *general* equilibrium analysis, developed his theory in terms of the long period. Basically, it is a mathematical demonstration that in the long period (a conceptual time period defined as the time required for all production inputs to be perfectly variable) a free market system will attain Adam Smith's optimal welfare equilibrium. The assumption and conditions necessary for this "ideal state" are so restrictive that the theory was considered of little practical significance. However, as we will see later, it played a major role in shaping the vision of economists in the mid-twentieth century.

These concerns, combined with the earlier views on competition, yielded a particular economics, but also a particular social philosophy. We term it the "free enterprise" or "laissez faire" tradition within economics. This was the dominant view of economics until the 1930s in both England and the United States. We can summarize it under a few propositions held by these economists.

1. People are motivated primarily by self-interest described best by Adam Smith as an "innate propensity to truck, barter, and exchange."
2. A free market economy, through the forces of competition, converts that self-interested behavior into the common good by forcing firms to produce what consumers demand and to do so in the most efficient way.
3. A free market economy requires freedom of choice — of where to invest, of what job to take, of what product to purchase, and so on.

4. Problems in the economy, including poverty, are due either to governmental interference with the free market or are the result of physical and human nature. The scarcity in physical nature requires time to overcome. The perversity of human nature means some people will always fail and thus be poor; some people are lazy, immoral, or improvident.
5. Public authorities can and should do little besides enforce the rules of the game and provide those goods—i.e., defense—that the private sector is unable to produce.
6. There is an inherent stability in the market economy, and since supply will create its own demand, that equilibrium stability will generally be at a position of full employment.

ECONOMIC THEORY AS SOCIAL PHILOSOPHY

In the case of the free competition-laissez faire view of the economy, the technical and analytical became intermingled with personal interests and underlying world views on society. Thus this tradition, as is the case with the other traditions, is also at least partly a social philosophy.[15] As a social philosophy, or ideology, the laissez faire economic theory that had been dominant in the industrialized West served two essential and related functions. It acted to restrict the scope for "scientific" inquiry and it served as a policy stance for molding society in its image, while legitimating certain aspects of the status quo.

On the level of restricting or defining the scope of economic inquiry into the causes of the failure to ensure life-sustenance, laissez faire economic theory focused attention on the niggardliness of physical nature and the improvidence of human nature. Universally applicable hypotheses were devised which transcended institutional, systemic, and historical variations. The theory focused potential economic research upon and, in effect, constrained attention to the behavior of individuals and households. Thus, people were poor because they had made the wrong decisions on questions such as family size, lacked the necessary ambition, or simply had bad luck in their choices. This provided a universal explanation for poverty which exonerated particular economic institutions from blame.

Concentration on the actions of atomistic actors camouflaged the existence and exercise of power in an economic system and the fact that poverty was perpetuated if not created by social institutions that benefit certain social classes at the expense of others. Ultimately, the theory became a conservative defense of the status quo. Poverty, caused by the improvidence of human nature, can be reduced only by educating people to overcome their natural indolence. Changing economic structures will not make any difference, except to the extent that existing social institutions misdirect the decision-making ability of rational individuals. The individualist/rationalist tradition of the West, with its emphasis on achievement and attribution of responsibility to individuals, lent credence to free market views.

Economics developed primarily in the individualist societies of England and the United States. Explaining poverty by an appeal to human nature fit very well with the values of an individualist, achievement-oriented culture. Hard work, thrift, and prudence always have been seen as the keys to success. Failure has been attributed to a lack of these values. Systemic causes of the failure to ensure life-sustenance to all have been ignored; instead, blame is placed on personal characteristics.

If self-esteem is lacking, that again has nothing to do with the society, but is a result of the failure of the individual. In hard times, when one loses a job for instance, there is no societal obligation. The individuals must pick themselves up and enter the job market to find any job which is available. Freedom must be exercised.

Government must avoid any interferences in the stability of the economy and its natural tendency toward equilibrium at full employment. Cyclical ups and downs of the economy might be necessary to reallocate resources more efficiently, but government intervention in past cycles merely made things worse.

Freedom must also be fostered, and government interference with its exercise in the economy must be avoided. Thus the effort to control the growth of markets such as the stock market during the 1920s should be avoided, for freedom of choice in a competitive economy will lead to the best possible economic results.

During the 1920s this strain of economic philosophy became linked with a conservative Republicanism best exemplified by Calvin Coolidge.[16] And the boom of the 1920s with high growth rates, increases in consumption, the creation of ever newer financial mechanisms, and growth of the financial sector seemed to validate this economic and social philosophy. Reality conformed to the model's assumptions and there could be no questioning such a success story.

THE DECLINE OF LAISSEZ FAIRE ECONOMICS

This theory of a free market economy dominated the thought of economists and policymakers until the 1930s. In the 1980s it has been resurrected. What caused the eclipse of laissez faire for fifty years? Certainly a major factor was the Depression, which belied the claims of that social philosophy both as to the causes of poverty and to the claims of full-employment stability. In addition it seemed apparent that the theory did not account for four major problems in the real world economy: monopoly, externalities, unequal opportunity, and unemployment.

The market economy as it actually developed turned out to have an Achilles' heel: competition tended to destroy itself. Competition turned out to be a footrace with the winner getting larger and larger and the losers dropping out of the race. This occurred during the 1920s, but was unremarked in the euphoria of the period. Thus the U.S. economy became characterized both by largeness and by a high concentration of firms in each industry. As a result, price competition was replaced by competition in advertising and product differentiation. To the classical economists, competition was the key force ensuring that the market economy was efficient, so the decline of competition was a severe blow to the credibility of laissez faire theory and led to calls for government intervention to restore competition through antitrust and procompetition policies.

The second problem with the free market that laissez faire theory failed to deal with is externalities. An externality is a cost or benefit not included in the market price. For example, a firm's cost of producing an auto is $3,000. With a $1,000 markup, the sales price is $4,000. However, in producing the auto the firm dumps waste in the local river that will cost $500 to clean up. This $500 is a cost to those who use the river for swimming, fishing, or whatever. As industrialization and density of population increased during the growth of the U.S., so did externalities. Thus, again, there came calls for government intervention to correct the market failures and to account for these external costs.

Economists also realized that for a free market to be efficient and at the same time to allow self-esteem and real freedom, some degree of equality of opportunity was necessary. Inequalities in income, power, and wealth made claims to equality of opportunity highly dubious. While there was ostensibly a high degree of freedom of choice, this was true only for those in the upper levels of society. Someone without skills or a stable job had few decent choices: a little more to eat or a few more clothes, to continue in a dead-end job or try to get some type of dole, to vote for someone who would neglect her interests or to abstain. And, of course, the poor family's child had little equality of opportunity as compared with the rich family's child. Again, this realization led to calls for public policies that would tend to equalize economic opportunities.

The most serious problem that plagued the free market economy was recurrence of massive unemployment. To worry over the efficiency of resource allocation in the face of large-scale and prolonged unemployment seemed as important as rearranging the deck chairs on the Titanic. When the U.S. unemployment rate hit 25 percent in 1933, economists and policymakers were ripe for a new vision and a new social philosophy. In the public's eye the fundamental problem was that after 150 years of economic growth under a free-market economy, two thirds of the population was still "ill-housed and ill-fed." The easy assumption about the individual causes of poverty rang hollow as millions of hard working persons suddenly found their life-sustenance severely threatened.

The New Deal/Keynesian economics concensus that emerged out of the 1930s provided a theory and program to save the market economy by utilizing government intervention to correct the first of its four failures — unemployment.* It is to that story that we turn next in Chapter 3.

*The other three failures of the unfettered market system have been dealt with — however inadequately — piecemeal during the past forty years.

3. The Triumph of Keynesianism: Forty Years of Placid Progress?

When the classical and neoclassical analyses failed to provide acceptable answers to the Depression and other problems such as monopoly, externalities, and equality of opportunity, there was a vacuum. And policymaking, like nature, abhors a vacuum. In the process of recovering from the Depression, a new analysis and set of policies took form, based on the work of the English economist John Maynard Keynes. His followers, the Keynesians, inherited the influence and respect which had been the neoclassicals' before them. They also inherited responsibilities for the economy.

For Keynesians the crisis of the 1970s was as chilling as a cold shower, particularly coming on the heels of the self-assuredness of the 1960s when most were convinced that all major macroeconomic questions had been solved.

This chapter traces the development of economic theory and policy from the thirties, when a new era in economic understanding commenced, to the late sixties, when the curtain on this era seems to have dropped. There was a gradual but rich accumulation of economic knowledge that permeated the thought of the majority of economists and government policymakers throughout this period. During these four decades understanding of the economy increased, the followers of this "new" economics multiplied, its detractors faded, the government's ranks were filled with its proponents, and all was well with the economic world—or so it was thought.

UNSTABLE BACKGROUND—STABLE ADVANCE

In many respects the period from 1930 to 1970 was hardly placid. These middle forty years of the twentieth century saw the first days of a depression in the Western world that threatened the collapse of the entire free market economy. Unemployment in the U.S. rose sharply, hit astronomical figures, and then refused to drop, averaging 18 percent from 1930 to 1939. Glaring inequities of wealth and income became stark realities in the face of bread lines and widespread poverty. Life-sustenance was a dream for many. There was a rash of mortgage foreclosures that expelled countless small farmers from their land and sent them west out of desperation only to find that bitter taste of *Grapes of Wrath* and to lose the pride and self-esteem they had. All of this occurred in the midst of an absurd idleness of capital equipment, despite the obvious need for production.

The problems of this first critical period were then exchanged for new ones in another cataclysmic event: World War II. This truly world-wide war ravaged the whole of Europe, much of Asia, and left few "neutral" countries unscathed. While carried out mainly on foreign soil, the war nonetheless had a major impact on the lives and the livelihood of North Americans.

The fifties provided something of a breathing spell in spite of the Korean war and three Eishenhower recessions, and the final decade of these forty years brought the first days of Camelot, attractively bedecked with the apparel of an upswelling idealism and the belief in the possibility of a better world and a better life for all peoples. But while engaged in an all-out war on poverty at home, Camelot and the Great Society were caught offguard and were destroyed in the distant swamps of Vietnam. What had initially been nothing more than an annoying "police action" escalated into a full-scale national war, continued to bedevil the great idealists, and finally drove them ignominiously out of office in 1968.

Yet from another perspective, these four decades comprised a period of placid progress. This was the case for the sometimes lauded and sometimes scorned profession of economics, for these were years of increasing knowledge of the American economy and improving ability to control it and avoid major disruptions like the crash of 1929 and the depression of the thirties. These were the halcyon days of the Keynesian economists, for it became undeniable that government could have a beneficial stabilizing impact on a growing economy. And while support for Keynesianism may have been tentative in the 1930s, the recurring and unquestionable reinforcement of the Keynesian approach prompted even Richard Nixon, himself an inheritor of Republican laissez faire policy, to concede that "we are all Keynesians now." So a seemingly impregnable Keynesian house was built, from its fledgling days during the Depression years to its triumphal achievements of the sixties. What follows is the story of the construction of this edifice which some economists are even now working busily to rebuild; but others work at odds with them, for it is upon the ruins of the Keynesian mansion that others can hope to lay the foundations for a new and different structure.

CONCEPTION AND CONSTRUCTION OF THE KEYNESIAN STRUCTURE: THE STORY UNFOLDS

The story begins in October and November of 1929, the months of the stock market crash and the initial phase of the Depression. Then followed the three-year period when bank failures would become commonplace (9,000 out of the 24,700 banks in existence in 1930 had gone under by the end of 1933),[1] when jobs would dissipate as if into thin air (unemployment rose to 25 percent in 1933),[2] when debts would become insufferable, and when prices would begin to drop (wholesale prices in the U.S. dropped 16 percent by the summer of 1930). This price drop was a major obstacle to recovery because the businessman's expectations of profits, which regulate his orders to manufacturers, were lowered further since no one could foresee when, and at what level, the fall would come to an end.[3] It also meant that the real value of debts rose, making repayment more difficult. It was a time for concern and gravity, for these conditions were extremely serious even if only temporary in nature. But that was perhaps the most frightening and foreboding aspect of it: the system could apparently do nothing to help itself. The traditional economists of the day all believed sincerely that the free market economy was self-regulating, self-stabilizing, and self-sustaining. They were therefore at a total loss to explain this seemingly perpetual downspin, and even less able to prescribe appropriate remedies. It was not until 1933, when Franklin Delano Roosevelt assumed the presidential helm, that the deterioration in living conditions and economic understanding began to turn itself around. This was certainly not because Roosevelt had been blessed with a vision of the intricate workings of the economic system, but because as a creature of his times he realized, along with his counterparts in European capitols, that only one economic agent could possibly provide an avenue of escape for the system, and that was the government itself.[4]

It had now become acutely obvious that the isolated, atomistic activity of individual producers and consumers was not going to generate the motive force for economic recovery, at least not in any acceptable time frame. Although there had been a long history of government involvement in the economy, Roosevelt, as is well known, proceeded to involve the government in previously unacceptable areas. To mention a few examples: during the Roosevelt years the government checked industry's abuse of labor by establishing minimum wages and maximum hours. Labor unions were endorsed and protected in the wide-ranging National Labor Relations Act (Wagner Act). Various public works projects were supported with the government employing people in activity previously handled exclusively by private industry. Public utilities came under strict and far-reaching regulation to prevent abuse of their monopoly position. The government intervened in agriculture to protect farmers by introducing legislation to support prices. The Social Security Administration was organized. And finally, the government began to play a major role in the extraction and use of the nation's natural resource and power supplies, as evidenced in the Tennessee Valley Authority.[5]

And even as Roosevelt was hard at work getting the government intimately involved in the economy, John Maynard Keynes was busy laying down the intellectual underpinnings of this approach to recovery. Roosevelt was aware of neither the depth and substance nor the potential impact of Keynes's work when the two met in 1934; he nevertheless was practicing the very types of prescriptions suggested in Keynes's revolutionary volume *The General Theory of Employment, Interest, and Money*, which came out in 1936.

Indeed, Roosevelt's reaction after the meeting with Keynes was, "I saw your friend Keynes. He left a whole rigamarole of figures. He must be a mathematician rather than a political economist." Keynes's reaction was similarly laudatory; he said that he had "supposed the President was more literate, economically speaking."[6]

The General Theory

What Keynes argued in his book had always been considered damnable heresy, for where economists had believed that free market economies were self-sustaining, Keynes was now arguing that such laissez faire systems were inherently unstable. Why were free market economies so susceptible to this debilitating capriciousness? The answer, in essence, is rather simple. The classical economists before Keynes's time had assumed and had even abstractly "proven" that through the medium of markets tens of thousands of economic participants would go about their daily economic activities in such a way as to achieve, unknowingly, a full employment economy. But Keynes now turned the tables on such thinking and argued that such theory was patently ridiculous. Indeed, during the Depression one was hard pressed to argue that markets worked well enough to ensure a healthy economy.

One of the cornerstones of Keynes's theory was his treatment of investment. Classical and neoclassical economists believed that the level of investment was closely tied to the interest rate so that as the interest rate dropped investment would increase. In an economy tending toward recession, the interest rate would drop, investment would increase, and a recession would be prevented. Keynes, on the other hand, argued forcefully that investment decisions were much more closely linked with what he called "animal spirits," a term which suggests unquantifiability, but which in large measure reduces to a concept of profit expectations, or business optimism. Keynes had ample evidence for his case in the Depression, for even though investment was sorely needed and the interest rate had fallen below one percent, there were still no takers. No sane business person would invest, regardless of the interest rate, if convinced that the project would incur losses.

In addition to this argument about the interest rate and investment, Keynes rejected the classicist notion that wage reductions would lead to increases in employment. Investment decisions were not based primarily on labor costs and neither were short term hiring practices. In addition, wages were a part of aggregate demand. If wages fell, aggregate demand and thus sales would fall. If sales fell, profits would decline and thus firms would demand less labor. Again the Depression experience made these points appear obvious to all who were not completely wedded to a classical or neoclassical stance.

As a result of his analysis, Keynes argued that full employment was a special case of the more general less-than-full-employment equilibrium. Decentralized decision-making by millions of consumers and businesses would add up to full employment only by accident. To the mind of Keynes it was not at all surprising, therefore, that the economy was mired in muddy wallows with no mechanism to lift itself out.

Keynes, however, did not leave the economy to flounder. He instead proposed that the necessary ingredient for stability was appropriate government fiscal intervention, consisting of expenditure and/or taxation policy. He showed that such policies could have a "multiplied" effect on the economy so the government could ease the recession-racked economy back toward a full-employment equilibrium by providing the initial stimulus to restore confidence and return some much-needed purchasing power to the economic participants. As a result, any unemployment caused by deficient aggregate demand could be overcome simply by government action to increase aggregate demand. He realized that the policies would abridge in some degree individual economic freedom. But the steps taken were not very restrictive, and the danger of the overall collapse of the capitalist system was so great that this was not a major concern.

To gain a clearer understanding of how such a government program would work, let us use a hypothetical example. Suppose a town has several industries, but none of them is producing at capacity because they simply cannot sell their wares. As a result unemployment has risen. In an effort to forestall the inevitable and feared layoff, workers have allowed wages to be lowered, but the layoffs continue. Banks, which have excess money to loan out, reduce the interest rate to a very low level in hopes that some businesses will find an opportunity to invest the funds, create jobs, and start the system on the road to recovery. But there are no takers. The town's economy is stagnant and a spirit of pessimism and futility is pervasive. But the town council has an idea (let us assume this town is autonomous and thus has control over the money supply); they would like to restore some optimism in the people by giving them some of the purchasing power they no longer have. Suppose their plan is to hire some workers to build a much-needed bridge over the local river. To carry out this plan they will need workers, cement, steel, lumber, and assorted other products. For these industries there is now an increased product demand and in order to meet the new demand they must increase production by using up some of their plant capacity presently in excess and by hiring workers to operate the machines. This may not seem like a long term answer to the problem, but now the newly hired workers have received paychecks and they in turn go out to buy various goods that they have done without. The multiplier effect of the bridge expenditures comes into operation. Surprisingly, the cement, steel and lumber industries do not experience the expected fall in demand when the town council project comes to an end. Instead the workers are now refurbishing their homes, buying new furniture, appliances, and cars, and the industries find that they can continue their increased level of production. The people begin to feel that the bad times are behind them and the good times ahead. As optimism rises new investment takes place because now businesses anticipate realizing a profit over and above the interest rate on their loans, and unemployment is diminished further. Eventually, with the appropriate council policies the town will achieve a full-employment economy and the town citizens will have left behind the hopelessness and despair that was their city. Also, and importantly, the town's project will have paid for itself through higher tax income from the new activity. Thus there will be no deficit for the council to pay off.

This hypothetical town illustrates some crucial aspects in Keynes's prolific and creative writings. For our purposes, he contributed two vital concepts that permeated the new mainstream economic analysis until the seventies. First, he argued that the economy was by itself fundamentally unstable. Second, responsible and discretionary government intervention could restore and maintain full-employment equilibrium which would allow free markets once again to play their role as the most efficient means to allocate scarce resources. This latter claim came to be the basis of "Keynesian" analysis in the U.S. Our own work, and that of a group called "Post-Keynesians," take the first claim of instability as the point of departure.

It must be emphasized that the problem Keynes focused on was the immediate deficiency of aggregate demand that made full-employment production unprofitable. In that situation, government borrowing and spending of idle funds would set the economy in motion again. The policy analysis is clearly focused on the short run and does not deal with long run questions of growth. But with 25 percent unemployment, Keynes was justified in declaring "in the long run we are all dead."

The New Deal-Keynesian Consensus

Though FDR engaged the government more deeply in traditionally private-sector activities than had ever been done before, and though conditions were improving slowly, the real proof of the Keynesian demand-management propositions came with the monumental spending requirements of World War II. In short order the vacant factories were taken out of mothballs, dusted off, and retooled, and were soon producing the equipment needed for the U.S. war effort. Idle men and women were either handed a rifle to use or were put at the seat of a rifle-making machine. There was practically no unemployment. The war experience was thus the first piece of uncontested evidence that the government could have a major impact on aggregate demand and could offset the demand deficiency of the private sector.

Production for war, however, did not serve the daily needs of consumers in the U.S., and many feared that with the end of the war the economy would lapse back into its previous depressed state. But the high employment levels during the war had brought money into the hands of goods-hungry Americans, and they had not been able to spend it during the war because of the comprehensive rationing programs. Therefore, when the war ended, the pent-up consumer demand that had been building during the war years was unleashed and resulted in such a flurry of economic activity that the economy easily maintained its healthy full-employment position. Once again the experience bore witness to the primacy of demand and proved that a sufficient aggregate demand was the vital component for maintaining a healthy economy.

The story of the Keynesian ascension hit a lull in the 1950s. To start off the decade the power of aggregate demand was once again eminently clear as a recession during the Truman years was washed away by spending for the Korean War. But then began eight years of a nostalgic return to the principle of the balanced budget. President Eisenhower sincerely believed that "deficits were bad for the character, public spending was wasteful, and the national debt was a burden unfairly imposed by one generation on the generations which succeeded it."[8] Eisenhower believed the free market, based on individual economic decision-makers, would lead to the best economy possible. Such an opinion is exemplified in some comments made by George Humphrey, the Secretary of the Treasury: "I just do not believe that there is any group of men who are so smart that they can tell everybody in America what to do and be wiser than the great bulk of our people who are actuated by an incentive free choice system."[9] In other words, intervention in the economy would be kept to an appropriate minimum. There would be no effort on the part of government to maintain the economy at some approved level of growth, unemployment, and inflation.

Such an epoch of apparent reversals of Keynesian economics may be interpreted as a setback. And this would have been the case, no doubt, had the Eisenhower policies been the progenitors of a successful economic policy. But this was far from the truth, for in "seeking balanced budgets, free markets, active competition, and price stability, Republican policy had achieved instead deficits, inflation, recession, and lagging growth."[10] So Keynesian tactics, instead of suffering a strategic defeat, were vindicated by the failure of the non-Keynesian approach. The three recessions suffered in the Eisenhower years were thus powerful evidence that without government intervention in the economy, there would be continual instability, low growth, and social unrest. The Keynesian policy mix appeared to provide success on the desired goals of the economy.

The stage was thus set for the new vigorous and idealistic leadership of John F. Kennedy, who adroitly recognized the centrality of economic well-being in the lives of common Americans. This was not surprising, since it was the coincidence of the presidential race and the third Eisenhower-Nixon recession that paved the way for the narrow Kennedy victory in 1960. Naturally, Kennedy was well aware of the importance of understanding, monitoring, and controlling the economy in postwar society. For a political figure to be associated with economic health meant re-election and public praise, but to be associated with economic recession signalled the inevitable loss of the administrative reins and possibly the stigma of public disgrace as well. Kennedy, therefore, although somewhat reluctant at first, was eventually won over by the Keynesian theoreticians on his Council of Economic Advisers, and was instrumental in introducing in 1962 the tax cut finally passed in 1964. Such a tax cut would have been considered suicide by pre-Keynesian economists because it was issued in the throes of a sizable budget deficit and therefore, it was thought, the only growth engendered would be in the deficit. These dire consequences did not occur, however, for far from causing budgetary problems this tax cut appeared to kick off a long period of growth and low unemployment.* This was the first authentic Keynesian experiment, carried out in complete contradiction to pre-1930 economic doctrine. And it had all the appearances of a smashing success: output rose, unemployment fell, inflation was negligible, and the deficit was not worsened but actually improved by 1965.

The success of the experiment was important in developing the Keynesian approach to stabilization. Recovery from the Depression had relied upon increases in government expenditures to fuel demand. But now it was shown that changes in tax policy could have similar effects. So the economic policymaker now had two tools which could be used for the same end, and the potential was there for mixing them together so as to be more successful in fine-tuning the economy.

Through this experience Kennedy's successor, Lyndon B. Johnson, became extremely optimistic (from the viewpoint of today, overly so) about the ability of appropriate government activity to ensure a full-employment, rapid-growth economy. For Johnson such a doctrine of fiscal activity was just what was ordered, because his vision of the "Great Society" would never become reality without massive government spending efforts. Indeed the spending required by these programs combined with the increasing expenditures on arms for the Vietnam War reduced the unemployment rate to 3.3 percent in 1968. Johnson, however, balked at the suggestion of his Keynesian advisers that Federal spending was too high for the tax revenues being collected. Economists warned that, with the economy growing vigorously, unemployment very low, and a budding inflation showing signs of flowering, taxes ought to be increased to balance the levels of high spending. Keynesians argue that had the economists been heeded the inflationary pressure would never have built up to the extent that it did. But, alas, Johnson feared that news of a tax increase would dissolve support for

*This tax cut should be distinguished from that proposed and enacted in 1981 by "supply side" economists. The Keynesians propose personal tax cuts when there are idle capacity and stable prices. This provides an incentive to put idle plants back into production and satisfy increased demands. The supply siders see tax cuts as providing incentives for making new investments in plant and equipment.

the Vietnam War and his social programs. As a result he did not request a tax increase until 1967 and although enacted in 1968, it was too late to stem the tide of an advancing inflationary wave.[11]

Nevertheless, the 1960s was a period of growth and expansion, the longest single period of continual growth in the nation's history. This period was initiated by the Kennedy/Johnson tax cut and the economy was kept hot, perhaps too hot, by expenditures for the Vietnam War and the "Great Society." At the end of the decade, although plagued by a higher-than-desired inflation rate, there was still little doubt that Keynes had squarely hit the head of the macroeconomic nail when he suggested that the government was the key actor in the economy. Government had obviously been instrumental in bringing about a successful economic era, just as surely as it had been the cause behind the inflation of the late sixties. Still, with better management such errors in policy could certainly be minimized. Again the path to life-sustenance, self-esteem and freedom seemed to be marked out by Keynesian analysis.

The Coming of Age of the Council of Economic Advisers

In the previous paragraphs, we alluded to the new and increasing influence of the Council of Economic Advisers. Both Presidents Kennedy and Johnson turned to their Councils for advice on economic trends and policy proposals. It was this august group who engineered the 1964 tax cut and who finally convinced President Johnson of the necessity for increased taxes in the late sixties. Given its importance in economic policy-making, we should look briefly at the meteoric rise of the council to domination of national economic policy.

Presidents, monarchs, and other world leaders have rarely been able to handle the myriad duties of governing their lands without the liberal use of a corps of counselors. Two of the more famous historical figures were Machiavelli and Rasputin. On a less sinister level one might add Thomas More, Rexford Tugwell, Charles Schultze, Marina von Neuman Whitman, Murray Weidenbaum, and Arthur Okun. Marina von Neuman Whitman? Charles Schultze? Arthur Okun? Who are they and why do they deserve equal billing with the rest of this eminent group?

They are part of a new breed of advisers who have come to prominence in recent years in most, if not all, countries around the world. Perhaps Whitman, Schultz and Okun will never command the historical attention accorded the other counselors mentioned, but they represent a rising collective group which has gained progressively more power in national and international political and economic arenas.

These are the economic advisers, and in many ways, they are doing for the economic what Machiavelli did for the political: developing a framework in which economic considerations have an independent existence open to policy manipulation, but always under the guidance of professional economists. Marina von Neuman Whitman was on the Council of Economic Advisers under President Ford. Charles Schultze was an influential economic adviser during the 1960s and was named chairman by Carter in 1977. They and others such as the late Arthur Okun have found important niches for economists in the executive branch of government. A similar role has been staked out on the legislative side with the Congressional Budget Office under its first head, economist Alice Rivlin.

What process led to such an important role for economists? As the new Keynesian era dawned, and faith in automatic economic stability was shaken, those best equipped to monitor economic performance and suggest appropriate economic interventions were naturally those trained in economics. Therefore, when Congress passed the Employment Act of 1946, an act which had widespread support and which officially legitimated a role for government in attaining the main economic objectives, one of the provisions called for the appointment of a Council of Economic Advisers, a group of three economists headed by a chairman. The initially prescribed role for the council was to prepare the "Economic Report of the President." While operating in the shadows during the Truman and Eisenhower years, the Council began to gain more influence during the Kennedy administration and the remainder of the sixties.

Under Kennedy, who had realized that the state of the economy influences political success or failure, the role of the Council expanded substantially. It now began advising the President of trends in the national economy as well as on policies which might aid in attaining growth and stability.

At the same time the new advisers were improving their capacities for this role. One of the main developments was new, highly sophisticated mathematical models to represent the U.S. economy. Such models combine the best in economic theory with massive amounts of economic information or data. Using the techniques of statistics and the capacities of the ever more powerful computers, the economy can be represented in a series of equations. Of course it must be a simplification in some degree, but the claim was that the simplifications of a good model were only in unimportant areas, so the results would not be distorted. From their beginnings in the fifties, the models became more complex and detailed and by the late sixties there were several models of the entire economy with some hundreds of equations. They can be used by the policymaker to simulate a policy maneuver and determine the probable results. Alternatively, an appropriate goal for the economy can be defined and policy actions that will achieve that objective can be isolated from the model. Consequently it is not necessary to use the real economy as a guinea pig, for what works in the model ought to work in the economy and ill-conceived policies need not burden the public. Thus the policy advisers could experiment with these model economies until they found just the right mix of policy to attain the desired goals.

The main agents in these developments were the Keynesian economists who have supported an active governmental role in stabilizing economic affairs. The activist doctrine was ideally suited to the politician and the statesman, for in politics nothing succeeds like success, and here there was promise of success in the sphere of life that increasingly dominates the thought pattern of the citizens living in our high mass consumption society. It is no wonder then, that economists and their "simple" models became the handmaidens of the politicians and first the Council and then the Congressional Budget Office became central players in national policy development. The strength of this process was shown most obviously during the Nixon administration when advisers such as Alan Greenspan and Herbert Stein, who would never admit to Keynesianism, continued the central role of the Council in economic policy. Indeed, their use of it was so clear and successful that Congress felt unable to play an independent role in such an important area. Thus was born the Congressional Budget Office.

It was not until the Reagan Administration of 1981 that the status and importance of traditional economic advisers was challenged, but that is a component of the chapter which follows.

As the Keynesian star reached its zenith in the 1960s and as intellectual interest in macroeconomic problems waned, the Keynesian task seemed to be reduced to slowly perfecting the analysis and use of policy. Since the Keynesian approach had now assumed the mainstream position, it also took over in the classrooms where a new generation of macroeconomics students focused on the lessons, the issues, and the achievements of the Keynesian approach.

The first lesson was gleaned primarily from the Second World War and the Korean War experiences, but not by everybody. It should have been abundantly clear that the stimulation of demand during the wars was a major factor in overcoming the lingering malaise of the Depression in one case and a threatening recession in the other. The strict orthodoxy which once again became the cry of the 1950s generated the painful lesson of three recessions. In this period, just as the Luddites of England tried to effect a return to their cherished old way of doing things by smashing the new technologically superior machines, so too the conservatives trained in the classical wisdom tried to return to an economic theory whose application showed it no longer appropriate nor accurate. The new leadership of the 1960s was willing to take account of the economic lessons taught by the wars. The heresy of a tax cut to stimulate demand was attempted, and it provided the economy with the stimulus needed to accelerate the recovery from the 1960-61 recession. At the same time, government expenditures were monitored in a new fashion, where the dominant consideration in determining the final level of expenditures was the state of the economy and need for demand stimulus rather than some fixed level keyed to tax receipts. This resulted from, and served to reinforce, the paramount importance of aggregate demand in the economy. This was the focal point of practically all Keynesian analysis.

But this did not mean that there were no issues left for Keynesian analysis. The dominant one was the appropriate tools for demand management. This question sparked the lengthiest debates of the 1960s. While Keynes had emphasized fiscal policy and his followers heightened this emphasis, experience showed that monetary policy was certainly not passive, and so could not be ignored as irrelevant. In fact, monetary policy had a key role in certain instances such as the credit crunch of 1966 when restrictive policy raised interest rates and paralyzed construction activity. In addition, special problems were posed by the fact that monetary policy was vested in the Board of Governors of the Federal Reserve System, not in the executive. Coordination of fiscal and monetary policy became a concern, particularly when the philosophies of the Board and the administration differed, not an unusual situation since the seven governors were each appointed to fourteen-year terms.

Just as monetary policy was not as passive as had originally been thought, likewise the operation of fiscal policy raised a series of issues which Keynesians had to deal with. For example, tax laws could not be altered without time-consuming legislative processes. It was thus possible to recognize the need for a tax action in one year, but to be unable to effect that action until the next year, when it may have been too late. Furthermore, to be effective, tax changes had to be permanent, otherwise consumers would tend to ignore their effect on disposable income and not perceptibly alter their consumption patterns. Finally, since businesses base investment decisions primarily on criteria other than tax rates, tax cuts to business in the form of accelerated depreciation and such had very little impact on the level of investment, and therefore a minimal impact on the economy as a whole. Naturally, this has not diminished the fervor with which businesses lobby for "job-creating" tax cuts, nor has it lowered public faith in their efficacy. But complete success in fine-tuning the economy could not be obtained until such problems with policy implementation could be solved. Such problems were amenable to research and improvement. But there were some other areas that had more serious implications for the Keynesian mainstream.

A Cloud On The Horizon: The Ominous Phillips Curve

While the proponents of Keynesianism had discovered much about the inner working of the economic system, there were areas that went almost completely untouched. The first of these was the supply side. Having placed primary attention on demand, the more arcane questions relating to long run supply decision and incentive effects remained largely unexamined. The second major omission was the behavior of prices. When prices were considered by Keynesians they tended to be treated as a subsidiary component of demand analysis. The theory assumed that if demand were too high there would be a tendency for prices to rise; but it was also implicitly assumed that if prices were rising, unemployment would be exceptionally low. Therefore, the simple response would be to impose contractionary policy, thereby cooling off an overheated economy by lowering aggregate demand.

The paucity of Keynesian curiosity in these two areas is not too surprising when one remembers that Keynesian economics was a child of the Depression. Supply was not an issue, because in the thirties the producers' willingness to produce was restricted primarily by the shortage of demand. Also in that period, there was absolutely no danger of inflation, and so the question of aggregate price movements was relegated to a back burner.

Therefore, the environment in which Keynesianism was raised offered little chance of learning how to cope with either supply shock phenomena or major price increases that were not demand-related. In the seventies these omissions of the early years caused the mature Keynesian analysis initially to demur and then to scramble for ad hoc explanations of apparently unexplainable phenomena.

While the seventies exposed these Keynesian weaknesses and continued to threaten the very heart of the theory, one cannot claim that the Keynesians had not been warned. The first intimation that there might be more to a stable and growing economy than mere demand management was introduced in 1958 by the Englishman A. W. Phillips. He noted that there was a definite relation between wage increases and rates of inflation which was not confined to periods of full employment.

This implied that there was a tradeoff between unemployment and inflation across the broad range of states of the economy. Phillips found that lower rates of unemployment were generally associated with higher rates of inflation. This meant that fighting inflation by restricting aggregate demand was going to create unemployment and possibly even trigger a recession. This appeared to pose a political choice — either more inflation or more unemployment — that was very discomforting.

This tradeoff appeared to result from the fact that in reality the economy did not mirror the perfectly competitive model underlying both neoclassical and Keynesian theories. The economy had large areas of monopoly power, labor and natural resources were not highly mobile, and other inflexibilities slowed down the adjustment mechanisms of the market system.

Robert Solow and Paul Samuelson, two of the foremost counselors of the sixties, investigated this phenomenon and found that a rate of unemployment of 3.5 percent would require a rate of inflation of 4 percent and unemployment of 2 percent would lead to 7 percent inflation.[12] Thus life was made a bit more complicated. The sanguine view that Keynesian tools were equally effective against both inflation and unemployment was no longer tenable: some mix of these two undesired phenomena would have to be chosen. The estimates indicated that the mix would be acceptable in the American context, but it was still a cloud on the Keynesian horizon.

THE END OF ORTHODOX KEYNESIANISM

As is well known, the cloud on the horizon has built up into a storm and is even now menacing the most stalwart Keynesians. While in the sixties the counselors could offer such benign alternatives as 5 percent unemployment and 3 percent inflation or 3.5 percent unemployment and 5 percent inflation, in the seventies the alternatives were more likely 12 percent inflation and 7 percent unemployment or 8 percent inflation and 9 percent unemployment. Such choices are akin to choosing between suicide and execution. Neither is very palatable.

In the mid-1960s Robert Solow of MIT confidently announced that macroeconomics had, for the most part, lost the interest of academia, because there seemed to be few unanswered questions remaining. The Keynesian house appeared securely built and able to provide an intellectual shelter for the economist. But just as the best-built roofs eventually leak, so the cracks of overlooked problems and unanswered questions grew. And the events and problems of the 1970s threatened the very foundation of the analysis, making Keynesianism much less fashionable.

In the next chapter we will outline the "new" house that has attracted a large number of prominent economists in the U.S. and has shown potential for winning the hearts of Americans. This is the newest version of the old laissez faire economics, a varied group of analysts we shall refer to as conservative economic individualists (CEIs).

From listening to them one gets the impression they knew all along that the Keynesian house would collapse. It was just a matter of time. In many ways the CEI approach is nothing new, but rather is a hearkening back to the classical laissez faire doctrines of social freedom and free unregulated enterprise that ruled before Keynes. But before examining this new house we must examine the quality of the repair work on the Keynesian's harried abode.

Not all the old Keynesians are willing to abandon what they feel are the soundest of economic footings available. It is true, they admit, that the last decade has presented them with a barrage of unpleasant and unexpected conundrums, but there is nothing here so drastic as to warrant the wholesale abandonment of a generally sound approach to understanding the economics of American society. So before discarding the remaining Keynesians as the last of a dying breed, they should have the opportunity to respond to the caustic criticism that they have been subject to over the last few years.

In general the Keynesians claim that the decade of the seventies has been an unusual decade in which totally unexpected events cropped up, events which dramatically increased the instability of the economic system. One of the preeminent Keynesians, Franco Modigliani, a highly respected economist from MIT who firmly believes in the ability of the government to promote economic stability and growth, says the following:

> The serious deterioration in economic stability since 1973 must be attributed in the first place to the novel nature of the shocks that hit us, namely, supply shocks. Even the best possible aggregate demand management cannot offset such shocks without a lot of unemployment together with a lot of inflation. But, in addition, demand management was far from the best. The failure must be attributed in good measure to the fact that we had little experience or even an adequate conceptual framework to deal with such shocks; but at least from my reading of the record, it was also the result of failure to use stabilization policies, including too slavish adherence to the monetarists' constant money growth prescription.[13]

Modigliani says that supply shocks have been one factor in the apparent Keynesian ineptitude, and errors in demand management have been the other. To these, other Keynesians would add the growing importance of inflationary expectations that have heavily influenced U.S. economic activity from all perspectives — business, finance, government, and individual.

Behind all these rejoinders lurks the cry, "Don't blame us, it wasn't our fault; we just happened to be here when external instability disrupted what we had learned." The Keynesians argue that there were shortcomings in their framework, which could be overcome, but any alternative approach to the economy would have fared much worse. Had any other economic structure — say, for example, that being constructed by the CEIs — been forced to weather the economic disruptions of the seventies, it would not have held up nearly as well as has the Keynesian. In fact, say the Keynesians, if the CEIs had held the reins of power in the seventies then the economy would be in much worse shape than it is now.

Now that the severe disturbances of the seventies are in the past there arises a cautious optimism that there will be a return to a stable external environment. The Keynesians are ready, therefore, once again to claim the forefront of economic policy if the CEI advisers to the Reagan government fail to cope with the 1980s. In the following sections we will explore in more detail the Keynesian defense, the nature of the problem, and the reasons why the Keynesians feel their economic theory is the most viable for the future.

Let us start with their analysis of the sources of instability.

Supply Shocks: Jet Streams, Anchovies, and OPEC

In the early seventies our economy was hit blindside by some tremendous shocks. For some reason the weather patterns in this period, largely dependent on the jet streams in the upper stratosphere, became temporarily disrupted and brought drought to large sections of world agriculture. Crop losses in many countries were high and world food supplies dwindled. On the home front there was no drought but American consumers still felt the bite of higher food prices. This locally unpleasant occurrence was due largely to the huge sale of grain to Russia and China and sales of other food goods to various countries adversely affected by the droughts. As food supplies all over the world fell, prices rose.

This food shock was exacerbated by the untimely disappearance of the anchovy schools off the Peruvian coast, because of a combination of perennial overfishing and changing ocean current. A scarcity of anchovies seems hardly to merit a prime spot in the Keynesian defense, but it is not mentioned flippantly. In fact, anchovies were a major source of protein in livestock and chicken feed, and when producers in the mid-seventies had to turn to soybeans, the price of meat and chicken rose accordingly. Now, however, the anchovies have returned and farmers have found other ways of feeding their animals, weather patterns have approached normality again, crops have been restored, and these particular supply shocks which hit us so forcefully have faded. But these were not the only shocks of the decade.

In 1973 in the energy field, as is all too well known, the Arab affiliates of OPEC (the Organization of Petroleum Exporting Countries) decided to embargo sales of oil to the U.S. and Europe. During and after the embargo, prices of oil shot up. Soon the price of oil had increased by 400 percent and as the oil cartel consolidated and exercised its power, periodic price hikes became the rule for the future as well. In the U.S. the effects were profound, for postwar growth had been directly founded on the base of cheap energy sources. One immediate effect was that businesses passed along their increased costs to consumers and general price rises became the rule as other businesses and workers tried to recoup their losses. As policies were enacted to try to fight the rising inflation, workers were thrown out of their jobs and the seeds of stagflation started to bear their fruit. After 1973 the rising price of energy continued to be a prime cause of the unabating inflation, according to Keynesians.

The combined effect of the oil shock and the temporary food shock accounted for 60 percent of the inflationary binge of 1974. In 1979 OPEC enforced another grand price increase. Once again, Keynesians argue, their policies helped the economy adjust to these shocks. In fact, by the early 1980s the economy had adjusted so well that the energy savings resulting from smaller autos and other conservation measures had led to a substantial, if temporary, oil glut. Keynesians assert that if periodic oil shocks can be expected to recur then it is crucial that the government learn how to manage fiscal and monetary policies so that the ill effects of the shocks are minimized. Keynesians contend they have the best program for achieving this. Such shocks will hurt economic performance under Keynesian policy control, but other approaches will do worse. Nonetheless, there is hope that supply shocks will be fewer in the future.

Now let us examine the second component of the Keynesian defense.

Policy Problems: Errors, Shortcomings and What to Do About Them

While these unexpected shocks wreaked havoc on the U.S. economy, there have also been a number of policy failures. In a 1977

Wall Street Journal article Paul McCracken said, "Our problems of recent
years are not, as has sometimes been alleged, that economies no longer
respond to fiscal and monetary policies. Economies were responding
only too faithfully, but to the wrong policies."[14] With regard to the
sources of misguided policies we already mentioned the reluctance of
President Johnson to impose a necessary tax increase in the late sixties.
But this mistake was not due to any lack of advice on the part of his
Keynesian advisers, and they are hesitant to accept the blame for this
inflationary policy maneuver (or nonmaneuver if you will).

Besides contrary-minded presidents Keynesians have also had
their troubles with the Federal Reserve Board. Because the operation
of the Fed is separate from the operation of other government offices,
neither the Keynesian advisers nor the President himself can insist that
the Board behave in any prescribed manner. This throws a monkey
wrench into the works of coordinating monetary and fiscal policy, for
the Fed controls the former while the President and Congress control
the latter. Now if the Fed were populated with Keynesians this problem
would diminish, but in fact the Fed has not been dominated by people
of the Keynesian persuasion. Chairman of the Board Arthur Burns was
certainly no advocate of government intervention in the economy and
neither is the present Chairman, Paul Volcker.

Ample evidence of the failure to coordinate policy was given in
October, 1977, when the country was treated to an executive office
statement decrying the monetary restraint of the Federal Reserve. Less
than a week later Arthur Burns delivered a speech which characterized
the Carter policy on the economy as weak and ineffective. Similar exchanges also occurred between Paul Volcker and the Carter administration. Even the Reagan administration has differed with Fed
policy.

The ineffective use of monetary policy in the seventies was hit by
Modigliani. His prime example was the 1973-74 supply shock, and the
coincident decision of the Fed to maintain a fairly constant money
supply growth rate. According to his argument, this made the subsequent inflation and recession much worse than was necessary. Had the
Fed increased the growth rate when the shocks hit and then reduced it
again when the initial shock had passed, the repercussions would have
been substantially smaller than they were. Perhaps inflation today
would be much less than it is, and lost output could also have been
minimized.

While these rebuttals may seem to reduce, to some degree, the
Keynesians' guilt for poor policy, their activist stance still is called into
doubt by the current instability. This is so in spite of poor monetary
policy, for it is incumbent upon them to develop the rationale for effec-

ive monetary policy and to convince the country and the Federal Reserve Board of its correctness.

If the extent of policy problems ended here, then certainly the Keynesians would still be standing tall. But in fact their problems go much deeper. Perhaps the most significant barrier to appropriate policy implementation is the question of whether fiscal and monetary policy can be controlled to a point where policymakers can make effective use of them. All too often there have been wide divergences between planned taxation or expenditure levels and the actual levels. By 1977, in fact, it had become commonplace for the Office of Management and Budget to report shortfalls in federal expenditures. In other words, the level of planned government expenditures was set at some amount, but actual expenditures were significantly below this amount. At one point it was estimated that real disbursements were running at least 20 billion dollars below what had been programmed. Such an inability to control outlays could obviously make a mockery of the Keynesian insistence on the stabilizing role of fiscal spending.

In much the same way the money supply is no easy quantity to control precisely. Not only is there hot disagreement over what constitutes real money, but even when some measure of money is chosen, there is no guarantee that the Federal Reserve Board can control the amount of that version of money. At one point in 1977, for example, the chosen measure of money supply (M1 = cash + demand deposits) had grown over a six-month period at a rate greater than 9 percent, despite the stringent efforts of the Fed to restrict this growth to 6 percent. Part of the reason for the apparent inability to control the money supply in the short and medium term is that the Fed has not been able to deal with the many new forms of credit as they relate to "money." In 1979 there was some attempt to come to grips with this problem, by imposing credit restrictions, but their rapid lifting revealed the lack of certainty on the part of the Federal Reserve Board on how to deal with this factor. All of these financial innovations — money market funds, deposit-sweeping, overdraft accounts — mean, in the words of Frank Morris, President of the Federal Reserve Bank of Boston, "we can no longer measure the money supply with any kind of precision."[15] In the long run it still appears that money supply can be fairly well controlled, but the wild and apparently uncontrollable gyrations in the short and medium run can have a significant impact on the performance of the economy; so the solace of long run controllability may be scant indeed.

A third aspect of the problem is the time lag between the onset of a problem and the use of appropriate policy tools. When lags are prevalent there is no guarantee that policy action will have the desired effect on the economy. In fact, if the lags are long enough the actions may serve to do exactly the opposite of what they are supposed to.

Before we listen in on Keynesians' assessment of these difficulties, there is one more apparent failure that must be mentioned. This is the inaccuracy with which the highly touted mathematical models have predicted future economic trends. In the seventies, the models were of little help. While one was predicting a downtown another was predicting an expansion, and when the future "arrived" it was realized that the economy had done neither. When there were disruptions or when it looked as though the economy was headed for some rough times, we would be certain to hear news of the projections of the economic models. The *Wall Street Journal* would survey the predictions of the various models and generally find that the models did not differ greatly in the short run, but beyond two years or so the variation in predictions was substantial. And any one model could give very different predictions if some of its embedded assumptions about the behavior of the economy in the face of external events were slightly changed. Thus the experience in the seventies with the models produced in the sixties was disillusioning; and the role that models could play in assisting the Keynesian economists has come into doubt.

It may seem that this section, supposedly devoted to the Keynesian defense, has continued to catalogue Keynesian shortcomings instead. In part this is due to the state of Keynesian economics. Until there is more distance from the seventies, these economists may not be sure themselves how seriously their framework has been damaged. Keynesians do admit there are troubles with lags, they admit to problems in carrying out both fiscal and monetary policy, and they recognize the general ineffectiveness of their mathematical models, but they are not willing to give all up for lost.

The response of the Keynesians to these admitted difficulties is of a general nature. They suggest that as time goes on and problems arise, new mechanisms will have to be developed to deal with them. Thus it would be beneficial to create a situation whereby monetary policy could be coordinated with Keynesian fiscal policy. The likelihood of the two policy tools being at odds with each other would then be reduced significantly.

How to control fiscal and monetary variables effectively is a bit more of a problem for Keynesians, but by closely studying the character of money, by finding better mechanisms through which to implement fiscal actions, and by studying carefully and comprehensively the effects of policy actions, these barriers can be gradually overcome. The argument then relies on the hope that the learning which characterized the sixties will return in the eighties after the interim of the seventies where Keynesian analysis seemed to have faltered due to the unusual nature of those years. Now that stability is returning, goes the argument, Keynesians will once again be able to master the dynamics of our economy and be better able to judge the efficacy and logistics of policy maneuvers.

With respect to lags, the Keynesians are less secure. Policymakers can work to minimize the importance of lags, to some extent, by trying to reduce them, but they will never be done away with completely. Therefore, Keynesians are willing to resort to vigorous policy actions only when there are strong and continuous trends in one direction or the other. In a currently popular macroeconomics textbook Rudiger Dornbusch and Stanley Fischer make this point by saying that "there are still clearly definable circumstances in which there can be no doubt that the appropriate policy is expansionary or contractionary. An administration coming to power in 1933 should not have worried about the uncertainties associated with expansionary policy. . . ."[16] Other suggestions of circumstances requiring stabilization policy are wars and periods when unemployment rises too high. They offer the year 1975, when unemployment was 8.2 percent and on an upward trend, as one such instance.

With respect to fine-tuning, however, Dornbusch and Fischer are equivocal. They are reluctant to abandon the whole concept, but they make no hard and fast case in favor of it either. "The major lesson . . . " (of the issues discussed in the previous paragraphs), they say, "is not that policy is impossible, but that policy that is too ambitious in trying to keep the economy always at full employment (with zero inflation) is impossible. The lesson is to proceed with extreme caution, always bearing in mind the possibility that policy itself may be destabilizing."[17] Finally, they propose cautious use of monetary and fiscal policies that are understood and the effects of which are known with a high degree of certainty.

Inflationary Expectations

The newest and potentially most damaging problem to the Keynesian approach is inflationary expectations. The new conservative economic individualists argue that Keynesian policies have built expectations of inflation into the structure of the economy. While the Keynesians are not ready to agree with the CEIs on the source of inflationary expectations (CEIs say excessive monetary growth is the source), they do admit that inflationary expectations can become a problem.

The concept of expectations is not at all new to the Keynesians, but has a long and honorable place in Keynesian analysis. In fact, in stability in the economy has long been attributed to business expectations and their effect on the rate of investment. When business expectations were less than optimistic, the government was expected to act to restore an optimistic outlook. Keynesians also considered the role of expectations among workers as a key factor in determining the aggregate level of employment.

In the late sixties and seventies, however, events combined to create a set of expectations among businessmen and workers that contained an inflationary bias. This not only leads to perpetually rising prices and wages, but it also engenders inflation-hedging behavior. Financiers tend to invest in sectors where inflation is the highest so they will get the highest return on their investment. Businesses hedge by purchasing and stockpiling material, and consumers remove their money from bank accounts and buy either consumption goods or inflation hedges such as real estate. As a result of this reaction to inflation and its expected continuation, the Phillips tradeoff is less favorable than it was in the early and mid-sixties. Presumably unemployment can still be reduced to traditionally low rates, but now only at the expense of higher inflation. Any policymaker today would be elated at the Solow-Samuelson tradeoff of 4 percent inflation for 3.5 percent unemployment!

But even though the problem of expectations is not new to the Keynesians, the solution to inflationary expectations may still be a difficult problem. Keynesians shy away from the painful medicine of slowing money growth and inducing a recession which the CEIs say is the only way. Instead they tend to favor wage and price guidelines as one way of dealing with these expectations. If workers know their incomes and if prices are forced to remain stable, after some time the various groups will come to expect stable prices and their expectations of inflation will be reduced.

It is interesting to note that the most recent round of wage and price controls initiated by then President Nixon in August, 1971, was implemented with precisely this idea in mind. Arnold Weber, who headed the main commission entrusted with administering the controls, made it quite clear in his description of the period that the successive "phases" were designed quite consciously to reduce inflationary expectations.[18] The controls of the early seventies, however, were anything but a complete success. Although they initially restrained inflation from 4.5 percent down to 2 percent for 1972, the easing of the controls brought with it such a burst of inflation that any temporary reduction seemed to have been to no avail. So even though expectations were dampened for a time, they surged back with greater force than before when the lid was taken off. The long-run effectiveness of wage and price controls, therefore, remains in doubt.

Do wage and price controls hold any hope for the future? That is hard to say. Theoretically it seems as if the controls should work if carried out properly. Given the recent mixed experience, one wonders if they can be effective. Indeed the failure to control expectations may signify a diminished likelihood for the success of price controls in the future. After all, if people have learned to expect a burst of inflation after controls are lifted, they will probably behave accordingly, which means that the probability of success of any temporary control program is low.

A SUMMING UP

The Keynesians have three rejoinders to offer those who criticize them and who contend that their message is obsolete. Supply shocks, policy errors, and expectations, say the Keynesians, are the culprits of the economic malaise that has infected our country. Each of these explanations is plausible, but it does not seem as if the Keynesians are oversupplied with reassurance for the future. We may hope that no more supply shocks will threaten us; we may hope that policy errors can be reduced as bureaucratic flaws are weeded out and a better understanding of policy effects is gained; and we may hope that policymakers will learn how to deal with expectations. But all of this fills the economic cup of the future with just a little more hope than the typical American wishes to drink in. It would be more comforting to hear a little more certainty and a little less hopeful speculation. But then, just maybe, the Keynesians are right.

So far we have focused on Keynesian attempts to correct only one of the four major flaws of a free-market economy — unemployment — and the resulting stagflation of the 1970s. Keynesian failures in this area obscure substantial, if mixed, successes in correcting the other three flaws: externalities, unequal opportunity, and monopoly.

Keynesian economists joined the fight to correct the worst externalities in our economy. As a result we breathe cleaner air, enjoy purer lakes and rivers, and work with greater safety. The undoubted benefits, however, were tarnished by costs of implementation. Costs of production were increased by anti-pollution and safety regulations. In addition, the bureaucracy created by regulation was quite inefficient and caused a public outcry that helped defeat the Carter government along with his Keynesian advisers.

A whole series of policies, that were at least coincident with the Keynesian era, expanded equality of opportunity. Voting rights laws gave blacks equal access to the political system. Equal employment laws banned job discrimination against minorities and women. School systems were required to equalize per-pupil expenditures where before they had been heavily weighted in favor of the well-to-do. Head Start tried to reach the young to help them overcome the lack of opportunities caused by disadvantaged backgrounds. These programs were seen as making a "free"-market economy more free by increasing equality of opportunity. The clear benefits were once again obscured by the public outcry against certain programs, particularly busing and affirmative action. In addition, welfare programs tended to be confused with those aimed at equal opportunity, to the detriment of both.

In terms of the fourth major flaw of a free-market economy — monopoly — Keynesians paid lip service to competition but did little to stem the tide of industrial concentration. In fact, the greatest merger movement in American history — that of conglomerate mergers — took place during the 1960s and 1970s with little evidence that it is yet ended.

Needless to say, these difficulties have not demonstrated the superiority of alternative theories, at least not to Keynesians' satisfaction. Their view of how the economy operates remains intact. With its origins in the Great Depression, Keynesianism's basic world view is characterized by a belief in the inherent stability of and the tendency toward substantial market failure within an unregulated market economy. This view fits comfortably with an optimistic belief in the efficacy of active intervention by government through the use primarily of fiscal policy. It is easy to understand why Keynesians are reluctant to accept evidence that by implication contradicts their basic vision of how the economy operates.

It is interesting to note that despite the inconclusiveness of the evidence, the CEIs are winning the debate, and the Keynesians are becoming more conservative and less interventionist. There are several reasons for this development.

One reason for the CEIs is that their policies have not had to face, until the Reagan administration, the test of being implemented. The Keynesians, by contrast, suffer from their identification with an activist government — one which takes responsibility for the stability and growth of the economy — at a time when it cannot deliver acceptable results.

A second advantage for the CEIs is that, since empirical tests are inconclusive, and since both groups are believers in the free-market system, the burden of proof is always on the Keynesians to show why government is needed. Each time government economic policy fails it is interpreted as evidence not only against Keynesianism but also for the CEI world view. Therefore, Keynesians are always at a disadvantage when debating the CEIs because of Keynesian acceptance of the free-market system.

This forces Keynesians to take a more conservative stance. More and more Keynesians are calling for government deregulation, the use of market incentives for government programs, a less activist fiscal policy, and so forth, all without convincing empirical evidence, but certainly in harmony with their belief in free markets.

Clearly the Keynesian record is mixed. The balance of success appears to depend on who is doing the evaluation. But having reached the inner circles of the government, the Keynesians cannot be expected to pull back in quiet splendor to review the decade of the sixties as grandparents might savor home movies of times gone by. In fact, much of the rhetoric from high level economists and from the White House itself during the Carter years retained heavy vestiges of the Keynesian influence. This is now changing. The economic advisers in the entourage of Ronald Reagan tend to be of the CEI school. But if, as we anticipate, the CEIs promote policies that are quite out of step with what the economy and the country need, then shortly Americans will again be on the prowl for new economic understanding. They may turn once again to the Keynesians. So the Keynesians wait patiently, readying themselves for a return to Washington.

4. The Assault on the Keynesians: Free Enterprise Once Again

THE RETREAT TO SIMPLICITY

The world of ideas is only slowly adjusting to the growth in the importance of the electronic media, especially television, and only recently are economists beginning to utilize this vehicle for communicating their ideas to a wider audience. Two of the prime examples of such efforts are television series which were also serialized into books, one by John Kenneth Galbraith entitled *The Age of Uncertainty,* the other by Milton Friedman and Rose Friedman, *Free To Choose.*[1] If one were to survey discussions or writings on contemporary economic problems, the theme of the Galbraith series would appear to capture the ethos of the age: new problems, failures of traditional solutions, and the list could go on. And Galbraith richly embroiders on the complexities of the age.

But Galbraithian complexity is reduced to clear simplicity by the Friedmans: most problems arise from government economic intervention, with the solution being its removal and a return to unbridled individual freedom.

If the ratings are any indication, simplicity won out over uncertainty. And that is in large degree the story of this chapter. For in the face of uncertainty and complexity, it appears that the public wants simple answers, solutions that comprehend, explain and resolve in a few short and simple ideas. That is one of the lessons of the election of Ronald Reagan in 1980. His economic proposals combined a traditional program of Republican austerity—which was not popular because it always resulted in more unemployment—with a simple solution to the low-growth, high-unemployment problems—the supply-side effects of tax cuts. Thus a simple, painless solution to stagflation was proposed: end inflation without lowering growth or employment. Despite its inherent contradictions, this simple program was effective in winning for Mr. Reagan the highest post in the country. In so doing the dominance of the Keynesian orthodoxy was eliminated with one stroke. And the story of how this return to a theory of the past was engineered is the topic of this chapter in which we present the approach of the "Conservative Economic Individualists" (CEIs).

As a starting point, we should recall that in the 1960s the Keynesians had cornered the simplicity market. In that era, excessive unemployment would be combatted by a little more government spending and/or a little less taxation. If there was high inflation the opposite steps would solve that. These easy-to-use and seemingly flawless tools were all that was needed to keep the U.S. economy progressing along a smooth and steady path of growth. In the 1970s this simple logic lost credibility, for in this period one became hard-pressed to trust simple Keynesian solutions to both high inflation and high unemployment. In that decade the confused Keynesians had little to say. All too often they lamented that the economy was not as simple as they had once thought and many resigned themselves to studying the various complexities they now perceived to pervade economic life.

But when the intransigent 1970s struck where were the deposed Classicists and Neoclassicists? They had also had a simple view of economic life that offered simple solutions to contemporary problems. They had contended that markets did, in fact, work and what the government must do to maintain stability is very simple — nothing. But they had been largely discredited by the Great Depression because as economic counselors they had been poorly prepared either to explain its occurrence or to propose avenues of escape, other than cutting wages and toughing it out. However, though attrition of laissez faire economists during the thirties was high, belief in unregulated markets and market systems remained the sustaining vision of a number of economists. For the most part they retreated to live in the obscurity of a few academic retreats and to reevaluate their theoretical and policy stance and find mechanisms for dealing with its shortcomings. One such bastion which was to take on substantial importance later was the University of Chicago. Melvin Reder has described developments there and how certain events such as the departure of the Polish economist Oscar Lange allowed Chicago economics to develop in its particular fashion.[2] The role of Milton Friedman was quite important in this. But the resurgence of free-enterprise economics received a major impulse in 1963, when Milton Friedman, later a Nobel Prize winner, and Anna Schwartz published a book entitled *A Monetary History of the United States, 1867-1960*.[3] Of central importance was the fact that the book offered interpretations of the Depression and other recessionary periods which placed the blame squarely on the shoulders of the government and its control of the money supply. The Depression, they argued, was the direct and inevitable result of a drastic decline in the money supply from 1929 to 1933 resulting from mistaken government policy. The book was cogently argued and forcefully presented, and free-market economists now had reason to claim that the system had actually been self-stabilizing all along. Only government errors had caused the catastrophe of the 1930s. Even though the Friedman-Schwartz claims were far from universally accepted, the vindication of pre-Keynesian, laissez faire economics was now well underway.

Friedman soon had a broad group of followers and collaborators who not only adhered to his interpretation of macroeconomic phenomena, but also supported his doctrines of free enterprise, free choice, individual liberty, and so on. Before long they became known as "the monetarists," because of their emphasis on the money supply as the strongest and most reliable determinant of the level of prices and of economic activity. But this group of reincarnated Classicists espoused much more than just proper monetary control, so the monetarist label is misleading. Because they hearkened back to the pre-1930 economic ideas that opposed all subsequent change in the political economy, we should call them conservative. Because they advocated free unregulated enterprise, free markets, the sovereignty of the individual consumer, and individual choice as the measuring rod for all public policy, we find it appropriate to entitle them economic individualists as well. Thus we use as our description of the group, "Conservative Economic Individualists" (CEIs).

Throughout the 1960s when the economy was performing exceptionally well, Conservative Economic Individualists were definitely on the outside, acting as gadflies to point out difficulties with the Keynesian analysis. For the most part their points were technical, but they were maintaining and developing their own analysis in the universities and later in research institutes such as the American Enterprise Institute.

With the deterioration of the economy in the 1970s, the CEIs had their opportunity to become once again the leaders of conventional economic wisdom. During the 1970s, while the Keynesians were expending their energies trying to apply patching material to their structure, and at the same time trying to convince people that the structure could, in fact, be repaired, the CEIs remained in the opposition, but always making the claim that no solution to the problems would be forthcoming until the Keynesians had been discarded and the CEIs had been restored to their proper role at the center of economic policy.

With the election of Ronald Reagan as President, the 1980s promise the CEIs another chance to prove that their interpretation of the economy is the correct one and that the country should follow their advice. Let us briefly introduce that interpretation and that advice.

CEIs have never believed that sustaining full employment by government actions is either possible or desirable. At the fundamental level they believe that the present crisis is caused by too much government intervention in the economy. As Milton Friedman has said, "We are suffering from inflation and recession produced by government attempts to promote full employment."[4] They reason as follows. Growth of government and inflation are the twin evils that threaten economic welfare and personal liberty. The establishment of full employment as a national priority generates irresistible political pressures to achieve that goal, and the resultant policies set off the flames of inflation and create an increased need for government control. Moreover, the inflation can then proceed to trigger a recession. Inflation frustrates people's plans, destroys their confidence, and creates the type of uncertainties which lead both businesses and consumers to cut back on their spending plans.

In addition, CEIs argue that the ever-growing macromanagement functions and social security measures of the federal government create a burgeoning bureaucracy and politicization of economic decisions which in turn generate inefficiency, a loss of incentive in the private sector, and a pandering to the marginal voter by politicians with promises of ever more government programs to replace private activity. The only answer is a sharp reduction of social welfare programs that affect personal incentives, a transformation of activist macromanagement into fixed rules, and the acceptance of the necessity of short-term unemployment to cure inflation.

The CEI framework was turned into a salable political program by the addition of two new, or renewed, elements. The first was a conservative treatment of poverty which brought more coherence to the usual approach to the question. Rather than simply blaming the poor and looking for personality or attitudinal failures on their part, CEIs see the culprit in the continuation of a culture of poverty as the government. The social welfare programs which developed during the 1960s and 1970s—food stamps, medicaid, and so on—create a psychological dependence on the government and sap the incentives and energies of poor people.[5] Of course the same is true for the rich, whose incentives are suppressed by high taxation. But here is a rationale for reducing government programs which has its roots in the classical tradition and which is not openly an attack on the life-sustenance of portions of the population.

The second component is "supply-side economics." It starts again from the assumption that government programs and taxation sap incentives to business and to savers and workers. Thus a program of tax reductions can have very powerful effects in stimulating the economy, increasing output, and increasing productive capacity. Inflation will fall with increased output. In the process, of course, consumers will have more to spend as well. This component of the program served to shift attention from the oft-noted recessionary effects of efforts to fight inflation, and the possibility of having the best of all worlds was once again opened. And the mechanism was appropriately quite simple: less government activity and lower taxes.

While not all CEIs would accept these add-ons to the program, this was the form in which it was sold and bought by the American public. The core of the CEI program remains a return to the free market, limited government activity, limited discretionary stabilization activity, and stimulation of rugged individualism. But it will have to live with the new components, and evaluation of its performance will have to include their effects.

Let us now examine the CEI program in greater detail.

CEI INTERPRETATIONS OF THE CURRENT CRISIS

CEIs believe a free-market economy is self-stabilizing and self-equilibrating. If there are unavoidable disruptions that shake the economy from its steady growth path, then the market mechanism will quickly push the economy back toward its equilibrium position. According to the CEIs, the terms "boom" and "recession" would have little importance in national affairs if the economy were allowed to work on its own. Some take this one step further, even questioning whether the economy's poor performance warrants the commonly applied categorization of a crisis. Certainly the CEIs agree that the 1970s have brought a series of noticeable disruptions. The rise of OPEC, the failure of the Bretton Woods Agreement on exchange rates, the coincidence of high inflation and unemployment, the rise of the multinational corporation, the flight of business to Third-World countries, and declining productivity are all components of the deteriorating economic climate of the 1970s.

Nevertheless, many CEIs question the existence of a crisis on three grounds. First, they contend that the relevant statistics are structured so as frequently to overestimate the dimensions of current problems. Second, many of the phenomena which appear crisis-related may be nothing more than transitional symptoms of an economy undergoing change. No economy is static and it must always adjust to new operational parameters (e.g., higher energy prices, new technological developments). Therefore the seeming difficulties may actually be representative of a healthy and mature, but constantly changing, economy. Third, in a few years, when the CEIs reduce governmental intervention in the economy, things will begin returning to normalcy again. According to this view it is not the economy that is in crisis, but it is government meddling that is keeping an otherwise healthy economy from self-stabilization.

One wonders, however, if the insouciance displayed by the CEIs is a bit overdone. Surely they recognize that the U.S. economy is in trouble. Jack Kemp and David Stockman's "Dunkirk" memorandum in the early days of the Reagan administration recognized the existence of a crisis even if blaming it all on government intervention in the economy. To be sure, the CEIs are aware of the current state of affairs, but their assessment of "no crisis" is based on one central factor: the government must disassociate itself from any direct active relationship with the economy. If that were to happen, then what appears to be a crisis would soon disappear because of the CEIs' *faith* in the market's ability to stabilize itself.

In the CEI view the futility of traditional government stabilization policy has been more than evident during the 1970s. In desperation Richard Nixon imposed wage and price controls in 1971 in hopes of curbing inflation without the usual rise in unemployment. But when the unpopular controls were lifted in 1974, inflation soared as businesses and unions tried to recoup what they felt they had lost in the control period. Saddled with this high inflation, Gerald Ford declared inflation "public enemy #1" and embarked on his "Whip Inflation Now" campaign. In order to bring down the double-digit inflation of 1974 to acceptable levels, Ford reduced the annual growth of the Federal Budget from 11 percent to 5.5 percent. Inflation declined to the 7 percent level, but at the same time unemployment shot up to over 8 percent. In 1976 the state of the economy became a major campaign issue for Carter and Ford, Carter exclaiming that an 8 percent unemployment rate was unconscionable, and Ford defending his policies of moderation in Federal spending. After winning the election Carter immediately undertook to alleviate the unemployment problem. In 1977, the first year of the Carter presidency and the second year of a business expansion, the Carter administration raised Federal spending by 5 percent (over and above inflation) and sustained a 25 billion dollar deficit. Furthermore, the Fed allowed the money supply to grow faster than it had during the Ford years. But with inflation at 7 percent and unemployment at 8 percent, the government faced a catch-22 situation; no combination of fiscal and monetary policy was clearly optimal, for how do policymakers choose between two alternatives that are clearly not consistent with the goals of the economy? Neither Ford nor Carter had good solutions, partly because they were innocent victims of their economic advisers and the advisers could come to no viable consensus. So while Carter's policies tended toward traditional Democratic positions and helped reduce unemployment to around 6 percent, inflation took off again and by the first quarter of 1980 had reached an annual rate of 18 percent.

In the last days of the Carter administration, the bewildering vacillation on stabilization policy as well as on many other questions reflected the uncertainty prevailing as to which problem was the more serious, inflation or unemployment. There was nothing in the Keynesian toolkit to combat them both at the same time. When in October, 1979, the Fed opted to change its money-supply-growth target from interest rate maintenance to a steady growth rate of the money supply, interest rates skyrocketed to 20 percent, investment slowed (especially in the housing sector), and the long-awaited recession hit, causing unemployment to rise to 8 percent by June of 1980. Meanwhile, realizing the grave consequences of their policy switch, Paul Volcker and associates retracted and allowed the money supply to increase once again at a faster rate. By 1980 the government, according to traditional Keynesian economic wisdom, could do no right. Whichever way it turned, it only exacerbated one of the twin evils, while not greatly alleviating the other.

The accession of the Reagan administration brought a new consistency to economic policy, as both the monetary and fiscal authorities ostensibly were pursuing contractionary policies. This resulted in one of the shortest recoveries on record after the 1980 recession: by the second quarter of 1981, the economy slipped into recession again, a long recession which pushed unemployment rates to postwar highs while bringing down inflation below its recent historical levels. But again it was an unsavory mix, even if policymakers were now ready to make their choice clear.

But in all of these situations in the CEI view, the real cause of prolonged stagflation was government policy which prevented the economy from correcting itself. According to CEIs, government meddling in the international sector has also increased the problems of the domestic economy. They argue that international economic activity ought to enjoy the same freedom as that in the domestic economy. This translates into elimination of trade barriers in the forms of tariffs and quotas, and it also signifies the paramount importance of truly flexible exchange rates between national currencies. Presently, however, the U.S. protects many domestic industries from foreign competition and has traditionally intervened in exchange markets to maintain the value

of the dollar. Although the Bretton Woods Agreement, which legiti-
mized government intervention to maintain rigidly fixed exchange
rates, collapsed completely in 1973, the government refused to allow
the dollar to float freely as the CEIs would prefer, until the advent of
the Reagan Administration. Even though the official international exchange policy was to let the dollar float, the government still intervened
regularly in a technique known pejoratively as the "dirty float," interfering with market adjustments.

The CEIs thus respond to the claims of "crisis" in two ways. First,
they deny the existence of a crisis, arguing that whatever aberrations
presently exist are necessary transitional features of a changing economy. Second, they amend this assessment by berating the government
as the perpetrator of many of the crisis-stage phenomena that we have
experienced through the 1970s. If the government had reduced its
activist role back in 1970 when the thin Keynesian veneer of apparent
activist successes began to peel away uncovering the center of Keynesian ineptitude and faulty logic, then it is likely that many of today's
problems would have subsided long ago as markets worked to repair
themselves.

But CEIs go beyond criticism of policy to a technical description
of the economy. Let us look at its main elements: the Phillips tradeoff,
the natural rate of unemployment, crowding out, and rational expectations.

The Long-Run Phillips Curve

CEIs recognize that the key Keynesian dilemma was the coincidence of high inflation and high unemployment. They argue that their
theoretical understanding of a free-market economy provides a clear
and simple explanation for this as well as a solution.

The core of their reasoning can be found in the CEI analysis of the
previously discussed Phillips Curve tradeoff. Even before the 1970 experience with stagflation, Milton Friedman, in delivering the 1968
presidential address to the American Economic Association, outlined
the CEI view that any reliance on the relationship between inflation
and unemployment for creating policy was misleading. The reason for
this is quite simple; as Friedman said, "there is always a temporary
tradeoff between inflation and unemployment; there is no permanent
tradeoff."[6] The CEIs agree that the government may, for a short time,
succeed in reducing unemployment through policy maneuvers, but this
can never last. In other words, the government will be unable to hold
the economy for an extended period of time in a position that markets

will not tolerate. Successful policy can control inflation, and this should be its focus. Then unemployment will adjust to its "natural" market-determined level. Policy should not choose among tradeoffs.

To understand the dynamics of this problem let us consider the behavior of consumers, labor, and business managers in a hypothetical small country. Several industries have plants in the country and numerous small businesses exist that serve the needs of local consumers. Let us suppose that unemployment is 5 percent while inflation is zero. The government decides that 5 percent unemployment is too high; 4 percent would be better, and officials would even be willing to suffer a little permanent inflation if unemployment could be kept down to 4 percent. So the government decides to increase the money-supply growth rate slightly. When the money-supply growth rate increases banks have more to loan out so they lower the interest rate on loans. With lower interest rates than before consumers are more likely to take this opportunity to buy a new car, put an addition on the house, take a long vacation, and so on. In any case spending goes up. But when spending goes up the industries must produce more to meet the demand. The plants will soon put up signs announcing that they will be hiring. But to their surprise no more workers flock to their gate than before. As always, they experience a fairly steady proportion of their employees quitting to look for new jobs and they have just about the right flow of replacements. To boost output they must have more workers, so they increase the wages to make the job more attractive. Thus fewer people quit to look for new jobs in other places and some people who were not in the labor force enter in response to the higher wage.

But the industries adjust in another way, by raising prices. Demand is good, wages have increased, and there is every reason to take advantage of the buoyant economy. As prices in these core industries shoot up, it is not too long before other local businesses raise their prices too. The general price level edges upward and inflation has begun.

Now it is not too long before the workers who have been receiving higher money wages find they have gained nothing since the prices are higher and they can purchase no more than before. Workers who were tempted into joining the labor force by the apparently higher wages now drop out again and regular employees begin to quit their jobs to look for better ones, and the unemployment rate inches back toward 5 percent. Policymakers are bewildered at their failure.

But the implications for the unemployment-inflation tradeoff are readily perceived. There are short term changes in the unemployment rate only when workers are tricked into thinking their wages are higher or lower than they really are (in terms of purchasing power). Now if the politicians do nothing, then prices will once again stabilize, real wages will return to their market determined level, and unemployment will once again return to 5 percent. If, however, they persist in their efforts to keep unemployment below 5 percent the money supply-accelerator pedal will need another push. The same process will recur. Workers, however, do not remain foolish for very long. They soon realize that the increased wages offered by local employers will only offset the rising price level and before the employers even offer to raise wages workers are already demanding it. Suppose the price level has been rising about 2 percent per year, then workers will automatically demand a 2 percent wage increase, and they will have no incentive to work more since the 2 percent increase just keeps them on a par with the rising prices. Unemployment will stay at 5 percent. Now if the government wishes to keep unemployment down they will have to get inflation moving even faster than 2 percent to fool the workers into working more.

Each time the government raises the money-supply growth rate, unemployment will drop for a time, but gradually inflation will increase and unemployment too will push upwards again. If eventually the inflation rate approaches, say 15 percent, then workers will automatically demand a 15 percent wage increase, and inflation is thus built into the workings of the economy. Inflation will inch even higher, but the base or natural unemployment rate will not change. The vaunted Phillips tradeoff is thus no tool that should interest policymakers, for in our hypothetical country the citizens have seen no tradeoff at all; as inflation went up unemployment was supposed to drop, and that did not happen.

Whenever the government undertakes to reduce the unemployment rate below this "natural rate," it will succeed in doing nothing in the long run except raising the inflation rate. The same approximate rate of unemployment will prevail at practically any rate of inflation, and that inflation rate is set by monetary policy. The CEIs explain that since the government of the U.S. has continually tried to maintain unemployment below this natural rate, it should be no surprise that inflation has been so high during recent years.

So while the Keynesians feel themselves in a state of crisis, the CEIs believe they fully comprehend the coexistence of high inflation and what is perceived to be high unemployment. Thus the CEIs explain not only the causes of stagflation but the reasons Keynesian stabilization policies are ineffective.

The natural rate of unemployment plays a central role in the CEI argument, and we should examine it more closely.

The Natural Rate of Unemployment Hypothesis

The level of unemployment in the economy is set in what economists call the labor market. The key factor as noted above is the real wage rate that will be paid. The negotiations between owners of labor, workers, and purchasers of labor, employers, result in a supply and a demand for labor that will set this real wage rate. More importantly, this negotiation which takes place in the market and allows the situation and needs of both sides to be expressed, will also determine the amount of employment in the economy. Such a market-determined amount of employment, combined with characteristics of the labor force, also sets the rate of unemployment in the economy. Thus when CEIs speak of the natural rate of unemployment, they mean that rate that would exist if a competitive market operated effectively in setting the level of employment.

What is that natural unemployment rate? There is a slight problem in defining it, because it is not observable; there are quite obvious deviations from the market-determined rate. So it becomes quite difficult to pin CEIs down. It would seem plausible that the natural rate would be something less than 6 percent, meaning that at prevailing real wage rates, less than 6 percent of the labor force would choose to remain unemployed.

In the 1950s and 1960s a 4 percent rate of unemployment was considered "full employment" (the natural rate), but in the 1970s that rate seemed all but illusory. Could it be that the "natural rate" has jumped a full 2 percent? A quick review of the seventies shows that unemployment was appreciably below 6 percent in three years and dipped slightly below 5 percent only in 1973. Is it possible that 6 percent of the labor force chooses to be out of work? Why would people openly choose not to work when jobs are available? To these questions the CEIs have a number of rejoinders.

First of all, as referred to briefly in our earlier illustration, there are times when people choose to leave their present jobs and search for another. Since most jobs must be found during the hours of eight to five, workers often cannot look for a different job without quitting their present occupation. The time it takes them to find another job is a period of unemployment. In technical jargon such workers are referred to as frictionally unemployed, because they are people between jobs. Statistics have shown that such job searching generally takes less than fifteen weeks, so one might sincerely question the gravity of such unemployment. In fact, CEIs have argued that as more workers switch jobs, the economy benefits since workers will tend to move to jobs where they are more productive.

CEIs do recognize another type of unemployment which is structural in nature. Since the U.S. is a changing economy there are times when some jobs become obsolete and as a result the workers trained in these skills can no longer sell their talents on the market. If they cannot adjust and learn new skills they might be unable to find work and these unfortunates join the ranks of the unemployed. This is called structural unemployment because the workers are willing to work, but they cannot find an employer in need of their abilities. The CEIs, however, tend to downplay this source of unemployment, because there are always jobs for the unskilled available as well as for skilled workers, and if one is willing to take one of these jobs and to lower wage demands far enough, one can obtain employment. Structural unemployment is a regrettable feature of a technologically dynamic society, but one that is substantially outweighed by the benefits of the progress itself.

For the CEI, these are the two types of unemployment that exist, and the second is of doubtful importance. Generally speaking, if someone is out of work, the CEI believes it is because that person makes that choice. But if such frictional unemployment is the only kind of unemployment of any import, why would it change from 4 percent to 6 percent in a relatively short period of time? The CEIs give two reasons. The first involves the composition of the work force. CEIs are quick to cite the fact that the proportion of male workers twenty-five and older in the work force has fallen from 60 percent in 1955 to 46 percent by 1975. This indicates a rise in the proportion of both women and young workers. Not surprisingly, women and young workers are characterized by a much less stable work pattern than are older males. Male workers are generally family breadwinners and the security of a long-term job is a desired asset. For youngsters and females the absence of the same familial financial burden permits a little more freedom in exercising a predilection to change jobs. Nor is it astonishing, then, that the proportion of people between jobs (by their own choice, remember) has risen over the years as the labor force has changed. Thus the natural rate of unemployment has naturally risen.

Policymakers, therefore, ought no longer to view 4 percent as some magic target level of unemployment that signifies that all is well with the economy (4 percent is in fact the unemployment rate that the Full Employment and Balanced Growth Act of 1978 [Humphrey-Hawkins] targets as its measure of "full employment"). How, then, does the government know what unemployment rate should be the target? It doesn't, and shouldn't! It should simply eliminate policies of economic control and let the market work. Whatever unemployment rate results will be the natural rate, the rate which can be considered the sum total of the free choices of workers themselves.

The second reason more people than ever are choosing to be unemployed is a direct result of government intervention. Before the government intervened, the unemployed received no wages for the simple reason that they performed no work. Now, however, with high unemployment benefits which in some cases last up to fifty-two weeks, it pays not to work. When unemployment is "subsidized" in this way workers can afford to be much more choosy in accepting new jobs than they had been previously. CEIs claim that workers will therefore remain out of work when acceptable jobs are available. Again, the increase in workers who choose to remain unemployed is perfectly predictable. It is a rational response of the economic decision-maker to changes in the incentive patterns generated by the structural arrangements of the competitive labor market.

There is another government policy designed to assist the poor that has also worked against the poor by increasing unemployment. Minimum-wage legislation that raises the bottom wage above that which many employers can afford to pay has swelled the ranks of the jobless. Instead of hiring workers, more employers mechanize because it becomes cheaper to do so. Many teenagers and women who would ordinarily be willing to work for less than the minimum wage are therefore left with nothing when, without the minimum wage laws, there would be jobs available for them. So the rise in unemployment rates in the 1970s is the result of natural market forces, and it certainly requires no new government initiatives to deal with it. Also, if unemployment temporarily increases to 9.5 percent, that is a short term result of past bad policy, and the rate will soon drop to its natural rate. If it doesn't drop, the natural rate must have increased.

The Crowding-Out Hypothesis and Monetary Policy

The CEIs also argue that fiscal policy is ineffective as a stabilization tool. Deficit spending for the purpose of stimulating the economy, they say, is nothing but a hoax. Suppose, for example, that the deficit was financed by printing new money. (All deficits, of course, must be financed somehow.) In this event the same sort of process as that described above occurs. Spending increases (some or all of which will be in the government project), inflation rises, and soon workers demand inflation-compensating wage hikes. We quickly are back to where we started, but with a higher inflation and a greater government involvement in the economy. This latter result also comes about if the government deficit is financed through borrowing on the open market or through the selling of bonds. Here the government demand for loans will increase the interest rate and effectively reduce the amount of financing available to private businesses. Therefore, as government business activity grows, private sector business declines; funds become more difficult to obtain, since the government is a competitor.[7] This is popularly known as the "crowding-out" hypothesis; i.e., government crowds business out of the financial markets thus reducing private investment which in turn reduces productivity and economic growth. So an activist fiscal policy could only be detrimental.

Monetary policy does have a role, but not the role the Keynesians would assign it. First of all, it is claimed that the Fed can control the money supply, and if there are difficulties with that, they derive from technical mistakes by the Fed. The latest explanation for the continued difficulty in this regard is the failure to use "contemporaneous reserve accounting" in dealing with banks, an arcane dispute which does not need to concern us here. In addition, the Fed does not need to create the money that the Federal executive's programs would require; it can set the money supply according to its view of the economy's needs.

But there is a problem with monetary policy. Its effect is subject to lags in the same way as fiscal policy, and so discretionary monetary policy should be avoided. In its place should be a "monetary rule," an agreed-upon rate of growth of the money supply which the Fed makes its target. The rate should be keyed to the growth in productivity in the economy and the increase in the need for money for transactions in a growing economy.

This is indeed the policy which the Fed adopted in 1979, thereby rejecting any efforts to set interest-rate targets. In subsequent years, this policy has raised a series of additional problems, not the least of which is the radically higher interest-rate structure which accompanied this decision. But the CEIs believe that such a policy will operate well, the Fed will not destabliize the economy, and the rate of inflation will be determined by the growth of the money supply. If that is low enough, so will inflation be, and unemployment will settle at its natural rate as long as fiscal policy does not disrupt the economy and crowd out private spending.

The Rational-Expectations Hypothesis

In recent years an even more rigid variant of the "stabilization policy is ineffective" position has emerged: the Theory of Rational Expectation. Its outline is as follows. Since businesses and unions are getting larger and since they are increasingly hiring highly educated personnel capable of anticipating, analyzing, and predicting governmental actions, there is little reason that any significant group will be fooled about how the economy will perform. Unions and businesses rapidly perceive an inflationary act on the part of the government, e.g., an increase in money-supply growth, and they adjust their wage and price decisions accordingly. The net result is that no one will be tricked and fiscal and monetary policy will be rendered totally ineffective, even in bringing about short-run increases in employment above the natural rate. Some trenchant observers have suggested that in this innovative approach even Friedman has been "outfriedmanned," because while he has argued that such policies are effective in the very short run, these new analysts discredit even the short run effects.

Again it is very hard to test the claims of the rational expectationists, especially if they allow the possibility of unanticipated inflation because of some outside shock to the economy. But the hypothesis becomes less credible in the light of recent experience when unemployment increased rapidly by over two percentage points and inflation fell dramatically. Unless one is willing to claim there were rapid changes in the natural rate of unemployment, the evidence on the short-run tradeoff seems unassailable. Nevertheless, this analysis may become more relevant as each sector in the economy is concentrated in fewer hands and as more sophisticated methods of predicting the future economic climate are developed.

Conclusion

The CEI position, beneath the technical claims, is quite simple. The claims of crisis are overblown. If only competitive markets were allowed to function properly, there would be no crisis — minor problems, yes, but no lasting symptoms. Crisis hunters who point here and there at what they feel are indicators of an economic malady, who lament the inadequacy of the economic system and prescribe patchwork remedies that only create sweeping inefficiencies all too often persuade befuddled policymakers to enact their ill-conceived proposals.

Hence, for CEIs the economic problems — inflation, unemployment, and low capacity utilization — are either caused very directly by government policy, are developments reflecting natural tendencies of economic change, or are the expected situations given the various and sundry shocks sustained by the U.S. economy. Generally speaking, if the government were not a leading participant in economic affairs, any apparent deterioration in economic performance would only be representative of an unimprovable market system moving back toward equilibrium after sustaining an unavoidable shock (e.g., the rise in energy prices, or a severe drought). There would be no indication here of a deep-seated crisis.

From the textbook point of view the CEIs seem almost flawless, once one accepts their initial assumptions about the behavior of people (i.e., that self-interest is the drive and motivation behind every economic action) and the performance of markets. And yet, even though their textbook analysis seems sound, it is also undeniably clear that reality deviates from their claims in many ways. Economic performance corresponds with their claims only if one gives very flexible interpretation to their technical claims such as the natural rate of unemployment. The competitive market model of the economy is violated more often than not. Technical problems in controlling money continue. The vaunted stability of the economy certainly is not notable as CEI policies are implemented by the Reagan administration.

Nevertheless, there is consistency and a certain strength in CEI analysis, and given their assumptions, one is soon persuaded to give some credence to many of their claims. Certainly the theory as politically packaged in the 1980 elections appealed to many Americans looking for simplicity in the face of uncertainty.

Let us move now to the broader underlying CEI program, leaving behind for a time the technical underpinnings.

THE BROADER CEI CONTEXT

We have been focusing on stabilization policy but the CEI position is much more far-reaching than those technical issues. It cannot be repeated too often that the heart of the CEI position is that a market economy operates optimally when left alone, government is incapable of improving the economy, and most of our economic problems are caused by government intervention.

We have seen this argument in detail in the case of macroeconomic policy for stabilization. We can gain additional insight into the CEI framework by examining their approach to the three other major problems in the real world economy besides unemployment: monopoly, externalities, and unequal opportunity. Remember it was the failure to deal with these four problem areas of a market economy that caused the eclipse of laissez faire economics for fifty years and the ascendancy of Keynesianism.

The Other Economic "Problems"

With CEI analysis the very existence of the problems is called into question. The CEIs' worldview sees the economic complexity of reality through the lenses of supply and demand, equilibrium and maximization (subject to constraints) by rational, atomistic agents. Universally applicable hypotheses are devised which transcend institutional and historical variations. As a result, the theoretical world of the CEIs by its very nature is one in which externalities are of minimal importance, power is widely diffused, and personal inequalities are due to free choice — by rich and poor alike.[8] Reder describes this as holding "tight prior equilibrium" assumptions.[9] As a result, monopoly and externalities are generally assumed to be unimportant, or partial evidence is found which calls their importance into question. Monopoly power, if it exists, is not viewed as institutional or endemic to modern industrial society. To the extent that it does exist, it is largely traceable to governmental interference in the economic system. Externalities are minimized by labeling them "neighborhood" effects and making the theoretical claim in the Coase theorem that market forces provide an incentive to pay to limit externalities, thus minimizing externalities and making any policy steps unnecessary. Finally, CEIs have developed elaborate theories to demonstrate that people freely choose what happens to them.

Simply to deny the existence of major problems is not finally a satisfactory response. But there is an additional argument. It claims that government attempts to correct these alleged problems fail to do so and in the process create new problems, particularly in the area of incentives. The catalog of examples is long indeed: occupational health and safety regulations increase production costs, reduce productivity, and do little to improve health and safety; environmental standards and conservation measures increase costs, lower productivity, and eliminate jobs; consumer protection regulations increase costs and violate individual freedom of choice; minimum wage laws create unemployment among the unskilled; social welfare measures undermine individual self-reliance and the incentive to work; public education restricts free choice and relegates the poor to inferior education. Furthermore, the large government bureaucracy necessary to run these programs is costly, unproductive of economic output, full of waste and inefficiency, and it generates burdensome regulations and paper work for private industry. Finally, these programs and the resulting bureaucracy require high taxes which discourage productive investment in the private sector. That, in turn, lowers the growth of productivity and economic output.

So the problems are either non-problems or governmentally induced.

The Underlying Philosophy

One of the strong points of CEI analysis is the internal consistency of its logic, whose roots go back to the eighteenth century. This consistency is most clear in the libertarian strain of the CEIs, a strain tracing directly back to the classicists of the eighteenth and nineteenth centuries. Classical liberalism (of Smith and Mill) assumed that the chief threat to individual liberty was government and the surest road to progress along with the best protection of liberty was reliance on individual initiative within the context of a free-market economy.

Modern liberalism (the New Deal/Keynesian consensus) sees the chief threats to individual liberty as large private power centers — particularly big business — and the poverty and lack of opportunity which make liberty empty of meaning. Thus government must curb that private power and promote prosperity and opportunity.

Modern conservatives still see the state as the chief enemy of individual liberty. But the threat to liberty from the power of large corporations does not arouse conservative concern.

Modern libertarians share with classical liberalism the distrust of governmental power, but they would push the logic much further than the typical conservative. For example, Milton Friedman opposes all licensing — whether of physicians, lawyers, or whatever — by the state as inefficient and infringements on individual liberty. He believes that if individuals are left to look after themselves in all spheres of life, the best of all possible worlds will ensue. No one can dictate to the individual what his or her needs and wants are, and no one should. A natural social harmony is believed to exist when each individual is permitted to pursue his or her own ends.

In terms of the goals of the economy specified earlier, it is quite apparent that CEIs place primary emphasis on the third, freedom. And they rank it far higher than most other goals. The CEI definition of freedom should include consumer sovereignty for certain, and at a theoretical level should also include citizen sovereignty and worker sovereignty. At a practical level, however, there may be problems with the latter two. Voters may choose means of protecting themselves and may actually vote to interfere with markets and competition, and they may be able to sway politicians. This may require some constraint. Also, many efforts toward worker sovereignty — worker management, worker ownership, job enrichment, etc. — are seen as inefficient. The hierarchical corporation structure is thought highly efficient in harnessing productive enterprises to their proper task, profit maximization.

But much of the appeal of the CEI philosophy is that, despite the prominence given to freedom, there is complementarity between it and the other goals. The invisible hand of the market system will take the individual choices and meld them together into an efficient economic system which will deliver the maximum amount of goods for the resources available. The attempt to provide life-sustenance will be successful.

And self-esteem comes from operating as a rational, maximizing individual. All will do the best job they can and earn the most income they can, and this will provide self-esteem.

Society functions well only because the self-interest of each individual is benefitted thereby. There is no inherent view that people ought to live in a society for the sake of society, for no person has any moral obligation to his or her neighbor other than that agreed to in a mutual contract. Since individuals are sovereign, and since any decision to coexist with others arises only from the perception that one will be thereby enhanced, the CEI rejects any limits on individual decision-taking. Consequently the philosophic objection to government intervention in the economy is that it is an affront to natural human rights. CEIs detest the burgeoning government bureaucracy and they are outraged when economic decisions become politicized, for many decisions may tend to be made on the whim of the marginal voter. The individual falls prey to the fickle vacillations of the average citizen, and is no longer able to undertake his or her fundamental right to make personal economic decisions.

Because of their focus on individual liberty and their faith in the free market, CEIs do not feel the need to discuss equity at any length. In a decentralized competitive market system each person earns in accordance with what he or she contributes to production. Hence, effort, ambition, and innate skills are rewarded; laziness, foolishness, and stupidity are not.

Conclusion

CEIs and the classical liberal tradition they represent place ultimate importance on the freedom of the individual to determine his or her own fate. Their policy stance is founded on the belief that the theoretical model of competition can be utilized to provide empirical proof that a laissez faire-market economy maximizes both individual freedom and economic welfare. Milton Friedman, in his usual trenchant manner, provides a short summary of the CEI position:

> The central planners want planning by them for us. They want the government—by which they really mean themselves—to decide "social priorities" (i.e., tell us what is good for us); "rationalize production" (i.e., tell us where and how we should work); assure "equitable distribution" (i.e., take from some of us to give to others of us).

> Such planning, from the top down, is inefficient because it makes it impossible to use the detailed knowledge shared among millions of individuals. It undermines freedom because it requires people to

obey orders rather than pursue their own interests. I am for planning, too, but planning by each of us separately in light of our individual, though shared, values, coordinated by voluntary exchange in free markets. Such planning, from the bottom up, enlists the interests of each in promoting the well-being of all. Government has its role — to provide a stable legal and monetary framework, enforce contracts and adjudicate disputes and protect us from coercion by our fellow citizens.[10]

Adam Smith could not have said it better. Two hundred years of change in the economic world are irrelevant to the economic theory of the CEIs. No Rockefellers, no multinational corporations, no imperialism, no environmental destruction; just many small buyers and sellers engaging in production and exchange, and thus maximizing their freedom and economic welfare. If we could only get government to tend to its proper business, all would be well. This vision of the world may be beautiful, but it *is* a vision, and a vision which the authors of this book feel to be completely at odds with the realities we must operate in.

CEI PROPOSALS FOR PRODUCTIVE REFORM

By now the reader should have a good indication of what CEIs would propose in the way of policy reform. A synopsis of their reform program, as seen in the Friedman quotation above, is sounded in the oft-heard refrain, "get the government out of business." Since CEIs view the economy as governed by certain natural laws which are, for all practical purposes, immutable, the government has no business fiddling with them, and can do nothing but harm anyway. CEIs claim that without government intervention, the economy would stay very close to a self-determined natural rate of unemployment, would function without the menace of inflation, and would adjust quickly to any unanticipated demands made upon it. Therefore, the policies proposed by those economists of the CEI tradition are, at least in some sense, antipolicies, for they seek to remove instead of install. This is a luxury which came with the minority and outsider position the CEIs suffered (enjoyed?) until recently.

Their specific policies can be quickly detailed.

Limiting the Role of Government

CEI proposals to limit the role of the government in the economy logically follow from the criticisms of Keynesian policy discussed in the previous section.

First, CEIs call for a general reduction in government expenditures to reduce the size of government, to reduce its impact on the economy, and to allow greater room for private sector activity. Wherever possible, necessary public functions should be transferred to lower levels of government.

Second, they urge cuts in social welfare expenditures on the grounds that they reduce individuals' incentive to work and are a major source of waste and fraud in government.

Third, they propose that government programs and legislation which contravene the workings of the free market be repealed. Examples are minimum wage laws, import tariffs and quotas, rent controls, farm price supports, and subsidies to the ship-building industry.

Fourth, they call for deregulation—i.e., the elimination of regulations on business activity that increase the cost of production and lower productivity. Examples are occupational health and safety laws, consumer protection regulations, control of airlines and trucking, and environmental protection requirements.

Finally, they propose a general tax cut to pass on to the taxpayers the savings from the above proposals. The size of the tax cut is constrained by the need to maintain a balanced federal budget (more on this later).

Stabilization Policy

On the key question of stabilization, any arbitrarily chosen target goal of full employment has to be abandoned. The government has very little influence on the unemployment rate, and a target simply justifies ever-increasing government expenditures and consequent inflationary pressures. The government is no longer, therefore, to be seen as the front line against recession, and the size of government expenditures must be severely limited so that the private sector can operate freely in attaining society's goals.

While fiscal policy alternatives are to be reduced to nonexistence, monetary policy cannot be handled quite so summarily. Since monetary shocks have been behind every major recession and expansion in the U.S., CEIs believe that the road to economic stability follows stable growth of the money supply. Activist monetary policy cannot realistically hope to counter recessionary or inflationary tendencies, and in fact, anything other than steady money growth will cause instability rather than cure it. Monetary policy should therefore never be used to regulate economic activity, but should pursue a steady rate of money expansion related to the normal rate of economic growth. In this way individual decision-makers will not spend resources anticipating Federal Reserve actions, but will know exactly what to expect from the monetary authorities.

Excessive money growth is the root cause of any inflation. If monetary authorities had not increased money growth to prevent a recession by accommodating expansive fiscal policy, we would have no inflation now. For the CEIs, the question is how to bring that inflation back to zero without initiating a paralyzing recession. The only certain cure for inflation is reduction in the growth of the money supply, and they argue that we will have to accept substantial unemployment until the fires of inflation are dampened. This is the strategy which generated the 1981-82 recession, and with unemployment reaching postwar highs, it is clear that the campaign to slow inflation has been quite costly.

The final component of stabilization policy proposals sees coordination and agreement among the major free-market countries to exert strict control over international liquidity, to regulate the international money supply just as the domestic money supply is regulated. In this fashion all the countries of the world can depend on a stable international monetary structure, and the stability of the entire international economy can be insured.

The anticipated result from these policies would be a sharp expansion in economic growth which, combined with a constant rate of monetary growth, would eliminate inflation over time and reduce unemployment to its "natural" level. At the same time freedom of the individual would be preserved by reducing government intervention and relying instead on the private sector.

These are radical proposals which would hurt some vested interests, would cause a number of substantial short-run problems, and whose long-run success is far from agreed upon by any but true believers. How could such a set of policies actually be enacted? In the U.S. case, the election of 1980 opened the door, but only after traditional CEI analysis was packaged with a new panacea. Let us examine it.

The New Component: Supply-Side Economics

Most of the above policies are vintage Adam Smith, but something new and salable was added with "supply-side economics." In addition to cutting government expenditures and deregulating the economy, supply-siders want massive tax cuts (even if they cause short-term budget deficits) to provide incentives for new savings and investment which will increase productivity and aggregate supply in the long run. This will create jobs and lessen inflationary pressures.

Supply-side economics has an ambitious version and a more modest one. The ambitious version argues that a reduction in tax rates (not offset by an equivalent reduction in government expenditures) will increase real output by enough to increase actual tax *revenues* even with the lowered *rates*. It will do so by operating on the supply side of the economy.

Keynesians made a similar argument based on the demand side of the economy. That is, if there were unemployed resources in the economy a tax cut would stimulate demand, putting the idle resources back to work and, thus, increasing real output and tax revenues. Supply-siders, in contrast, start with the assumption that there are no unemployed resources, but that more resources would be offered for sale or hire if the real rate of return were higher. A tax-rate cut would increase the after-tax rate of return to productive resources, thereby causing more of them to be supplied. Over a short period of time this would increase real output and thus tax revenues.

There are two key assumptions in this line of argument. Both of them are empirical issues. First is the belief that a tax cut will provide the incentive for people to invest more in productive plant and equipment and to supply more of their labor. Second is the assumption that the magnitude of the effect is enough to result in increased tax revenues. For the time being we will grant the first assumption. The second one, however, is very dubious. There is little empirical evidence one way or the other, but the large increases in output necessary to generate an increase in tax revenues are improbable.

Because of this difficulty the modest version of supply-side economics merely says that a cut in tax rates will increase real output though tax revenues will decrease. But even this modest version is not obviously true. Again it depends on the magnitude of the effects. As Professor Herbert Stein, a non-supply-side CEI, has written: ". . . if the increase in private sector saving is less than the decrease in public sector saving (the increase in the budget deficit resulting from the tax cut) private investment will be crowded out and there is no reason for counting on an increase in the long-run growth rate."[11]

An extreme version of supply-side economics, popular within the Reagan administration, maintains that inflation can be stopped without unemployment by utilizing tax-rate cuts to increase aggregate supply. They argue that since inflation is simply the excess of aggregate demand over aggregate supply, why use Keynesian demand constriction (which creates a recession) when you can painlessly increase supply? This version resembles "voodoo" economics, given the magnitude of the effects required. For example, demand has been growing at 10 to 12 percent per year and the supply of output by 2 percent with the result of 8 to 10 percent inflation. Even if the growth of supply doubled to 4 percent per year, which is next to impossible, there would still be 6 to 8 percent inflation remaining in the absence of a major downturn in demand due to a recession. In addition, the cut in tax rates would increase total demand immediately while supply would increase only over time. In the meantime the increased demand from the tax cut would make inflation worse.

Our evaluation of the whole CEI program is in the next section but it is worthwhile to conclude with Professor Stein's summary view of supply-side economics: "Supply-side economics may yet prove to be the irritant which, like the grain of sand in the oyster shell, produces a pearl of new economic wisdom. But up to this point the pearl has not appeared."[12]

ARE THE CEIs RIGHT?

Critiquing the economic theory of the CEIs is difficult because it is social philosophy as well as economics. The structure of laissez faire theory makes it particularly difficult to verify or falsify any of its constituent propositions. Its survival and attractiveness derive from the theory's tendency to shift from interesting empirical, though false or misleading, propositions to true, though empty, tautologies. For example, from the *truism* that people seek their economic advantage, CEIs deduce the *empirical proposition* that productive investment and work effort are reduced by taxes and similar government measures that reduce the rate of return. However, when confronted with evidence that investment rates over the period 1948 to 1980 *actually* were stable or even increased slightly in the face of escalating tax rates and government regulations, they retreat to a comparison of *potential* effects: in the long run if tax rates and other burdens were increased enough, eventually productive investment and work effort would fall. Thus, an apparent empirical falsification can always be sidestepped by comparing a long-run, abstract potentiality (impact of tax rates on the supply of productive resources) with concrete data (tax rates, etc.). Tautologies take forms such as the proposition that increased government spending means less resources available to the private sector. This is merely a statement about the rules of arithmetic rather than a proposition about empirical reality. Whenever conflicting evidence is raised, laissez faire theory retreats to this type of true but empty tautology, and its ability to avoid falsification certainly accounts for some of laissez faire theory's renewed vitality.[13]

Thus the CEIs' version of neoclassical economics is insulated from falsifiability. What remains, therefore, is a social philosophy from which policy prescriptions for the "good society" are derived. But this social philosophy seems particularly inappropriate for solving today's socioeconomic problems. The modern economy is characterized by interdependence among its economic actors. Externalities are the rule, not the exception. Firms are not simply price-takers; they are dependent upon each other's price and quantity decisions. Power is necessary to market new products, attain government favors, and compete internationally. General Motors, ITT, and IBM, not the corner newspaper dealer, typify the "representative firm" of today.

The perfectly competitive model of the CEIs has little of relevance to say in the face of today's urgent socioeconomic problems other than to exhort us to believe that the problems will all evaporate if we simply return to a laissez faire government policy. Technological change will not undermine competition, external diseconomies will transform themselves into minor "neighborhood" effects, power will dissolve, bureaucracies will break up, and to eliminate job dissatisfaction people will equate the disutility of work with the utility of income.

If the CEIs' theory is insulated from falsification the policy proposals are susceptible to critique and evaluation. One major advantage that CEI economists have had is that their policies have not had to face the test of implementation. The Keynesians, by contrast, suffered from their identification with past government policies—at a time when it was impossible to deliver acceptable results. Now, however, CEIs plan on reshaping the structure of the American political economy that has been built up over the past fifty years. What evidence is there that they will be successful?

There are three reasons to doubt that CEI economics, as implemented under the Reagan administration, will solve the economic crisis: first, the paucity of empirical evidence as a basis for analysis; second, its own internal contradictions; and finally, its uncritical faith in the efficiency of private business.

In terms of empirical evidence, there is very little to give confidence that CEI policies will work. One economic model had been touted in the literature as showing the beneficial effects of a CEI, supply-side program on saving, work effort, and investment. An earlier version was scrapped by its sponsor and there is little information to indicate successful implementation of the new version.[14] Indeed, it seems that supply-side CEIs have had some difficulty in formulating a macro model. David Stockman of the Office of Management and Budget found that when his expenditure and taxation plans were fed into the Congressional Budget Office model, the results were unacceptable (budget deficits of seventy and eighty billion dollars). Stockman turned to an economic model developed at the Claremont Economics

Institute but that, too, proved not to suit his needs. Finally, he teamed up with aide Lawrence Kudlow to construct what has been described as "a framework for constructing general economic 'scenarios.' "[15] The various assumptions in the "framework" apparently produced what Stockman had been after — an indication that implementation of the Reagan program would lead to growth of 4 percent a year and by 1983 a balanced budget and inflation rate of 5 percent. Including these claims as assumptions, however, is far from providing evidence in favor of such beliefs, and the economy is now paying the price for such sleight-of-hand.

There is another implication to the story of David Stockman and economic policy-making in the Reagan administration. We had spoken of the role of economic advisers during the Keynesian days. There has been a major shift in the situation with the Reagan administration. Economists play a much smaller role in actual decision-making. Indeed, seats on the Council of Economic Advisers were filled very slowly, and the Chairman of the Council has not been a significant nor an influential force on economic policy. The first chairman was placed in a number of rather awkward situations such as justifying the shift in administration stance vis-à-vis budget deficits. Early in the Reagan period, and based upon Stockman-type projections, the budget was to be balanced by 1983, or 1984 at the latest. However, by January, 1982, this had become an untenable position. It was left to Weidenbaum of the Council to explain why it was not important to balance the budget, but rather was important to reduce the deficit as a percentage of GNP. So the Council appears to be following rather than leading, certainly a factor in Weidenbaum's resignation.

The economic policy leaders appear to be a combination of savvy government hands such as David Stockman who know the operation of the government and of the budget, along with staff persons brought in from businesses and who therefore should know how to run the government as a business. In addition, and for varying lengths of time, analysts who had written for publications such as the *Wall Street Journal* and who had provided the ideological basis for the supply-side program, were in positions in the OMB and the Treasury where they would have an influence on policy.

But we find here a very subsidiary and very new role for economic advisers. It will be interesting to see if this mode is more successful than the previous one, and what impact that will have on policy-oriented economists.

Turning to a much larger context, some relevant information can be gained from the experience of countries which have attempted their own version of CEI policies. In general the experiment does not give rise to hope. Britain has fared so poorly that even the *Wall Street Journal* has attempted to distance itself from identification with the Thatcher government. In Chile and Uruguay and Argentina, not to say Israel, there may have been some success in getting the economy to grow, but inflation has not come down below the historical rates, unemployment has generally risen, and the wave of bankruptcies continues to ripple. Indeed if we look at the successful countries of the world, Japan or Germany, for example, they seem to have followed quite different types of programs. Available evidence hardly gives reason to place our reliance on CEI policies.

In addition to lack of empirical evidence, a second reason to doubt the potential success of CEI policy proposals is that the approach—unlike the theory behind it—carries within it a number of internal inconsistencies. The first is its new claim to the old "trickle-down theory," that if income is distributed to the wealthy who will invest it, the resulting increase in supply will finally lead to an improvement in the welfare of the poor. Indeed in an unguarded moment David Stockman termed supply-side economics "a Trojan horse to bring down the top (tax) rate."[16] If there is one lesson of Third World development economics, it is that this simply does not occur. The wealthy have not invested and, under trickle-down regimes in the Third World, incomes have shown no tendency to become more equally distributed. In many cases, the incomes of significant sectors of the population have actually deteriorated over time. There is evidence that either an absolute or a relative deterioration in income has disincentive effects and actually lowers workers' productivity. Business firms are very careful about their internal relative salaries because of the impact on work effort, but here we have a program which expects the poor and lower middle class to work harder as their relative income position worsens.

The second contradiction is the emphasis on deregulation of industry, based on an assumption that competition and its theoretical benefits are the likely outcome of deregulation. But if the market being deregulated is characterized by an oligopolistic structure, very different results may occur.

To see the difficulties with this position we have only to turn to the airline industry which was rapidly and effectively deregulated over the period 1978-81. The results of the exercise are less than successful. It is difficult to parse out the various effects of increased jet fuel cost, recession, etc., but there is little evidence that the magical results hoped for have actually materialized. Prices of airline fares were very stable during the 1970s, rising only 33 percent from 1973 to deregulation (in the face of massive increases in fuel prices). But then they took off at a pace at least double the consumer price index, increasing 29 percent in 1979 and over 30 percent in 1980. At the same time, there was major deterioration in the service to small communities, little effect on the load factor for the industry, concentration of the industry as mergers were undertaken, a drop in passenger revenue miles, and finally deterioration in profit results. This forced Braniff into bankruptcy, and a number of other airlines have been placed in danger of a similar fate. If this is the experience that we are to expect from further expansion of deregulation efforts in the economy, it does not bode well for the success of CEI policies.

The third problem with CEI analysis derives from its uncritical faith in the efficiency of private business. Economists are myopic regarding the business firm. They *assume* the firm efficiently allocates its internal resources in the pursuit of profit. The free market gives signals that lead all firms to allocate resources in such a way that the common good is attained. Problems occur when *external* factors interfere with market forces, e.g., market interventions by labor unions, government, and OPEC.

It is claimed that these external factors account for reduced productivity and lower capital investment. However, in Japan, Germany, France and other countries, the same external conditions exist without lowered productivity. In fact, in most of these countries business firms face harsher constraints from OPEC, government regulations, and labor union demands than their U.S. counterparts do.

There are many factors accounting for lowered productivity but one of them must be lowered R & D expenditures by business. An article in the *Harvard Business Review*[17] claims that falling productivity and lowered R & D expenditures can't be blamed on government, unions, etc., but that the responsibility rests squarely with the U.S. corporation and the type of manager that makes his or her way into the upper echelons. At present it is the financial analyst rather than the production specialist who reaches the top, and this leads to an indifference and inability to compete on technological grounds, the very area where the dynamism of the economy is generated and the sources of long-run competitiveness appear. American managers' preoccupation with short-run profit results leads them to decisions that deemphasize R & D and investment in new technologies which only yield their fruits in the long run. The reality is that foreign competition is winning the economic race because of new and better products and techniques.

Another side of this is the inability of firms to deal creatively with workers. Finally, after many years of pressure from the unions, General Motors is adopting programs which encourage worker participation in production decision, and which assume that workers can con tribute more than muscle power. The initial results have been quite favorable. Only the narrowness of vision of the business firm has prevented earlier action on what is certainly one of the key lessons of the Japanese experience.

Our conclusion is that the CEI economists both misunderstand the problems of the economy and provide a set of policies which are unlikely to have a beneficial impact.

CONCLUSIONS AND PROGNOSIS

A few years ago, when we wrote the first draft of this chapter, we concluded by giving the CEIs some credit for inspiring a healthy critique of Keynesian policies, but we also predicted that the CEI role had been largely that of a gadfly and that they would probably never obtain the reins of power. That prediction was wrong. Continued high inflation created a wave of support for any would-be leader who expounded answers other than the ones being advocated by those in power. Since the CEIs base their economics on values at the core of many patriotic Americans, and since the CEI explanations and solutions are relatively simple, it is not surprising that increasing numbers of the dissatisfied public turned to them in search of an America they think they once had. In a time of national crisis one is easily swayed by nostalgic pleas to "make America great again," the way it is said to have been when conservatives walked the high echelons of government office.

President Reagan voices practically all the CEI criticisms and proposals contained in this chapter. (He has favored a return to the gold standard, which CEIs do not approve.) And although it is unlikely that he will be able to institute a full and complete slate of CEI programs, we may nevertheless soon see if Conservative Economic Individualism represents and engenders the sort of social order people will be fond of living in.

Some have said that such nostalgia is only one necessary step on the inexorable road to new answers and new social possibilities that have not, as yet, been tried in America. When things go badly, people often return to solutions that worked somewhere back in the hazily remembered past. Britain too has engaged in the same sort of quest, as evidenced by the election of conservative Margaret Thatcher. As yet she has not been able to cope with the myriad problems facing her country. It is doubtful that Ronald Reagan and his CEI advisers will fare better in this country.

But in spite of this perhaps inevitable setback, world-wise economists cannot sit back idly and watch the world spin by them. They must continue to study, analyze, create, and speculate on new and possible approaches to all of the current problems. If our guess is correct, the crisis will not go away under the Reagan presidency and program of "antipolicies." Therefore we must be ready to respond, when failure becomes imminent and obvious, with new ideas to age-old problems that continually crop up in the ever-changing economic environment.

This we try to do in the remaining chapters. Chapter 5 outlines the attempts to explain our present crisis through the use of long-run cyclical analysis. Chapter 6 evaluates the Marxian argument that it is the inherent contradictions of a market economy that are keeping us in perpetual crisis and that the only solution is a socialist transformation of the economy.

In the remaining chapters of the second part of the book we attempt to present an alternative analysis of what is causing the crisis in the U.S. economy and what can be done about it. This will require a reconsideration of its institutional structure.

PART TWO

Two Challenging Critiques

5. Cycle Theories:
Watch and Hope

Implicit in all of the previous theoretical structures is a belief that steps can be taken to improve the functioning of the economy. Either government should do more or government should do less, but there are policy directions which are suggested and which can provide some expectation of changed performance.

But not all theories of how the economy functions have such implications. One stance, that of the cycle theorists, is that the course of the economy is determined by factors that are beyond manipulation, and so policy of any sort, even the undoing of current policy, is impotent to affect the economy's performance. A second stance, that of the Marxists who will be treated in the next chapter, is that there are steps which could be taken to deal with the economic ills, but they are so radical that they would require a fundamental change in the system. Such a change would threaten important powers in the economy and so could not be implemented as part of a conscious policy.

Our own position is that there are pragmatic approaches to dealing with the situation of the U.S. economy. However, for a complete understanding of possible reactions to the current dilemma, it is important to deal with the frameworks that take a very different stance.

THE CYCLE OF CYCLE THEORIES

Although we could return to the Greek or Roman traditions or to traditions of other cultures for the genesis of cycle theories, the starting point for theories of *economic* cycles is the work of the Russian author Kondratieff, whose major piece appeared in English in 1935.[1] The timing of its appearance and widespread dissemination is hardly an accident, and its popularity has mirrored the performance of the economy ever since. It was dismissed by Russian encyclopedists as "wrong and reactionary"[2] and by English philosophers as "blasphemy."[3] Finally it was ignored by American economists for decades after Garvey's "definitive" review article found its statistical basis defective. Improved economic performance pushed it further into the shadows. A turning point in the life cycle of this idea was apparently reached several years ago, and interest in the long waves is on the upswing. Prompted by the current slump, economists of widely different political persuasions have looked again at Kondratieff's views in the hopes of finding some clues concerning the origins and probable outcome of present difficulties. Geoffrey Barraclough used it quite effectively as a means to organize the views presented in nine books on economics in the middle 1970s.[4] And that is just a small part of the cycle-theory work that was being carried on.

In addition to Kondratieff, many other analysts have used cycle theories to explain economic phenomena. Schumpeter and Kuznets were early writers in this genre; Rostow and Mandel are more recent examples. Their common claim is that there are long waves in economic life, and that simple policy prescriptions cannot counteract them. They differ substantially in their suggestion of the cause of the cycle, and no one of the explanations is very satisfactory. One other shortcoming in their contribution to understanding our current situation is that they provide no way of telling exactly where we are in the long cycle. So they could imply extreme optimism for the future, or extreme pessimism. But with these limitations in mind, let us examine cycle theories for the insights they do provide.

ANALYTICS OF CYCLES

The interest and excitement which Kondratieff's hypothesis of long waves in economic life engendered come from the identification of these waves with economic cycles. It is important, therefore, to understand the concept of an economic cycle.

The Concept of the Cycle

Although there are a number of esoteric definitions, the one adopted by the National Bureau of Economic Research is a good starting point:

> . . . a cycle consists of expansions occurring at about the same time in many economic activities followed by similarly general recessions,

contractions, and revivals, which merge into the expansion phase of the next cycle; this sequence of changes is recurrent but not periodic. . . .[5]

The connectedness of the sequence is important. The values of the economic indicators cannot simply be random fluctuations about the mean (or moving mean) of that indicator. There must be a rhythm, a systematic variation in the level of economic activity, even if it is not a precise regularity.

This idea is sometimes expressed by saying that the cause of the depression phase of a cycle is the prosperity. A Russian critic of Kondratieff expressed the idea in this way: "To prove the existence of the major cycles it is not sufficient to find swings of long duration. You must prove that the causes of the upswing necessarily originate the factors which bring about the depression."[6] And Oskar Lange says that "To prove this theory [i.e., of long-range cycles] it would be necessary to show that there exists a causal relation between two consecutive phases of the cycle. . . ."[7] The root attraction of the idea of cycles is expressed very well in Lee:

> [the cycle idea] implies a regular succession of *similar* fluctuations, constituting some sort of *recurrence,* so that, as in the case of the phases of the moon, the tides of the sea, wave motion, or pendulum swing, we can forecast the future on the basis of a pattern worked out from past experience, and which we have reason to think will be copied in the future.[8]

Finally, there is contained in the concept of cycles the idea that the different phases of the cycle are self-reinforcing. Once a down-swing begins, it feeds on itself, creating further movement in the same direction. Once an upswing has begun, it too is cumulative.

These distinctions should be enough to separate the idea of a cycle from related ideas. A cycle is different from a trend, because the values of economic variables tend to recur; it is different from random fluctuations because there is a systematic variation in the values of these variables over time. And a cycle is different from swings of economic activity in that they are internally caused and tend to be cumulative.

When we turn to a review of actual cycles, we find that they divide into a number of categories, distinguished primarily by their length.[9]

Varieties of Cycles

According to the National Bureau of Economic Research business cycles may last from more than one year to ten or twelve years. As we shall see, the Kondratieff cycle is considerably longer. Nonetheless, even the NBER categories provide space for substantial variation. Several types of shorter business cycles have been studied. One is the major cycle, discovered by Juglar in the 1860s and so called "the Juglar cycle." Juglar himself reported that the cycles had a period varying from nine to ten years, but he did not claim the cycles had a precise or fixed length.

Juglar cycles have typically been associated with different rates of investment, although there are a large number of suggested explanations for them. In one view, the investment cycle corresponds to the life cycle of major product and equipment innovations. In order to embody a new technical innovation in process or product, substantial new investment is needed. When the new capital equipment is constructed, or the new product fully marketed, investment subsides, and the economy sinks back into a trough.

There is a shorter cycle as well. The minor or "Kitchin" cycle lasts from two to four years, although Joseph Kitchin, who discovered these short cycles in 1923, put the figure at forty months. These shorter cycles are associated with short-term adjustments, and are sometimes labelled "inventory" cycles, since they are thought to be the result of minor overaccumulation of inventories. As businesses produce slightly too much, they build up inventories; so they slow production to draw the inventories down. This pattern of marginal increases and decreases in the quantity of output gives the shorter cycles their rhythm.

Cycles of intermediate length have also been studied under the name "Kuznets" cycles. These are growth-rate changes in a wide variety of variables: output, population and size of the labor force, supply of money, stock of capital, etc. They are of intermediate length varying from fifteen to twenty years in duration. Associated with them, and sometimes also called "Kuznets" cycles are the cycles in construction. Once again these cycles average fifteen to twenty years in length. Building cycles originate when a strong "outside" stimulus, such as a wave of immigration, sets up a strong demand for housing. The financial institutions in the building industry facilitate speculation and uncontrolled construction after this increase in demand. The boom lasts until an oversupply of houses has built up, and the construction binge halts. Since houses are relatively durable, it is a long time before enough houses deteriorate so as to allow for a new upswing.

But most interest, especially in current writing, focuses on the long waves which are of considerably greater duration. Their period varies from forty to sixty years. They have been noted in the behavior both of prices and of production. The four authors we will deal with have long swings as their primary concern. Let us turn to an examination of them.

LONG-SWING THEORIES

Kondratieff

In "The Long Waves in Economic Life," Kondratieff admitted the existence of the Juglar and Kitchin cycles, but was most interested in demonstrating the existence of fifty-year cycles. He examined various indices of economic activity, concentrating on two: prices and production. Thus, he found that the wholesale price index for the United States, England and France exhibited no long-term trend, but did exhibit long wavelike movements about an average level. Data were available only from the close of the eighteenth century on, but they indicated the start of an upswing in 1789, a turning point twenty-five years later in 1814, followed by a prolonged downswing until 1849. In France and England, 1849 marked a turning point, while in the United States the turning point was delayed until 1866, after the Civil War. A downturn began in all three countries in the 1870s and lasted until 1896. The twentieth century opened on an upswing lasting until 1920, at which point Kondratieff detected the beginning of a new downswing.

Measured from trough to trough, then, Kondratieff's price waves lasted sixty years and forty-seven years respectively. There were similar long waves in the rate of interest, in wages and in foreign trade. But these last waves were obviously price-related movements, and so Kondratieff tried to demonstrate the existence of physical cycles by examining the production and consumption of coal and pig iron, and the production of lead. Since there was a long-term trend in production of these commodities, the cycles he found were accelerations or retardations in the rate of growth around this trend. There has been, however, considerable criticism of the Kondratieff cycles in production. Garvey argued persuasively that the choice of periods from which to estimate a trend line was arbitrary, and that the choice of dates for turning points was also arbitrary. With different choices, the Kondratieff waves in production vanished. He concluded that only the price waves were successfully established by Kondratieff.[10]

Nevertheless Kondratieff thought he had established parallel movements in a large number of economic indicators. This agreement prompted him to set up the following chart of the long waves:

First Long Wave:	Upswing	From end of 1780s until 1810-17
	Downswing	1810-17 until 1844-51
Second Long Wave:	Upswing	1844-51 until 1870-75
	Downswing	1870-75 until 1890-96
Third Long Wave:	Upswing	1890-96 until 1914-20[11]

Notice that he allowed for a five- to seven-year range in the dating of the turning point. Nevertheless, the dates for the general long waves closely paralleled the dates for the long waves in prices. The weakness of the data on the production series suggests that the turning points for the long waves were determined by Kondratieff primarily from the price series.

Several other characteristics of Kondratieff's long waves are important to note. First, they are alleged to be international in scope. Thus, data from all major capitalist countries are used; and in the case of the price series, they do reflect the long waves. Second, the shorter business cycles were affected by the long waves. The existence of a long upswing did not guarantee that no slumps would take place, but it did make the slumps less severe both in amplitude and duration. Similarly, on the downswing, years of depression dominate, even though there are some years of prosperity.

Granting Kondratieff's claims, the question remains as to the cause of the long waves. It is here that theoretical controversies abound. Leon Trotsky argued that the large trends which Kondratieff had discovered were exogenously determined.

> Their character and duration is determined not by the internal interplay of capitalist forces but by those external conditions through whose channel capitalist development flows. The acquisition by capitalism of new countries and continents, the discovery of new natural resources, and, in the wake of these, such major facts of a "superstructural" order as wars and revolutions, determine the character and the replacement of ascending, stagnating or declining epochs of capitalist development.[12]

In short, the argument was that these long-term movements were simply not cycles. The reason was that they were determined not by internal forces — the prosperity did not cause the depression — but by accidental combinations of unique historical forces. In fact, concluded the argument, they were a mere succession of trends, each more or less independent of those that precede and follow. To illustrate his point Trotsky produced a chart in which "long cycles are replaced by a succession of linear upward and downward trends of unequal duration and different slope."[13]

Kondratieff replied to this criticism by insisting that the long waves were as regular as the shorter business cycle. First, the long waves recurred at more or less regular intervals. While the length of the business cycle varies between seven and eleven years, i.e., 57 percent, "the length of the long cycles fluctuates between 48 and 60 years, i.e. 25 percent only."[14]

Second, he argued that the so-called external causes of the long waves were not really external at all. He listed four such causes: (1) changes in technique; (2) wars and revolutions; (3) the assimilation of new countries into the world economy; and (4) fluctuations in gold production. Changes in technique, for instance, are not independent of economic conditions. The impression that they are stems from the confusion of the process of discovery, which is indeed a creative act not determined by economic conditions, with the use of these discoveries. Once the new technical knowledge is available it is still necessary for the economic conditions to be ready for its use. In particular, the relative prices of labor and the new technology must be such that it is more profitable to invest in the new technology than to use more labor. Even where the new technology is capital-saving, it must be more profitable to introduce the new technology than it is to continue the old. And this criterion of profitability in turn relates to availability of loanable capital, and its rate of interest. Hence, it is correct to suggest that changes in techniques are not entirely exogenous factors.

A further point reinforces this. Although the act of discovery is indeed a unique creative act, the probability that a new discovery will be made does seem to be proportional to the number of people working on the project, and to the amount of social resources these researchers have at their disposal. Hence, although economic conditions cannot *determine* a discovery, they can increase the likelihood that such a discovery will be made.

Kondratieff is less convincing in the other cases. He argues that most wars have an economic basis, though he presents no compelling reason why religion or race are inadequate explanations for some wars. He also maintains that the opening up of a new country to the world market is economically determined. The discovery of the new country may not be so determined, he says, but its entanglement in the world economy is. Again he does not present a clear mechanism which would explain this economic determinism.

Finally, he makes the point that gold production is very much like the introduction of a new technique: the discovery of gold may be accidental and creative but its production is based upon how profitable it is to dig it out of the earth. Hence, it is more likely that gold production will take place when gold has its highest purchasing power, i.e., when prices are low. Hence, gold production is not independent of economic forces.

Kondratieff's major point was that all these factors could be explained internally (endogenously) to the economic system; and so even if they caused the long waves, it had not been shown that long waves were the product of external, accidental forces. He also made another,

more controversial, point, claiming that it was the long waves themselves which produced the changes in technique, the wars, the opening
up of new countries and the increased production of gold. In critiquing
the Trotsky view Kondratieff said, "they reverse the causal connections
and take consequence to be the cause."[15] It is one thing to argue that
these four factors are conditioned by economic events: it is quite
another to maintain that a long wave itself has causal power, and this
earned Kondratieff's hypothesis the title of "blasphemy."

He had a third and most basic reply. Kondratieff charged that his
critics "see an accident where we have really to deal with a law governing the events."[16] The claim that the long waves were governed by laws
implies that one could derive a theoretical understanding of them. Unfortunately, Kondratieff did not proceed very far with a development
of "an appropriate theory of long waves." But his point was that the long
waves exhibited the characteristics of lawlike phenomena; they were
recurrent, more or less regular, sequences of changes in economic life.
Chance or accident would not explain the recurrences or the regularity.
Hence, Kondratieff felt entitled to claim that the phenomena of long
waves were lawfully governed despite the absence of a fully developed
theory which formulated laws governing the waves.

However, as reported in Garvey's review paper, Kondratieff did
develop a theoretical model to explain the long waves, a model which
was never presented in English. Building upon the idea that the shorter
business cycles were produced by periodic reinvestment of fixed capital
with an average life expectancy of ten years, Kondratieff developed the
idea that the long waves were simply the economic reflection of the life
cycle of "basic capital goods." To this category of "basic capital goods"
belong big plants, railroads, canals, large land improvements, and the
training of skilled labor. Investment in basic capital goods proceeded
in spurts rather than continuously, and so the basic capital goods produced by one spurt of investment were allowed to deteriorate until the
next round of investment. The upswing of the cycle corresponded to
the initial spurt of investment, while the tapering off of investment in
basic capital goods corresponded to the downswing of the long waves.

To explain why the investment process was discontinuous, Kondratieff argued that investments in basic capital goods required large
amounts of loanable capital, and that these amounts were available only under certain conditions: (1) high propensity to save; (2) large supply
of loan capital at low rates; (3) its accumulation at the disposal of
powerful entrepreneurial groups; (4) a low price level. Thus, large
amounts of loanable capital were available only at the bottom of a
downswing. Once the upswing started, Kondratieff explained, it would
come to a halt because interest rates would rise and there would

develop a shortage of loanable capital. However, nothing in the theory explained why an upswing must start. Kondratieff's conditions were only conditions for the possibility of an upswing. This ignorance of the mechanism which generated the upswings did not prevent him from asserting that there was nevertheless such a mechanism, and that the long waves did form a lawful process in which each phase created the conditions which produced the next phase.

In Kondratieff we see the general outline of long-swing approaches. As can be seen there are precious few policy implications. The best a policymaker can do is to watch the economy and hope that the upswing will appear to save the day.

A more elaborate attempt to explain the long waves was developed by Schumpeter, to whom we now turn; but he again gave little policy guidance.

Schumpeter

Joseph Schumpeter was undoubtedly one of the preeminent economists of the twentieth century. He wrote widely on a variety of economic questions. Perhaps the best indicator of his contribution is that whenever there are changes in the economy or doubts about its functioning, other economists are able to find important and helpful insights in Schumpeter's writings — though they may have been written over forty years ago!

Schumpeter also wrote on cycles, which he thought were important factors in the functioning of the capitalist economy and thus had to be dealt with.[17] Schumpeter's views can be usefully broken down into three parts: first, his historical reconstruction of cycles in the capitalist countries; second, his analytical model of the course of a typical cycle; and third, his notion of leading sectors as explanatory factors in cycle theory.

Historically, Schumpeter resolved the course of development in capitalist countries into the interplay of three types of cycles: the long wave Kondratieffs, the middle range Juglars, and the short term Kitchins. His first Kondratieff runs from 1787 to 1842, and contains several Juglars. The second Kondratieff ran from 1843 to 1897 and also contained several smaller Juglars. The third Kondratieff has an upswing ending at World War I, and contains one complete Juglar.

In general, Schumpeter sees Kondratieffs as composed of six smaller Juglars, which are in turn broken down into three Kitchin cycles. This does not follow from any imposed theory, but simply emerges from the data available to him. He also notes that the longer waves influence the shorter ones. For example, during an upswing the intermediate Juglars never sink very low, and their highs are successively higher, while in the long term downswing, the highs of the Juglars are successively lower and lower.

An important consequence of Schumpeter's view is that the actual values of various economic indicators will reflect the combination of these three cycles. Hence, a major turning point may be hidden from view because it occurred within an opposite phase of a smaller cycle. Another consequence is that the troughs of normal business cycles will be especially severe in the trough of a Kondratieff cycle, while the peaks will not be as high.

Schumpeter's analytical model contains two steps. In step one, he imagines the entire economy in a state of equilibrium, where firms set prices equal to average costs, profits are zero and there is no involuntary unemployment. Into this situation comes an innovation. An enterprising person or firm decides to develop it. To do so, a loan from a bank is required. This bids up the interest rate, and the enterprising firm bids scarce resources away from other firms. This causes a price increase. The new innovation is a success, imitators follow, and soon a boom is underway. At some point, the innovation plays itself out. New investment declines, loans are paid back, prices decline, and a recession eventually returns the economy to equilibrium.

This is step one — a two-phase model of boom and recession. The next step adds two more phases. The recession, in step two, forces the economy down past the equilibrium point into a depression. At some point this depression gives way to a revival which brings the economy back up to equilibrium.

A distinctive feature of Schumpeter's view is that cycles are not to be measured from peak to peak or from trough to trough; rather they are to be measured from the points where the level of economic activity reaches equilibrium "from below" at the end of a period of revival. Connected with this is the idea that the forces which bring the economy out of a depression — the revival forces — diminish in strength as the economy approaches equilibrium. Thus, Schumpeter does *not* maintain that the innovation process is the way the economy builds its way out of a depression. The innovation process begins from an equilibrium point — not from a deep trough.

Schumpeter provided no novel ideas on how the economy pulls itself out of the depression trough. He mentioned the need to let prices sink until investment became profitable again and the need to pay off debts before embarking upon a new round of investment. He also emphasized the psychological expectations of businessmen. His novel idea was that the whole process began and ended from equilibrium, and was guided by the innovation process.

For all three types of cycles, Schumpeter proposed the same mechanism. The only difference lay in the scale of the new invention: innovations requiring little investment generated the smaller cycles; huge innovations resulted in the long cycles. Schumpeter distinguished three different sectors within which innovation took place and whose life cycle paralleled the long cycles. First, there was a revolution in cotton textiles and iron which set off the first Kondratieff wave. Schumpeter called this the Industrial Revolution. Then there was the revolution in the construction of railroads, and in the use of steam and steel. This set off the second Kondratieff. Finally, developments in electricity, industrial chemistry and the internal combustion engine set off the third Kondratieff upswing.

The major problem for Schumpeter was why these great innovations should tend to cluster at certain times. His best explanation was a hypothesis of imitation: as soon as someone successfully showed the way, a rash of innovations would take place. But these clusters of innovations would not continue indefinitely due to limitations on the availability of investment capital.

Critics have noted several problems with Schumpeter's views. First, he associated the beginning of an upswing with the start of an innovation process. But the innovation process usually produces a decrease in prices in the innovating industry. It is hard to reconcile this with the fact that prices tend to rise during the upswing of a long cycle.

Second, although Schumpeter wanted to maintain that cycles were an inherent part of the economic process, and not determined by outside physical or institutional forces, his idea of the great innovator seemed to be just such an outside force.

Third, and in relation to this last point, one of the defining characteristics of cycles is their continuity — the fact that the prosperity breeds the depression. Schumpeter's view allowed for that sort of continuity, but also implied that the entire economy could perch at an equilibrium point indefinitely until the innovation process started again. The continuity between the revival period which dragged the economy out of the depression phase and the prosperity period was broken, and nothing about the revival forces would ensure that prosperity would follow. Hence, the continuity of the cycles was made to rest on the historical accident that someone developed enough nerve to initiate the innovation process.

So with Schumpeter we have a much richer treatment of cycles which corresponds well with performance in the pre-World War I period. There have been more recent efforts to find long swings in economic performance, and to them we now turn with Simon Kuznets's and Walt Rostow's analyses.

Kuznets and Rostow

Kuznets and Rostow do not try to explain the long wave phenomenon via a unitary theory. In addition to updating the work on long cycles, their contribution is to isolate a number of forces, and to examine their historical interplay. Their approach is also less mechanistic and more historical. But again they do not provide policy guidance.[18]

Kuznets examines trends in production, and discovers evidence that swings in the production of certain sectors correspond to the life cycle of certain innovations. However, in contrast to Schumpeter he finds that the initial stages of the introduction of an innovation are periods of price reduction, and not price increase. He does not proceed from this sectoral analysis to an aggregate analysis of prices and production.

In his later work, Kuznets developed the idea that long trends in various economic variables were linked to population growth. Housing construction and building of the railroads, for example, were found to be population sensitive, particularly to waves of immigration.

But these trends in the growth rate of various economic quantities were of shorter duration than the observed long waves and so Kuznets could not use them as an explanation of long waves.

Rostow builds upon work done by Kuznets and his followers by using several of the forces found to be significant in various parts of Kuznets's work. The first of these is the rise of a new leading sector in production. For example, Rostow maintains that around 1900 the growth of the old leading sector composed of the railroad and steel complex was decelerating, while the new leading sector of the automobile, electricity and chemicals complex was only beginning to emerge. Hence, the period of 1900 to 1914 was one of decelerating output per capita.

The second of these forces is the movement in trade and capital in response to shortages of raw materials and foodstuffs. For example, in 1896 there was a worldwide shortage of wheat, causing a price explosion. This immediately triggered an adjustment mechanism as production of wheat in Australia, Canada, Argentina and Russia increased. The increase in production was made possible by large imports of capital into these countries. The imported capital was used to build up the infrastructure, especially by means of railroad construction.

It is into this interplay of forces that Rostow introduces the third force — the large movements of population about which Kuznets and his followers said so much. The key factor which produced the large flows of immigration was the growth of the new countries in terms of both agricultural and construction activity. Another result of the migration was that the large numbers of people produced increased demand for still further housing and infrastructural development.

In this way, Rostow tries to reconcile the different accounts which have been given of trends in various economic quantities. He also tries to apply his historical results to the current situation. He suggests that the current high prices of raw materials and foodstuffs indicate that we are in the *upswing* of a new Kondratieff wave, and that the development of new countries which is associated with these upswing periods should be expected.

With Rostow, the idea that there should be a necessary connection between different trends is lost. The basic change from an old leading sector to a new leading sector which he presents as part of the deceleration of output from 1900 to 1914 is not analyzed. We are not told why this change took place. Similarly, the shortage of wheat which produced the price explosion in 1896 is not analyzed. Why did this shortage take place then? The net result of these unanswered questions is the feeling that the whole process was rather accidental, and could just as easily have gone the other way. It would have the same implication for our current situation; and again the policymaker would have simply to observe with little ability to affect the economy's direction. So Rostow implies that long waves have no inner necessity at all. This conclusion differs from Mandel's in that Mandel attempts to revive Kondratieff. Since Mandel is a Marxist, his framework will also provide a good transition into the Marxist analysis of the next chapter.

Mandel

The major accomplishment of Mandel's *Late Capitalism* with regard to the idea of the long waves is to present in summary form new statistical evidence suggesting that there are indeed long waves in the economic life of capitalist countries.[19] He uses the data to make the claim that the present economic crisis is likely to get worse, for we are now in the *downswing* of a Kondratieff cycle.

The statistical information he provides is all in terms of physical output, and thus supplements the price series which have generally been accepted as showing long-wave behavior. Using data from the United States, Great Britain and Germany, he finds fluctuations in industrial output which match the price fluctuations Kondratieff had found. (See the tables 5.1-5.4.) Most interesting of all is his projection into the future: since 1967, he says, we have changed from a long wave of expansion to a long wave of contraction, as can be seen by a remarkable reduction in the percentage growth of industrial product. This implies that capitalism is entering a crisis, a theme that we will deal with at much greater length in the next chapter.

Mandel, in explaining the long swing, does not simply credit the development of these waves to outside forces acting directly on the rate of profit. Instead, he proposes a version of Schumpeter's theory of innovations. Each of the long cycles was characterized by the spread of a different kind of innovation in the technology of productive motive machines. The first cycle, which lasted from the end of the eighteenth century until 1847, produced the spread of the steam engine, made by a manufacturing process. The second long wave began in 1847 and ended in the 1890s, and was characterized by the use of the machine-made steam engine. The period lasting from the 1890s to the Second World War produced the widespread use of electric and internal combustion engines. Finally, the period beginning during and after World War II introduced the generalized control of machines by electronics, and the beginnings of the use of nuclear energy. The peak of this period was reached in 1967, and we are now entering the downswing.

The mechanisms Mandel cites are the usual ones: as the new technology becomes more widespread, there is less and less of a need to invest huge sums in it; all the basic investments have been made. Hence, the force that gave the upswing its power is gone. There are, so to speak, no more fields to conquer. Hence, the boom turns into a period of decline.

A theory which relies upon large-scale innovations in motive machinery is an attempt to give a genuine explanation of the cycles. But it is incomplete, and insofar as it must rely upon external unique forces it is no longer an explanation of a cycle.

One attempt to amend Mandel's view was briefly sketched by David Gordon. According to his view, large-scale investment could not take place after the initial phase of building up the new technology had taken place because "so much had already been set in concrete and billed for future repayment."[20] These investments in motive machinery and, he adds, in infrastructure, thereby locked us into a pattern which could not be broken. The boom had to be followed by a period of recession until the old technology and infrastructure simply wore out.

Gordon adds at one point that this process is not simply a matter of physical decay. The class struggle must enter in as well. Only when the class struggle becomes intense and labor puts a profit squeeze on capital will it become profitable once again to embark on a huge investment scheme in some new form of technology, or some new type of infrastructural development.

With Mandel and Gordon we begin to get to theories which see cycles as inherent in capitalism and which look to Marxism for the explanatory theory. We will deal much more with these theories in the next chapter.

SUMMARY

A theory of cycles has to do three things according to Mass.[21] First, the theory must explain why the cycle gets started — and once started in a particular direction, why it continues to develop in that direction. Second, it must explain why this cumulative movement in one direction comes to a halt. And finally the theory must explain why there is movement back in the opposite direction.

At one extreme there is the view that each and every cycle has to be explained by one and only one type of cause, e.g., innovations. At the other extreme, there is the view that only a narrative of the exact historical events can explain each separate cycle. The correct view is probably in the middle: each cycle is a unique historical event, but it must share certain causal features in common with other cycles. Otherwise, there would be no cycles, but only a succession of trends moving in opposite directions. Hence, a theory of cycles must allow for enough generality to expose the common elements in each cycle without mechanically imposing upon each cycle a pattern which does not fit.

The Kondratieff theory is stimulating and obviously has important implications for our present malaise. But it finally is of little help to policymakers and to us. For it has no suggestions for steps to be taken to deal with the cycle, nor does it have a theoretical base that could tell us we are in a cycle until it is long past! Though it is an intellectually appealing approach to understanding our current economic problems, it is far less well developed than the Marxist theories of the next chapter. And finally, for our purposes, its implication that nothing can be done to deal with current problems does not appear correct. So we must move beyond the long swing theories.

Table 5.1

Annual Cumulative Rate of Growth of the Industrial Output of Great Britain

PHASE	RATE OF GROWTH
1827-1847	3.2%
1848-1875	4.5
1876-1893	1.2
1894-1913	2.2
1914-1938	2.0
1939-1967	3.0

Table 5.2

Annual Cumulative Rate of Growth of the
Industrial Output of Germany

PHASE	RATE OF GROWTH
1850-1874	4.5%
1875-1892	2.5
1893-1913	4.3
1914-1938	2.2
1939-1967	3.9

Table 5.3

Annual Cumulative Rate of Growth of the
Industrial Output of the U.S.A.

PHASE	RATE OF GROWTH
1849-1873	5.4%
1874-1893	4.9
1894-1913	5.9
1914-1938	2.0
1939-1967	5.2

Table 5.4

Annual Compound Percentage of Growth of Industrial Output

	1947-1966	1966-1975
U.S.A.	5.0%	1.9%
Original EEC six	8.9	4.6
Japan	9.6	7.9
U.K.	2.9	2.0

6. Marxism: Inherent Cycles and Inevitable Crises

There is one body of economic theory which is unlikely to play a central role in the policy debate of the United States: Marxism. The popular vision of Marxism is dominated by the scowling, stern, and determined frame of Leonid I. Brezhnev and by the bearded, cigar-smoking, fatigue-clad form of Fidel Castro. These men do not evoke sympathetic feelings in most citizens of the Western World, for the visions in Western eyes of Gulag Archipelagos and mass exodus of refugees from Cuba are far from the idyllic scenes promised by dedicated Marxist communists. Indeed, as part of the Western political struggle against the Soviet Bloc countries, Americans slowly, but inexorably, have learned to treat evil as synonymous with communism. Sadly, but understandably, Karl Marx himself is all too often thought to have been a perverted, evil, and maladjusted man, because he is often associated with the terrorism and revolution that rings the globe today. Still, there is a vast gulf between Third World revolutionary advocacy and the economic thought that originates in Karl Marx's innovative theories of the market (Marxists prefer to call it capitalist) economy.

If we could just slip on the raiment of semiobjectivity for even a short period of time, we would realize that Marxist interpretations and explanations of our current economic and social dilemma have a surprising degree of coherence and relevance. This may be uncomfortable for some, but really it need not be that troubling, for Marx was both an economist and a social and political theorist. In his economics he assiduously studied, reflected upon, and recorded all the mechanisms which he felt were essential to capitalism, and for our purposes it is unfortunate that his economics has been simply dismissed because it is popularly connected with guerrilla-led revolution. In fact, over the years more and more well-known (and often conservative) economists have begun to lend a sympathetic ear to some of Marx's work on the

111

economics of capitalism.[1] Part of this new interest stems from the well-developed economic theories with which Marxists claim to understand the dynamics behind the intermittent capitalist crises. It is in this spirit that we move forward into Marxist theories of the stagflation and social malaise of the seventies and eighties. Any complete understanding of the U.S. economy must take into account these Marxist insights.

Much of Marx's thought on capitalist economies centers on a dual tendency which is thought to be inherent within the structure of the system. The first part of this tendency is toward fluctuations from short booms to temporary recessions, the cycles of the last chapter. These short cycles are an inevitable aspect of capitalist growth. Because of their transitory nature such cycles are not very disruptive and there is, therefore, no compelling reason to decry them as unnatural or cataclysmic.

The second side of this tendency is substantially more serious, for a series of these short cycles could, over the long run, develop into an economic stagnation of critical proportions. In Marxist terms this is known as the tendency toward crisis. Crises such as these will not cure themselves, as will the shorter periodic fluctuations. In contrast with our earlier long-swing theorists, there is no tendency towards recovery and upswing. Instead, only major shifts in structural and social relations will relieve a crisis and allow the system to resume its normal, if somewhat altered, mode of cyclical expansion.

Most economists of Marxist persuasion claim that the U.S. is currently in one of the long-run stagnation crises which beset the U.S. economy every fifty years or so. A serious crisis threatened the nation shortly after the Civil War, lasting from 1870 until about 1890. The next severe crisis, which many of us (or our parents) still remember, began with the stock market crash in October of 1929. And now, beginning somewhere in the 1970s, we have entered a third major economic crisis, perhaps the worst of all in terms of long-run events.

In the first two cases capitalism was saved, but not without major institutional and behavioral revisions. The system was saved from complete collapse at the end of the nineteenth century by a proliferation of new monopolies that did away with the ravages of uncontrolled competition, by a surge in global expansion that reduced the costs of raw materials, by new technical innovations, e.g., the entirely new industry created by electric power, and by relatively progressive labor policies undertaken "voluntarily" by the newly created large firms.[2]

When capitalism floundered again in the 1930s, government took on the role of stabilizer under the guidance of the New Deal/Keynesian consensus and the government role grew along with the economy. Finally, the Marxists argue that before we emerge from the crisis of the seventies and eighties, the economy will undergo another major shift. Some predict that shift will be toward increased economic planning.[3] Others expect more substantial structural reform. But they all agree that whatever direction the economy actually moves in, one can be sure that there must be a dramatic change in the economic and social system before it can begin a stage of renewed vitality.

What clearly distinguishes Marxist economics from that of the traditional economics which is quoted in the newspapers, heard on radio and TV, and used for advising in Washington, is that traditional economics, as embodied in either CEI or Keynesian garb, claims that the economy can be kept on a stable growth path. CEIs believe it will grow of its own accord, and Keynesians believe it needs management; but neither group anticipates major crises to crop up periodically. Marxists, on the other hand, fully expect that any capitalist country, by its very nature, must not only go through cyclical fluctuations, but must also struggle through rarer but still inevitable crises of monumental proportions. It is this sort of crisis that we find ourselves mired in right now. So while many may be put off by the radical militancy of what is commonly known as Marxism or communism today, it would be extremely unwise to skate around the only fully developed economic theory that has predicted the periodic crises we have experienced throughout the capitalist era.

In this chapter, therefore, we will look at the Marxists' critique of capitalism, see why they confidently foretell capitalist crises, assess whether their explanation has any validity, and finally confront the Marxist call to reform. Our procedure is initially to discuss some of the core elements of Marxist theory in order to lay open its vision of the world. We will draw heavily on quotes from Marxist writers to ensure a proper presentation of their views. Second, the theory will be applied to events of the sixties and seventies to explain in Marxist terms why and how we have arrived at the current crisis. And third, we will take a brief look at the Marxist solutions.

ELEMENTS OF MARXIST THEORY

Although economics forms a large part of his general system, Marx is much more than an economist. Economics, sociology, political theory, history and philosophy are all mixed into his sweeping analysis. In this section only those portions of Marx's thought that are relevant to crisis theory are covered.

The general framework for Marx's analysis is his materialist interpretation of history. Marx rejects philosophies of history which are based on metaphysics or psychological laws of human nature. He denounces metaphysical explanations as meaningless mysticism. Psychological explanations are dismissed with the remark that "it is not the consciousness of men that determines their existence, but, on the contrary, their social existence determines their consciousness."[4]

Marx developed the view that the *general* shape of any given historical epoch was determined by the prevailing mode of production. By "mode of production" he was not referring simply to technique (which was included among what he termed the "forces of production") but also to the "relations of production"—the relations into which people entered with one another by reason of the various positions which they occupied in the productive process. The mode of production and the relations of production breed a superstructure of ideas and institutions. As Marx put it, "The sum total of these relations of production constitutes the economic structure of society, the real foundation, on which rises a legal and political superstructure and to which correspond definite forms of social consciousness. The mode of production of material life conditions the social, political, and intellectual life process in general."[5] However, Marx does not insist that all ideas and institutions represent passive adaptations to the mode of production; some cultural expressions might rise quite independently. He contends, nevertheless, that such autonomous noneconomic forces exert only a minor influence on historical development.

For Marx, social reality is more than a specified set of relations; it is the process of change inherent in a specified set of relations. In other words, social reality is the historical process. The process of social change is not purely mechanical; it is rather the product of human action, but action which is definitely limited by the kind of society in which it has its roots. "Men make their own history," Marx wrote, "but they do not make it just as they please; they do not make it under circumstances chosen by themselves, but under circumstances directly found, given and transmitted from the past."[6] Society is both changing and, within limits, can be changed.

Evolution in society occurs because the elements that make up the mode of production change. Different forms of society may accelerate or retard the development of these economic factors, but some change in the productive forces takes place under all economic conditions. In the early stages of a particular social system, the material forces of production are compatible with the relations of production and the superstructure of ideas and institutions. In this period the existing relations of production are "forms of development of the forces of production." But changes in the relations of production and the cultural superstructure lag behind the development of the material forces of production. And then, "at a certain stage of their development, the material productive forces of society come in conflict with the existing relations of production, or — what is but a legal expression for the same thing — with the property relations within which they have been at work hitherto." The existing property relations now "turn into fetters" on the forces of production. When this occurs then "begins an epoch of social revolution. With the change of the economic foundation the entire immense superstructure is more or less rapidly transformed."[7]

The class struggle is the vehicle of social change. Or as Marx expressed it, "The history of all hitherto existing society is the history of class struggles. Freeman and slave, patrician and plebian, lord and serf, guild-master and journeyman, in a word, oppressor and oppressed, stood in constant opposition to one another, carried on an uninterrupted, now hidden, now open fight, a fight that each time ended, either in a revolutionary reconstitution of society at large, or in the common ruin of the contending classes."[8] In medieval society the dominant relationship had been that between feudal lords and serfs. In the classical world it had been that between master and slave, the relationship of servitude between them depending on the fact that the master-class possessed, not only the instruments of production and the product of labor, but also the producer himself as a personal chattel.

In capitalist society the legal bonds which tied the producer to a lord or master no longer existed. The laborer had been emancipated, and before the law was a free agent, entering into a contractual relationship with an employer which was in form akin to any other market contract. In other words, labor for a master was no longer obligatory. Employment was by virtue of an act of sale of labor power on the market by free exchange. This marked the essential difference between the social relationships typical of capitalist society and those which characterized earlier forms of class society. With the market it appeared that free and equal contractual relationships had been substituted for a relationship of exploitation; that freedom and equality had been realized and the resemblance to the older class societies no longer remained. But Marx said, "The modern bourgeois society that has sprouted from the ruins of the feudal society, has not done away with class antagonisms. It has but established new classes, new conditions of oppression, new forms of struggle in place of the old ones." Or again, "for exploitation veiled by religious and political illusions, it [the bourgeoisie] has substituted naked, shameless, direct, brutal exploitation."[9]

In any social system as the relations of production mature and harden, while the forces of production continue to develop, the lines between the ruling and oppressed classes sharpen. The oppressed class,

which stands to gain by a modification of the existing property relations, asserts itself and attempts to secure political control. Since this
class is aligned with the all-powerful productive forces, its eventual success is guaranteed. A new set of property relations develops which is
appropriate for the expansion of the new productive forces. With the
change in property relations, the entire superstructure of ideas and institutions is modified and changed. All history, according to Marx,
follows the cycle of revolution, progressive evolution, the rise of and
need for resistance to institutional change as a part of further progress,
degeneration, and again revolution. What Marx says about capitalism applies to all previous social systems as well: "not only has the
bourgeoisie forged the weapons (the forces of production) that bring
death to itself; it has also called into existence the men who are to wield
those weapons — the modern working class — the proletarians." And
again, "The development of modern industry . . . cuts from under its
feet the very foundation on which the bourgeoisie produces and ap-
propriates products. What the bourgeoisie therefore produces, above
all, are its own grave-diggers. Its fall and the victory of the proletariat
are equally inevitable."[10] Marx contends that after capitalism has been
replaced by socialism and socialism by communism the evolution of
social systems will come to an end because class conflict will then have
been eliminated.

> In broad outlines Asiatic, ancient, feudal, and modern bourgeois
> modes of production can be designated as progressive epochs in the
> economic forms of society. The bourgeois relations of production are
> the last antagonistic form of the social process of production —
> antagonistic, not in the sense of individual antagonism, but of one
> arising from the social conditions of life of the individuals; at the
> same time the productive forces developing in the womb of bourgeois
> society create the material conditions for the solution of that an-
> tagonism. The social formation brings, therefore, the prehistory of
> human society to a close.[11]

This, then, is the Marxian version of the historical process:
economic factors play the decisive role in shaping the evolution of society, because the relations of production determine the ideological,
political, legal, and institutional structure of the community. Since the
forces of production are continually changing, the form society takes is
also subject to constant change, not in a simple mechanistic fashion,
but inexorably nonetheless. Indeed, one may identify four different
historical stages — primitive communism, the ancient slave state,
feudalism, and capitalism — each of which arose out of the previous
stage as a result of the conflict between the forces of production and the

relations of production. In each case the internal contradictions generated by this incompatibility led to the breakdown of the older system and to the emergence of a new one. In each instance, the agents of change were the social classes that were created by the particular mode of production that was used; the method of change was a struggle between classes arising from the internal contradictions of the system. Nor is the capitalist mode of production exempt. It, too, has created its internal stresses and strains. Like the previous stages, therefore, it will eventually be swept away, according to Marx, in favor of other forms — socialism at first, and then communism.

It was the secret of capitalism as a mode of production that Marx was concerned to probe; and he hoped thereby to reveal the specific character of the conflicts within this mode of production which could determine its place in history, its growth and movement and the future society that was destined to supplant it.

Marx's theory of *surplus value* provides the framework on which he bases his analysis of capitalism. The essence of capitalism, in his view, is the division of the population into two classes. "The epoch of the bourgeoisie possesses . . . this distinctive feature: It has simplified the class antagonisms. Society as a whole is more and more splitting up in-to two great hostile camps, into two great classes directly facing each other — bourgeoisie and proletariat."[12] One class, the capitalists, owns all the means of production; the other class, the workers, has only its own labor power to sell. The available supply of labor and the existing means of production are capable of producing a flow of commodities that is greater than that needed to maintain the labor supply and the means of production intact. The economy, in other words, is able to produce a surplus over and above the value of subsistence needs of the workers and the value of the raw materials and equipment used up in production. Marx calls this "surplus value." The surplus is expropriated by the capitalist class in the form of net profits, interest, and rent.

How does surplus value arise and why are the capitalists able to expropriate it? According to Marx, labor power, which the capitalists purchase in the market and consume in the productive process, possesses the unique characteristic of yielding more than its own value as it is used. This excess value that labor power creates is the surplus value that capitalists expropriate. Since labor power is a commodity its value "is determined, as in the case of every other commodity, by the labour-time necessary for the production, and consequently also the reproduction, of this special article. . . . in other words, the value of labour-power is the value of the means of subsistence necessary for the maintenance of the labourer."[13] The capitalist buys labor power at its value and since he "acquired the right to use or make that labouring power work during the *whole day or week,*"[14] he is able to force the worker to work longer than is necessary to produce a value equivalent to his labor power. Or, otherwise, "The value of the labouring power is determined by the quantity of labour necessary to maintain or reproduce it, but the *use* of that labouring power is only limited by the active energies and physical strength of the labourer."[15] The surplus value which is generated goes to the capitalist because "wherever a part of society possesses the monopoly of the means of production, the labourer, free or not free, must add to the working-time in order to produce the means of subsistence for the owners of the means of production."[16] But why can't wages rise above the subsistence level, above the value of labor power, so that the workers could obtain part of the surplus value? Marx's answer depends on his famous concept of the "reserve army of labor." The reserve army of labor consists of unemployed workers who, through their active competition on the labor market, exercise a continuous downward pressure on the wage level.

> The industrial reserve army, during periods of stagnation and average prosperity, weighs down the active labour-army; during the periods of overproduction and paroxysm, it holds its pretensions in check. Relative surplus-population is therefore the pivot upon which the law of demand and supply of labour works. It confines the field of action of this law within the limits absolutely convenient to the activity of exploitation and to the domination of capital.[17]

Marx maintains that only labor can create surplus value; but could it not originate from the raw materials and capital equipment utilized in production? Since the value of all commodities is determined by the amount of "socially necessary labor time" worked up in them, raw materials and capital equipment can only transfer this value in the production process. They have no value in and of themselves separate from the labor embodied in them. The capitalists who sell the raw materials and capital equipment obtain the surplus value when they sell them to other capitalists for use in production. The capitalists who purchase them get back merely the value they paid for them. Although Marx admits that better machinery increases surplus value, he holds that it is the embodied "socially necessary labor time" that is responsible, not the machinery.

The value of the total product produced in the economy during any period, then, is the sum of three components. The first part, which merely represents the value of the raw materials and capital equipment used up, "does not, in the process of production, undergo any quantitative alteration of value,"[18] and is therefore called constant capital (c). The second part, that which replaces the value of labor power, does in a sense undergo an alteration of value in that "it both reproduces the equivalent of its own value, and also produces an excess, a surplus-value, which may itself vary, may be more or less according to circumstances."[19] It is therefore called variable capital (v). The third part is surplus value (s) itself. Therefore total value (V) can be shown as V = c + v + s. Marx uses three ratios of these components of total value. The ratio, s / v, is the rate of surplus value or the rate of exploitation. He expresses this as a division of the working time into the period that labor works for itself and into the time that it works for the capitalists. If s / v is 50 percent, this means that it only takes labor ⅔ of the work day to produce its means of subsistence, and the other ⅓ of the work day is spent producing surplus value which the capitalists expropriate. The ratio, s / c + v, is the "rate of profit" on the total capital invested. Finally, the relation between constant and variable capital, c / v, is what Marx terms the "organic composition of capital."

The goal of the capitalist is to increase the mass of surplus value which he receives. It is not the production of goods for consumption or even for a particular profit. As Marx says:

> . . . it is only in so far as the appropriation of ever more and more wealth in the abstract becomes the sole motive of his operations, that he functions as a capitalist, that is, as capital personified and endowed with consciousness and a will. Use-values must therefore never be looked upon as the real aim of the capitalist; neither must the profit on any single transaction. The restless never-ending process of profit-making alone is what he aims at.[20]

With a given employed labor force the capitalist can increase the mass of surplus value by raising the rate of exploitation. There are three ways of doing this. First, by extending the length of the working day and with the value of the means of subsistence unchanged, the surplus labor time and hence surplus value is increased. Second, real wages can be reduced, but since real wages are normally at the subsistence level, this can be done only temporarily if the labor is to be maintained. Third, the productiveness of labor can be increased. This involves a change in the state of technology. The improved technique increases the total output produced by a given labor force, and thus increases the difference between total output and subsistence output.

In Marx's model technological improvements are endogenous and occur at a rapid rate. By the very nature of the capitalist process technological change must occur. The capitalist is constantly seeking ways to increase the mass of surplus value. Since the methods of lengthening the working day and reducing wages have physical limits the capitalists must rely primarily upon increasing the productivity of labor via technological improvement to increase surplus value. Each capitalist firm discovers that it can temporarily gain on its competitors by introducing more productive instruments. By doing this, it immediately lowers the cost of production, while the price of the product falls only gradually as other capitalists follow. Those who are among the first to introduce a new technique, therefore, gain extra profits. Thus each capitalist firm tries to get the jump on its competitors or, failing this, introduces new machinery merely to hold its relative position in the industry.

Marx believes that there is a strong tendency for technological progress to increase the quantity of machinery and equipment per worker. Thus, to take advantage of new techniques capitalists require a larger stock of capital. Another way an individual firm can increase its total profits or surplus value is to expand its output under existing methods of production. This requires an increase in the outlay on labor, raw materials, and capital equipment. Thus, whether the capitalist firm increases its total surplus value via technological change or simply an expansion of output, it finds that it must accumulate more and more capital. This, then, becomes the goal of capitalist activity. As Marx says, "Accumulate, accumulate! That is Moses and the prophets! . . . Reconvert the greatest possible portion of surplus value . . . into capital! Accumulation for accumulation's sake, production for production's sake . . . this [is] . . . the historical mission of the bourgeoisie. . . ."[21]

Marx viewed capitalism as a powerful engine of economic growth. The capitalist is driven by the system to accumulate more and more capital. But capitalism uses harsh and inhuman methods to accumulate this capital in the beginning. In one of his more emotional passages Marx says, "If money . . . comes into the world with a congenital bloodstain on one cheek, capital comes dripping from head to foot, from every pore, with blood and dirt."[22] In spite of the role it plays in generating wealth, capitalism — by its very nature — is not able to maintain sustained economic growth. It is plagued with both cyclical fluctuations and periodic crises. And in spite of the great increase in wealth, the great mass of people benefits little. Economic development continues: accumulation and more accumulation, but with the capitalists reaping most of the benefits and workers remaining near a subsistence level of existence. Life-sustenance is not delivered to all. Esteem and freedom are reserved to the elite that controls society. Where does it all end? What is the path which lies ahead of capitalism? In one place Marx says:

> As soon as this process of transformation has sufficiently decomposed the old society from top to bottom, as soon as the labourers are turned

into proletarians, their means of labour into capital, as soon as the capitalist mode of production stands on its own feet, then the further socialisation of labour and further transformation of the land and other means of production, as well as the further expropriation of private proprietors, takes a new form. That which is now to be expropriated is no longer the labourer working for himself, but the capitalist exploiting many labourers. This expropriation is accomplished by the action of the immanent laws of capitalistic production itself, by the centralization of capital. One capitalist always kills many. Hand in hand with this centralisation, or this expropriation of many capitalists by few, develop, on an ever-extending scale, the co-operative form of the labour-process, the conscious technical application of science, the methodical cultivation of the soil, the transformation of the instruments of labour into instruments of labour only usable in common, the economising of all means of production of combined, socialised labour, the entanglement of all peoples in the net of the worldmarket, and with this, the international character of the capitalistic regime. Along with the constantly diminishing number of the magnates of capital, who usurp and monopolise all advantages of this process of transformation, grows the mass of misery, oppression, slavery, degradation, exploitation; but with this too grows the revolt of the working-class, a class always increasing in numbers, and disciplined, united, organised by the very mechanism of the process of capitalistic production itself. The monopoly of capital becomes a fetter upon the mode of production, which has sprung up and flourished along with, and under it. Centralisation of the means of production and socialisation of labour at last reach a point where they become incompatible with their capitalist integument. This integument is burst asunder. The knell of capitalist private property sounds. The expropriators are expropriated.[23]

Marx undoubtedly hoped that his version of capitalism's demise would come true. His life was spent trying to promote this end. Whether it is a prediction that must follow from his model is doubtful. It would seem though, that the "expropriation of the expropriators" is not so much a prediction as a vivid description of a tendency. For, in Volume III, while speaking of the centralization of capital into a few hands, he says, "This process would soon bring about the collapse of capitalist production if it were not for counteracting tendencies, which have a continuous decentralizing effect alongside the centripetal one."[24] To conclude, here is a quotation from a present-day Marxist on this question: "In a real sense it can be said that Marx's entire theoretical system constitutes a denial of the possibility of indefinite capitalist ex-

pansion and an affirmation of the inevitability of the socialist revolution. But nowhere in his work is there to be found a doctrine of the
specifically economic breakdown of capitalist production."[25]

Regardless of the final outcome the two classes are always posed
in a fundamentally irresolvable conflict, neither side being fully con-
tent, and both sides always scheming about how to improve their own
position at the expense of the other.

The capitalists, however, always enjoy an advantage, for when
workers begin to gain, they have numerous means to keep labor in its
place. One result of this continual class conflict is economic cycles. We
will see why shortly. But one element which Marx did not foresee, and
which is crucial in the historical evolution of the capitalist system, was
intervention of the state in the economic system on behalf of other
groups of people, not just the capitalists. It is possible that this historical fact may have so changed the nature of capitalism that Marx's
analysis must be severely amended. Therefore, modern Marxists have
been forced to analyse the New Deal/Keynesian type of government intervention by developing a "theory of the state."

It is not too much of a simplification to reduce Marxist theories of
the state into a sort of grand conspiracy theory of how to keep laborers
in their place while keeping them from being discontented or at least
convincing workers that nothing better is possible. In his book *Fiscal
Crisis of the State,* James O'Connor illustrates one such interpretation.[26]
O'Connor maintains that there are two primary economic roles for
the state: accumulation and legitimization. Government expenditures
in the area of social capital correspond to the accumulation function
while expenditures for social objectives correspond to the legitimization
function. Social capital refers to government investment in physical
capital like highways and utilities and to investments aimed either at
improving labor skills or at improving techniques via research and
development. The best known social investment designed to improve
labor skills is the massive amount of money that must go into public
education.[27]

Aside from these expenditures which go directly to increase the
potential accumulation of capitalists are the explicit social expenditures. These include social security, unemployment benefits, welfare,
and medicare. Such programs are responses to expressed needs of the
working class. Through them the government, which is an agent of the
ruling class, in effect buys off the workers. Any incentives to rebel
against the system are effectively squelched as the government moves
an inch to satisfy the demands of the working class. But this is just a
sop, for workers still do not get what they deserve. In reality this type
of government expenditure merely legitimizes the continuation of a

system which caters to the needs of the capitalist. If a majority of the workers became rebellious, business would stand the chance of losing everything. So they allow the government to involve itself in such social affairs.

MARXIST THEORIES OF THE BUSINESS CYCLE

From the Marxist viewpoint the cyclical nature of the capitalist economy can only be understood historically. Furthermore, and more importantly, societies undergo their major upheavels during periods of crisis. Thus Marxists would say that we are about to witness a fundamental restructuring of the social institutional framework that orders all social and economic activity. Let us turn to the specific models of the business cycle used by Marxists.

Marxists propose three principal sources of inherent capitalist instability. The first of these focuses on the tendency for the organic composition of capital to rise over time. The second examines the inevitability of an aggregate underconsumption of goods. And the third analyzes the effects of the exhaustion of the reserve army of labor. All of these sources have one thing in common: each centers its attention on capitalist profits as the motor force of the economy. Because profits fluctuate between high and low rates, the level of investment-activity and economic growth fluctuate as well. The ensuing business cycles may not be highly disruptive at first, but they compound over time, with each downturn becoming more serious than the previous. Finally the steady progression of cycles builds up into a crisis, a situation where fundamental change must occur in order for profits to rise again, and for growth to proceed.

The Organic-Composition-of-Capital Thesis

An understanding of the trouble caused by the rising organic composition of capital requires a review of Marx's notion about the source of profits. Profits are the direct result of exploitation of the workers. A worker is paid, say, ten dollars per hour, but may create value at the rate of twelve dollars per hour. The two dollars per hour are the surplus and they are the owner's profit. To get total profits one multiplies the number of workers by surplus value produced by each. It is impossible to make profits except from the worker. Machines, for example, produce no extra value. If a machine costs $50,000, then that machine will, on the average, work to create $50,000 worth of output over its life, but no more. There are no profits, therefore, to be gained except through the employment of workers.

Now, because firms are motivated to increase their profits, they wish to increase the productivity of their workers. By so doing and by continuing the low wages, they can increase the rate at which workers are exploited. Instead of the worker creating a value of twelve dollars per hour, labor productivity may be pushed up to, say, fifteen dollars per hour. If wages remain below thirteen dollars per hour, then profits per worker will increase. Increasing productivity is essential to the competitive capitalist firm, for it must never allow its competition to get the advantage. And at first glance the drive to enhance productivity appears to be a lucrative venture. It has, alas, a serious drawback. When a firm engages in a productivity drive it usually opts to purchase more machines, allowing each worker to produce more output. As the capital in use rises, so does the organic composition of capital; that is, the value of capital in use rises faster than the value of labor employed. This process is accelerated if some workers are laid off due to the introduction of labor-saving technology. So even though productivity of each employed worker increases, the number of workers employed often falls, and the ratio of workers to total capital outlay always falls. Hence the base upon which profits are realized shrinks.

This can be seen by further examination of the above example. If productivity increases to fifteen dollars per hour, then the same level of production can be maintained with fewer workers. If wages rise to around thirteen dollars per hour, then profits per worker remain about the same; but profits on total outlays would decline since there are now fewer workers per machine. Even if demand for the product increases it is very possible that increased sales would not adequately compensate for the proportionate loss of the profit base.

Why, then, one asks, would firms introduce labor-saving technology? For many who are not well versed in Marxian thought and theory this seems a rather silly proposition. Everyone knows that new machines are introduced in order to increase profits, not lose them. Robert Heilbroner offers an explanation. He notes that the capitalist firm is obligated to mechanize in order to stay competitive. Says Heilbroner,

> He is only obeying his impulse to accumulate and trying to stay abreast of his competitors. As his wages rise, he must introduce labor saving machinery to cut his costs and rescue his profits—if he does not, his neighbor will. But since he must substitute machinery for labor, he must also narrow the base out of which he gleans his profits. It is kind of a Greek drama where men go willy-nilly to their fate, and in which they all unwittingly cooperate to bring about their own destruction.[28]

A second reason for substituting machinery for labor is to increase the qualitative control over the workforce. The need for more control over the work force could push firms to overinvest in machines regardless of a loss in profits.

But the effect of capital accumulation on the rate of profit clearly places limits on that process. Once a firm reaches the limit of capital accumulation, the only mode of further expansion beyond forcing the labor force to work harder is through an increase in technology which can increase the output per worker without reducing the number of workers. However, dependency on technology is an obstacle to expansion because technological innovation occurs slowly and gradually. Furthermore, many firms do not have the money to invest in technology. Dependence on technology also indicates the intrinsic instability of the capitalist system.

As the capital accumulation process proceeds, the profit rate will eventually fall so low that there is no longer sufficient incentive to invest. A recession begins, wages drop, and the weaker firms, whose profit rates have turned negative, go bankrupt. When upward wage pressures end, and when the stronger firms buy up the bankrupt ones at prices below their real value, profit rates can rise again and another expansionary period can begin.

While this was the earliest Marxist theory of the business cycle, it is also the weakest. Firms and industries with a high organic composition of capital do not necessarily have lower profit rates. The oil companies are a good example.

The Underconsumption Thesis

A second Marxist theory of capitalist instability is known as the theory of underconsumption and relies on an analysis of the dynamics of consumer demand. Here again firms are driven by the desire to increase profits. This time, though, they try to stretch profit margins by raising their prices. Once more they eventually do themselves in, because the general rise in prices has the effect of reducing the purchasing power, or the real wages, of their workers. As the real income of the laboring class declines, so too does their ability to purchase all the goods that are produced in the capitalist enterprises. In other words, aggregate demand shrinks, and when demand shrinks so does economic activity in general.

Two modern Marxists, Baran and Sweezy, refer to the problem of underconsumption as the inability of firms to realize full profits on total output.[29] As the real income of workers declines they will be unable to purchase the output when firms operate to capacity. There will be a surplus product, and firms can do one of several things to confront this surplus. First they may be able to take the surplus and find new markets in which to sell. This tendency, say many Marxists, is the source of much of the overseas development of multinational corporations. If this is not feasible, or if they cannot get rid of the entire surplus, they will have to cut back on production, reduce prices, or do a little of both. Workers thus lose their jobs, real income falls because of the unemployed worker, and a recession is at hand. Eventually prices may come down far enough so that real income levels are restored and internal underconsumption no longer bedevils the system. And as the potential of profits once again becomes a reality the same process will begin again.

Once again one wonders how firms could be so stupid. From a long-run perspective, any self-respecting business firm ought to recognize that it has little to gain from its attempts to increase short-run profits. But since each business firm operates individually in competition with its fellow firms, it is blinded to the larger picture. As a consequence, actions taken by single firms to enhance their own relative positions are compounded by similar decisions by competing firms to the detriment of all of them together. Marx described this quite well.

At some points it appears as if Marx thought it were possible to maintain a permanent and steady growth in the capitalist economy; but this would be possible only if everything went perfectly. For example, Marxist theory claims that capitalist firms are able to control both supply and demand. Supply is controlled via simple output decisions, and demand is controlled by business expenditures on investment goods, a category which includes wages in the Marxist schema. Marx formalizes the problem by conceptualizing it as a process which takes place over subsequent time periods. Production occurs in period one, but this production is purchased with the wages and capital expenditures of period two. So there is always a one-period lag in the consumption of goods. Now, suppose that productivity increases 10 percent in period two. The firm plans to give workers just enough wages to buy up all that was produced in period one. This means that the firm will have 10 percent profit in period two and will be able to invest that profit to increase productivity again in period three. The capitalist firm does not have to pay the worker for this year's product, but pays 10 percent less which will enable last year's market to clear. The system could thus enjoy uninterrupted expansion.

But this could only occur once in a million times, for such a delightful scenario would require perfect planning. And unfortunately, the capitalist system operates entirely too anarchically. Each individual firm operates autonomously. If one firm's planning is off, or if several firms just blunder, then the drop in demand could reverberate through the whole system and the permanent expansion would come to an end. The result is that the system will be subject to cycles of recession and expansion. As profits expand in the up cycle, investment will increase and the output capacity of the firm will rise. But eventually the firms realize that demand is not strong enough to purchase all their produced goods. They must cut back and a downward trend takes shape.

Empirically underconsumption would show up as too little consumption demand and thus too much saving for the available investment demand. So far in U.S. history this has not been a major problem. However, it will be interesting to see if the income distribution effects of the Reagan program might provide the basis for an initial underconsumption crisis.

The Reserve Army of Labor Thesis

The third theory of the business cycle is more convincing and realistic than the preceding two, when considered in light of the U.S. economy today. It refers to the labor market and what is known as the reserve army of labor. Whereas underconsumption theory centers on the effects of consumer demand for goods, the reserve army theory stresses the changes in the demand and supply for labor during the process of capital accumulation. During an expansion capital accumulates and the demand for labor increases. As demand increases, wage rates will also begin to rise since labor becomes relatively scarce. Furthermore, as labor becomes scarce, those working become relatively more powerful in their bargaining position and are able to demand not only higher wages, but better working conditions as well. Workers, of course, are always struggling to gain better wages and working conditions, but now that labor is scarce they start winning the struggle. If capitalists wish to continue production they either give in to their workers or they lose them to other firms. But as labor makes real gains, unit costs spurt upward and profit margins are squeezed to a point where the capitalist firm cuts back on production, an action that throws large numbers of workers back out on the streets. The solidarity of workers is thus splintered and each individual now concentrates more on finding or keeping a job than on winning more job benefits. Accordingly, as worker power jockeys back and forth, a cycle of recessions and expansions becomes the rule. Marx thought that in the long run the solidarity of workers would grow so strong that short-run unemployment would no longer destroy labor's unity. When this happened, capitalism would end, as workers would stay united to overthrow the system collectively.

Two aspects of the reserve army theory deserve special mention. First, the decline in the rate of profit is not traced back to basic instability in the process of capital accumulation. Rather, the profit squeeze results from workers' response to the process. In this scenario the source of instability is class conflict between labor and capital, and thus it is class relations which become the ultimate barrier to the progressive accumulation of capital.

The second point of interest is the particular way in which the workers use their power to squeeze profits. It is not so much the increases in wage rates that cut the profit rate, but worker demands for better working conditions. In fact, wages themselves may actually decline relative to profits, for gains in productivity may keep ahead of wage increases. Improved working conditions, however, constitute a considerable cost of production to the firm, and they cause costs to go up and profit margins to decline.

When these three theories of capitalist instability were conceived the final outcome was initially presumed to be the demise of the capitalist order brought about by the overwhelming solidarity and singularity of purpose of the mass of exploited workers. Cycles were considered to be characteristic, with each becoming more disruptive than the previous one, until finally the whole system would collapse in utter chaos. But as we all know, capitalism has not disappeared, and there is no compelling reason to believe it will topple and crash in the near future. Instead capitalism has adjusted to the pressures, meeting some difficulties with government regulations on business, and confronting others with some controlled income redistribution to the poorest members of society.

Nevertheless, and despite the absence of total collapse, there have arisen periodic capitalist crises. And in each of these crises the structure of capitalism has undergone major changes and the followers of Marx have been forced to revise the Marxist theory to account for the historical changes that have taken place. For the Marxists still feel that the theories of crisis are relevant, and they put down their roots in the three theories discussed. The dynamics of the capitalist system, however, have changed over time and new elements must be considered. In the following section we consider several of these revisions.

MODERN REVISIONS OF MARXIAN CYCLE THEORIES

The first major revision of the simple Marxist cycle theories was offered by Michael Kalecki, who reinterpreted the dynamics of the reserve army of labor theory.[30] According to Kalecki the working class enjoys a greatly enhanced class position in an economic expansion. Full employment, a consequence of expansion, leads to a changing worker psychology; no longer worried about immediate day-to-day job security, workers become progressively more militant and assertive. This tends to upset the balance of power between the classes, and the ruling capitalist hierarchy moves to reestablish its dominance. To this purpose the capitalist firms work in complicity with the state to engineer a crippling recession, thus destroying the workers' sense of job security and forcing them to worry more about their daily bread than about larger political issues. Cycles for Kalecki are, therefore, politically motivated, designed to restore proper labor discipline, not the profit margin.

The main difference between Kalecki's and Marx's cycle theories is that for Kalecki the primary causal factor is not the squeeze on profits. In fact, Kalecki argues that profits do not necessarily diminish during a period of sustained growth. In Kalecki's eyes the problem is maintaining a well-disciplined, nonpolitical, labor force.

But the issue of the profit squeeze has figured in the work of other contemporary Marxists. Two of them, Raford Boddy and James Crotty, have empirically investigated the existence or absence of falling profits in expansionary periods. Boddy and Crotty, however, make a revision of their own. They disagree with Kalecki because they find convincing evidence of falling profits, but they also differ from Marx in believing that rising wages, not improved conditions, are the main cause of diminished profit margins.

Boddy and Crotty divide the expansionary phase into two parts. In the first half of the upswing, investment grows and productivity surges upward. Wages increase, but not as fast as productivity, so profit margins increase too. Along with the expansion unemployment begins to drop, but the relative power of capital over labor is not diminished since workers must compete among themselves for the available jobs.

In the second half of the expansion, however, the ratio of profits to wages begins to decline. Rising wages have now caught up with and passed productivity increases, and profit margins decline accordingly. There are two reasons for this: first, say Boddy and Crotty, "in the latter part of the expansion, the depletion of building space requires that the composition of investment shift towards structures. Structures have a weaker impact than equipment on labor productivity."[31] As the expansion continues and available structural capacity is used up, the firm must construct new buildings. Since new buildings generally do not increase worker productivity as much as the new machines purchased in the first half of the expansion, productivity gains become slower.

The second reason for the declining profit-to-wage ratio is the now familiar one of the increased bargaining strength of workers. By the middle of the expansion, the economy approaches full employment and workers no longer have to compete vigorously with their peers for jobs. Indeed, Boddy and Crotty give evidence of surging labor militancy during the second halves of expansionary periods. Only through higher wages, they say, can the militant workers be appeased. Workers tend less and less to compete among themselves and they focus their collective attention on the owners of the firm. Boddy and Crotty remark that "falling unemployment rates lead to a unification of the work force because they reduce wage differentials between workers and even skill or job classification differentials, leaving the work force more homogeneous."[32]

There is, however, another way to deal with worker militancy: engineer a recession. Although corporate profits continue to decline in a contraction, the recession resets the dial of the economy to the start of the expansionary cycle, where industrial profits are the highest and increase the most. Thus, Boddy and Crotty picture a profit margin cycle imposed on the business cycle:

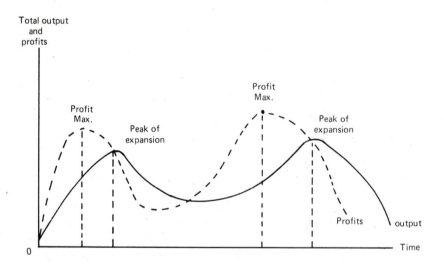

Boddy and Crotty's theory is related to the reserve army theory, and hinges on the incompatibility between full employment and profitability. It is important to note that the source of instability here is not capital accumulation, but labor's demand for better wages. Boddy and Crotty blame class struggle for capitalist instability. To blame class struggle implies that policy action controlling labor's wages might help stabilize the economy.

This implication raises strong objections from other Marxists who see capitalist cycles leading to socialist transformation, not to a more enlightened incomes policy. One of these, Howard Sherman,[33] believes the erosion of profits is really due to drastic increases in the prices of raw materials. Wages, says Sherman, always decrease relative to profits in upswings so they cannot possibly be the cause of declining profits. Because relative wages are declining, the problem of underconsumption sets in and combines with increasing costs of production, due to rising raw material prices, to diminish profit ratios.

In a rebuttal to Sherman, Boddy and Crotty give evidence that although the price of raw materials increases significantly during the first half of the expansion, those prices do not increase faster than output prices in the second half. Boddy and Crotty reassert that wages increase in the second half faster than prices and their data reflect this assertion. Sherman's response to Boddy and Crotty focuses on their interpretation of the capitalist system. He argues that they ignore the role of monopoly and consider the cycle only in terms of a competitive market.

Whether Boddy and Crotty, or Sherman, or somebody else has discovered the proper theory of falling profits may depend on one's conception of the competitive status of the economy. Boddy and Crotty build their arguments on a fundamental assumption of competition. Sherman criticizes them for this and points to the fact that monopoly and other market power structures must be considered since they now seem to be the rule of the day. He notes the Marxist view that society is in a continual process of change through time, and to take account of this, Marxists too must alter their theories, in this case to account for an economic structure dominated by monopolies.

One attempt to explain the function of monopolies in the modern capitalist economy, a report to the U.S. Congress by Howard Wachtel and Peter Adelsheim, explains how the pricing and output decisions of monopolies are fundamentally different from those of firms in competitive economies. They show that the effect of monopoly is to weaken further the impact of economy policy in stabilizing the economy, but at the same time show that monopolies can work to counteract the effects of the underconsumption problem.

In a perfectly competitive world faced with falling aggregate demand, if a firm began unilaterally to raise prices to maintain profit margins, it would lose its customers. If all firms raised their prices together, real wages and the purchasing power of workers would be reduced. This, in turn, could bring on an underconsumption crisis. But if firms are not competitive, they need worry much less about the former problem because of their power to set prices and control product demand. And as we have seen before, a firm that can set prices will tend to raise prices in the face of falling demand in order to keep profits high. Competitive firms would lower them to increase sales in the same circumstances. The usual description of such behavior is that firms now generally engage in some form of markup pricing.[34]

The growth in importance of large, non-price-competitive firms contradicts the usual policy assumption that prices will likely come down in a recession. Keynesians and CEIs have based much of their economic apparatus on the claim that a recession would cause prices to fall and that was the explanation for the 1980-81 and 1981-82 recessions. Wachtel, however, paints the picture much as do the Post-Keynesian Institutionalists.* With large firms predominant, a downturn will bring not only rising unemployment, but also rising prices — in a word, stagflation.

A recession, often considered by standard economists as the only way to restore economic conditions, affects large firms less even though they are the main cause and perpetuators of the slump. Instead, the working class, who have lost jobs and bargaining power, and the small businesses, who must contend with reduced demand, rising interest rates, and higher costs in general, are the innocent victims. When it becomes politically impossible to continue the recession, the government moves to strengthen the economy. In the meantime, workers have lost much time and much power and many small competitive firms have been driven out of business. The large firms, however, because of their internal financial structure and their market practices, are able to withstand a recession for relatively long time periods. When finally the government steps in, these are the firms that stand to be the major benefactors. Though inflation may not have been greatly damped by the recession, an expansionary phase begins and continues until big businesses once again need a recession to discipline labor.

Wachtel and Adelsheim's theory of markup pricing and monopoly behavior illustrates how a monopolistic economy is able to confront the basic instabilities caused by both the increasing organic composition of capital and by the exhaustion of the reserve army. By controlling prices and production and by turning recessions to their advantage,

---

*As a sign of its excellence, the Wachtel and Adelsheim study defies classification. We place it in the Marxist chapter because its basic theory, markup pricing, is derived from Kalecki and is complementary to Marxist crisis theory.

monopolies have been able to fend off the imminent capitalist crisis. But how does a monopolistic economy handle the problem of under-consumption? If monopolists raise prices beyond competitive levels in both expansions and recessions, then workers' real wages must at some point be cut to where they cannot purchase all that is produced. If it were otherwise, profits relative to wages could not be increasing. How have monopolists made up for this lack of demand? The answer is that they have gone overseas in search of new markets. Whereas competitive firms are normally too small to generate overseas operations, the larger and more powerful monopolies have deep pockets of resources from which to draw the initially needed investment funds. So while Wachtel and Adelsheim share many ideas with the other theorists in this chapter, they differ fundamentally in the view that monopoly has stabilized the economy and has allowed mechanisms to develop which can avoid the inevitable breakdown.

Which of these theories, if any, comes closest to explaining the experience of the past years? In the next section we will explore this question.

EXPLANATIONS OF THE CURRENT CRISIS

The theories just discussed deal primarily with the reasons for the existence of the business cycle in capitalist economies. Behind all of these theories, however, is the implicit notion that one day the cycles will build into an economic crisis and the demise of capitalism. But how can one know when this crisis has finally arrived? What are the undeniable signs? This was a problem with the long-swing theorists as well.

For contemporary Marxists a crisis is no longer an indicator of the imminence of capitalist collapse. Instead, periodic cycles build up the inherent contradictions of capitalism over time and eventually resolve into economic crises, crises which presage major change, but not necessarily total collapse. Crises in this sense are distinguished from normal cycles by three characteristic features. First, the economy behaves very differently in a crisis than it does in a normal recovery. For example, in a typical cyclical recovery one expects profits to increase by one or more of the mechanisms mentioned above, and this will lead to increased investment activity. One indicator of a crisis then may be the stagnation of the investment level when one normally expects it to rise. Second, a crisis is felt universally by the capitalist world economy; it is not just a domestic problem. Here one may expect the international economy to become very unpredictable and unstable. Third,

while cyclical periods generally do not unsettle fundamental social relationships, a crisis manifests a notable and significant change in the way
the two major classes relate to each other. If today we are in a crisis,
it must be shown that each of these three elements holds true. In order
to do that we must turn to the historical experience which has led up
to the 1980s.

In the nineteenth century the international capitalist order was
overseen by Great Britain. During this era the corporations of Great
Britain, the dominant actors in international affairs, took advantage of
their country's colonial expansion and reaped great profits from the
British colonies. But the British system of imperialism and colonial
governments attracted many competitors from France, Germany and
the U.S.; and by the end of World War I, Britain could no longer provide order in the competition among capitalist trading nations. As a
consequence, trade relations and international markets became quite
unstable during this period.

Due to its geographic advantage and increased industrial might
the U.S. emerged from World War II as the leading economic power.
In 1944 at the Bretton Woods conference the U.S. solidified its position
as the provider of economic order among capitalist trading nations.
New York replaced London as the financial center of the world, and
the U.S. dollar was to serve as both international money and a reserve
currency.[35]

This new position in the international economy made foreign
markets more accessible to U.S. business concerns. European countries
needed to build up reserves of U.S. dollars since the dollar had become
the standard currency for most of international trade. Thus, they
welcomed expansion by U.S. corporations as a source for building up
their reserve currency. Both foreign countries and the U.S. received
advantages from this expansion; the U.S. found other markets to consume their excess supply and foreign countries built up their reserves
with the influx of U.S. dollars resulting from capitalist expansion.
Given this scenario of mutual advantage, the U.S. accelerated its
penetration of the old European and Japanese empires. The U.S. built
up a system of military bases around the world which Marxists claim
was designed to maintain access to cheap raw materials and provide
military security to the multinational corporations. Those countries
which complied with U.S. imperialism received military assistance.
Governments which opposed U.S. penetration were overthrown. Examples are Iran and Guatemala. In this regard U.S. support of Britain
in the Falklands war with Argentina was a foregone conclusion.

Between the end of WWII and 1980 the foreign direct investments
of U.S. corporations grew from $10 billion to $213 billion. Domestic

opposition to imperialism was deflected through the accusation of communism and those who disagreed with foreign policy were blacklisted and humiliated. Marxists see the collaboration between government and business during this period of imperialistic expansion as support for the claim that the state serves the interests of the capitalist class. U.S. hegemony worked to protect business firms from the effects of low demand, using a combination of political and economic power.

However, the very nature of this expansion portended a long-run breakdown of power. The more investments were made in foreign countries, the greater became these countries' competitive stance among trading nations. Eventually Western Europe and Japan became capitalist rivals with the U.S., and the mutual advantage of imperialistic expansion collapsed.

In addition to the increasingly powerful bargaining position of Europe and Japan, Third World revolutionary forces were becoming more difficult and more expensive to contain. Perhaps the ultimate threat to continued U.S. hegemony manifested itself in the U.S. failure to maintain power in Vietnam. This defeat highlighted the ever more apparent U.S. inability to organize and control the competitive order of the world capitalist system.

The various forces threatening U.S. hegemony culminated in the breakdown of the Bretton Woods Agreement. Fixed exchange rates were replaced by a system of floating exchange rates. Floating rates can be very unstable because of the increased currency speculation and because many capitalist countries try to manipulate the exchange rates through banking practices and currency controls. Such instability has a profound effect on the quantity of foreign investment. In times of political and economic instability, such as those engendered by the move to floating exchange rates, financial assets are favored over capital accumulation. That is, corporations will delay their capital investments and await the reestablishment of international stability.

Such corporate behavior can easily be analyzed in the Marxist terms of underconsumption. During an expansion corporations find that they are producing an excess of goods. Hence, they look for other markets to absorb their surplus output. If these other markets are not stable and profitable, corporations will naturally choose not to invest until stability and profitability return. In the meantime they will attempt to build up their financial assets while waiting for stable market conditions to evolve. One repercussion of this drop in investment is an increase in the balance of trade deficit, for as corporations cut back foreign investments, exports also will decline. Hence, the stability of the international economy has serious implications for the capitalist system.

Also accompanying the decline in U.S. hegemony was the end of easy access to the raw materials of Third World countries. Third World nationalism and mutual cooperation combined with Soviet support to those opposing the U.S., severely restricting U.S. influence on international markets. Most important, the U.S. could no longer buy unlimited amounts of raw materials at inexpensive rates. The price of oil, for example, has risen more than tenfold in the years since 1973.

The importance of access to raw materials can best be understood through Sherman's analysis of the profit squeeze. Before the decline in U.S. hegemony, the price of raw materials would not increase during an expansion because the U.S. had control over unlimited amounts of them. That is, increases in demand for raw materials could easily be met without price increases. However, with the decline of U.S. ability to control the world economy, the supply of raw materials became more inelastic. Now, when demand for raw materials goes up, the prices rise, for Third World countries have gained more control over their resource deposits.

Marxists claim that imperialism and U.S. hegemony clearly enabled corporations to avoid the inherent capitalist problems of aggregate demand. Another way of controlling consumer demand focuses on the domestic economy, namely, the Keynesian method of demand management. Throughout the 1960s the government adopted a policy of expansion through spending. However, as the expansion continued for a number of years, corporate profits were squeezed. In this case much of the squeeze on profits was brought about by the exhaustion of the reserve army, for the unemployment level fell below 4 percent.

But if the government serves the capitalist class, as the Marxists say, why did they continue a policy of expansion? The answer to this question centers on the Vietnam War. From the Marxist viewpoint, the state was aiding the owners of production while fighting in Indochina, for they were attempting to protect and provide for imperialistic expansion. However, in doing this, the state simultaneously overstimulated the economy at home because it was not politically possible to increase taxes to pay for such an unpopular war. This policy of not allowing a recession to discipline workers not only led to declining profit rates for corporations, but also ignited the fires of inflation.

What was the corporations' response to the continued decline in profits? In order to meet the increased demand, capitalists needed to expand their capacity to produce. But the money needed to expand capacity output is derived from profits, and profits were declining. Thus, in order to meet the demand of consumers, corporations were driven to dramatically greater borrowing for investment.

The effects of borrowing in order to maintain corporate investments were not seen until the economy was allowed to go into recession and then begin another period of expansion. According to Boddy and Crotty, in the first half of expansion corporate profits increase and investment also increases as corporations expand their output capacity. However, when the expansion began, after the light recession of 1973, corporations were unable to put their increased profits into investment; rather, they had to pay off the debts they had incurred and the interest on those debts. Capital expenditures did not increase, and this circumstance prevented the growth in production and employment necessary for the recovery. Keynesian demand-management policies no longer worked.

In addition, Marxists suggest that after World War II the U.S. was able to sustain lower unemployment rates than in the prewar period mainly due to a social contract negotiated between organized labor and the largest corporate employers.[36] But this social contract broke down in the crisis of the 1970s. After the purging of the left-wing elements in the late 1940s, organized labor agreed to maintain labor discipline and refrain from actions which would threaten profitability, management prerogatives, or political stability. The largest corporations agreed to maintain economic growth and low unemployment rates in the organized sectors.[37] Increased unemployment rates during the 1970s reflected the breakdown of this social contract. Organized labor was unable to fulfill its part of the contract due to its declining influence among workers. Corporations were unable to fulfill their part of the contract due to the intensification of foreign competition and the other aspects of the 1970s crisis which forced a slowdown in the growth rate of real wages.

Also the rising influence of unorganized groups of workers and Sun Belt capitalists hastened the breakdown of the social contract. Since the 1960s, women, black, and Hispanic workers have demanded a greater share of the national income, while medium-sized and newer larger-size firms, operating out of the Sun Belt, have begun to compete for a greater share of economic and political power. Therefore, even if organized labor and the largest corporations had agreed to maintain the social contract, unorganized workers and Sun Belt corporations would have hindered its implementation.

With the breakdown in U.S. hegemony, the ineffectiveness of demand management, and the breakup of the social contract, U.S. policymakers made an initial turn to two other methods for stabilizing the economy and restoring corporate profit levels: controls and planning. In Marxist analyses both of these methods are impractical, and they will not stabilize the economy. Wage and price controls attempt to slow down the rate of inflation in the economy which is often blamed as the primary cause of instability in the economy. Although controls appear to restrain both classes in the system, radicals argue that they are aimed at the labor sector to slow down wage increases while allowing profits to increase, and thus are a weapon in the class struggle. They claim that increases in wages are visible and across-the-board changes, and therefore easy to control. In contrast, changes in prices are continuous and involve different increases for thousands of individual commodities. For example, the price changes of steel vary according to the different products produced, the size, and the weight of those products. Moreover, prices can be raised merely by changing the quality or quantity of the commodities. Hence, during the Nixon wage-price freeze consumers complained that the amount of coffee in a certain size container decreased, or the level of cereal inside a box of breakfast cereal declined while the price remained constant. Because price changes are less visible, they are harder to control. Wage-price controls become wage controls only. Once the labor class realizes the inequity of controls they will not follow them, and hence controls as a weapon in the class struggle will not work in the long run.

Economists also argue that, as a stabilization policy, controls do not solve the problem of inflation, but only postpone it to a future time. Instead of controls, then, economists have turned to state planning in order to stabilize the economy. Planning demands that domestic economic decisions be made by the state. As one might guess Marxists cringe at the mere suggestion of planning, for to put the economy in the hands of the state is essentially equivalent to allowing the business sector free rein over the whole range of economic decisions; for any agency set up by the state is most concerned with the interests of the business class.

Marxists argue that evidence of planning favoring business firms and hurting workers can be seen through two recent legal decisions.[38] The first involves the right of labor to strike over outstanding issues in contract negotiations. The issue surfaced during negotiations in the steel industry in which corporations convinced union leadership to accept a "no-strike" agreement, which means that outstanding issues of the contract would be submitted to binding arbitration. The "no-strike" agreement was subsequently upheld by the U.S. district court when the union, unhappy with the way the provision worked, contested its legality.

The second legal decision involves the right to stage a wildcat strike, a strike in which workers walk off the job without union sanction, over specific grievances during the term of the contract. A Supreme court decision in 1962 had prohibited any injunction against wildcat strikes. But in 1970 that court overturned the earlier decision so that arbitration, not strikes, would prevail. Public policy, in favoring business, had interfered with labor's most powerful tool for influencing the production process. But this didn't slow down wildcat strikes. Partly in response to the contradictions embodied in the social contract and partly to deteriorating working conditions (including a sharp increase in the injury-frequency rate in manufacturing), the proportion of wildcat to total strikes increased from 32 percent during 1961-67, to 40 percent during 1968-73, and to 43 percent during 1974-77.[39]

This Marxist analysis clearly leads to the conclusion that the economy is in a state of crisis. As stated earlier the three characteristics distinguishing a crisis are: (1) the economy is behaving differently than usual in recovery, (2) instability pervades the world economy, and (3) basic economic and social relationships change. The first of these conditions is manifested in the movement of investment as seen in the first timid and unsteady expansion following the 1973 recession. Resulting from a substantial increase in corporate debt needed to maintain production during the war in Indochina, corporate levels of investment did not rise in the expansion of 1974, nor again in the 1981 recovery. Profits were used to pay off interest on debts and also allocated to areas other than investment in the production process.

The second condition clearly holds, for the international economy is in substantial disarray. This results from the breakdown of U.S. hegemony which culminated in the Vietnam War and which led to the dissolution of the Bretton Woods Agreement. This dissolution has profoundly affected trading relationships between leading capitalist countries; the world economy awaits a new order. Recognition of this fact is symbolized by the work of the Trilateral Commission.

The third condition for crisis can be noted in changes in market structure and the subsequent changes in the organization of unions, which have followed the change from a competitive market to a market of conglomeration.

THE MARXIST ANSWER: A REDISTRIBUTION OF ECONOMIC POWER

Based on the above analysis, Marxists traditionally have proposed one policy: "Working men of all countries, unite!"[40] Marx himself envisioned the capitalist system ending in a revolution of the proletariat. However, present day Marxists do not definitely predict that the system will crumble in glorious revolution; but they believe that workers, through the organization of trade unions, will increase their power in the production process and will eventually take control of that process. Perhaps Marxists have cooled their traditionally drastic conclusions as a result of the changes which have evolved in the structure of the production process. In focusing on the relationship between the type of market and the level of unity among the workers in that market, an interesting connection can be detected.

Marx saw a capitalist system which was fairly competitive. Correspondingly, when unions sprang up they were organized according to the different competitive industries. The most effective unions organized all the workers of the relevant work force in a particular industry. If labor's struggle takes place through the medium of labor unions, the so-called working class is really divided up among hundreds of different industries. Labor is composed of hundreds of different groupings, each actively participating in its own private struggle, rather than joining in one group to struggle against the capitalist system in a unified way. Under this model of trade unions, Marx predicted that trade unions would not survive, for they do not work for the class as a whole.

In contrast to Marx, today's Marxists critique a system which operates through monopoly and oligopoly and multinational corporations. Wachtel indicates that there is a continuous movement toward concentration of capital as evidenced through the tendency of the concentrated firms to employ markup pricing in recessions. The effect that this change in market structure has on Marx's analysis potentially favors the position of trade unions. The horizontal integration of capital has transformed the structure of the market in such a way that there is a growing tendency toward fewer and fewer employers. Instead of many different industries formed according to product lines, corporate mergers have created a market characterized by increasing centralization and conglomeration. In theory, this type of market structure should help to create unity in the labor class. As the extent of horizontal integration increases, fewer but larger unions will be needed to direct a struggle against a smaller number of employers and industries, even though one employer might own several product lines. Given this trend in the economy, labor will have the opportunity to increase its power tremendously if workers operate much more as a class.

Clearly, today's unions have not seized this opportunity. But with the increasing tendency toward conglomeration on the business side, Marxists believe unions can remain effective and powerful only if they too organize across product lines and industries, and begin to seek a voice in the control of the corporations. It is this hope which has led

Marxists toward a policy of organization through trade unions rather than a revolution of the proletariat. No longer is the medium of trade unions doomed to failure.

In effect, then, the Marxists offer us no stabilization policy prescriptions that the government can be requested to implement, for the Marxists have no confidence in the present form of government. Instead of prescribing policy, they present a critique of the entire capitalist system, showing why capitalist economies are subject to recurrent business cycles and intermittent major crises. Roger Alcaly sums up the problem of capitalist instability in the following statement: "In the most basic sense, crises can be said to dominate the dynamics of capitalist development because capitalism is a system of production for profit rather than production for use."[41] When profits are not high, investors hold back, causing recession. When profits are high they invest and an exaggerated boom ensues. In this way instability is unavoidable in a capitalist environment.

According to Marxists this problem can only be resolved through fundamental social change. The pattern of ownership, the distribution and control of profits, and the locus of production decisions must all be taken out of the hands of the few. Marxists argue that capitalists will never take the initiative to carry this out on their own. Nor can the government be expected to sponsor such radical changes. Therefore, Marxists rely on the working class to unify and work forcefully through the creation of large and powerful labor unions. Labor must use its collective influence and power to demand participation in the decisions that are normally reserved for the capitalist.

David Gordon offers a choice and a challenge in the conclusion to a recent article:

> Assuming that the U.S. economy is substantially restructured during the 1980s, we face a critical choice: Will internal corporate systems of control become even more centralized? Or shall we finally begin to move toward more participatory and democratic systems of worker coordination and self-management?[42]

CONCLUSION AND PROGNOSIS

The immediate response to any demand for labor participation in management, particularly in investment decisions, is to write it off as ideological and impractical. But if the labor movement in the U.S. is to maintain its bargaining position in the struggle with large conglomerates, it will have to expand and reorganize in the direction described above. Perhaps the key to success in the effort to establish a position in corporate investment decisions is political influence. Working collectively through unions, labor must break away from its traditional tie with the Democratic party and help form a new political party. In this way the working class will assure itself of representation in the legislation of public policy. What labor needs now is education; workers must understand the structure of the market and its intrinsic instability in order for them to oppose that structure for their own good and for the good of the country.

The Marxists are the only group of economic theorists who have a fully developed theory that explains the business fluctuations and the recurrent economic and social crises. Right now, they say, we are suffering through one of the times of crisis. But these could be avoided, they tell us, if major changes in the social, economic, and political structure took place. First, productive resources must be owned by a much wider range of people, and labor must participate in the decisions of how to distribute profits. Second, stability in the world economy needs to be restored via international cooperation rather than competition and antagonism. And third, labor unions must be allowed and encouraged to evolve in the manner outlined above.

Few people, however, are willing to lend a very sympathetic ear, for while Marxists provide a coherent critique of the present crisis, their proposals are vague and sound like slogans. Moreover, the fact that the Russians, Chinese, and Poles claim to have built a socialist system in accordance with Marxist theory is a terrible albatross for American Marxists.

Capitalism has seen the U.S. through a great number of prosperous years. True, admit the Marxists, but the curtain is falling fast on the era of capitalism. If prosperity is to continue, and if progress is again to prevail, then an unbending allegiance to the free market system must fall by the way. Marxists warn that one day they will be vindicated and proven right. We shall see.

But whatever our views on the correctness of the Marxist analysis, let us appreciate it for the insights it provides as the only coherent theoretical structure which does not see recurrent cycles and depressionlike conditions as an accident. They are predictable from its framework.

Let us turn now from these theoretical frameworks which have dominated economists' thinking on the modern macroeconomy and its problems. We will start with our own theoretical stance, then look more closely at our contemporary economy, and finally in the last chapter offer our own menu of policies for dealing with the current problems.

PART THREE

The Alternative:
Post-Keynesian Institutionalism

7. Toward a New Political Economy: Methodological and Historical Considerations

Before beginning to develop our new directions in political economy, we can summarize our reasons for rejecting the old ways. Long-swing theories provide no guidelines for dealing with our problems, nor even a clear hold on where we are in the cycle. Marxian analysis holds out the possibility of useful insights in understanding the present crisis and directions for the future. But Marxism as an ideology is so uncongenial to the American temper that it has little hope of becoming the core for a new political economy. We will incorporate some Marxian analysis in the following chapters, but a political economy which can deal in a meaningful fashion with the present U.S. economy will deviate substantially from Marxism.

In our view, both Conservative Economic Individualism and mainstream U.S. Keynesianism are bankrupt theories. Whether they ever were applicable or just historically fortunate enough to seem so is not very important, because the present economic dilemma is a strong indictment of both. Neither appears capable of coping with the myriad problems today confronting our economy and our society. So we move on to new territory.

Perhaps the CEIs and traditional Keynesians are limited in that they simply do not understand (or more probably refuse to believe) that the economy does not work according to their claims. Business firms are mere profit maximizers, they say. Workers look for jobs that pay the highest wages and offer the most leisure with little regard to job satisfaction or personal fulfillment. The U.S. industrial economy is almost exclusively competitive in nature. Corporations borrow and invest almost entirely on the basis of the interest rate and expectations of a certain rate of return on their investment. Workers earn in accordance with what they contribute to production (i.e., no one is exploited). The list could go on, but the point is made. CEI and traditional Keynesian analyses distort greatly the nature of the real world. Certainly each of these statements has a small element of truth in it, and as a result each can be defended to an extent, but at the same time none of the assertions even begins to explain the functioning of the actual economy. People do not always act rationally, maximizing this and minimizing that. Small firm competition does not prevail in the United States. And noncompetitive firms do not act merely to maximize profits. Investment planning has relatively little to do with the interest rate, and large corporations attempt with some success to plan the sort of economy they will function in.

The obvious question arises: does it matter that the real world differs from the ideal one of these economists? CEIs and Keynesians respond that they do not claim that everything they say about the economy is completely true, but since their conceptions of people and their activity in the economic world capture most of the relevant information, their theories will perform adequately with respect to economic understanding and predictions of economic phenomena. In answer to the question, then, these economists would say "No, differences between the real economy and that of our theory do not invalidate our theory." As Milton Friedman has said so frequently: the reality of the theory's assumptions is unimportant. It is the ability to predict correctly that counts. Let us investigate this claim.

FORMAL THEORY, PREDICTION AND STANDARD ECONOMICS

Both traditional theories claim to be "positive economics." Positive economics, with its logical positivist model of explanation, has found wide acceptance among economists since the publication in the 1950s of I. M. D. Little's *Critique of Welfare Economics* and Milton Friedman's *Essays in Positive Economics.*[1] Predictability is the crucial element in positive economics. Economic science is advanced by logically deducing a hypothesis from a general theory. These hypotheses act as predictions of correlational relationships in the real world. That is, the "positive science investigator" pursues a testing of the degree of correspondence between his or her predictions and the empirical evidence provided by the real world. A high degree of correspondence or a "good fit," acts to confirm the theory (or at least keeps the hypotheses among the not-yet-falsified); a low level or lack of correspondence indicates a flaw in the theory. It is by testing that disputes are resolved, and if the predictions derived from one model prove "better" than the corresponding predictions drawn from another, the former is tentatively selected as preferable. In every case, the theory preferred is the one which best explains the observable phenomena of the economic world. Thus, empirical testing is seen as the key to theory selection in economics.

Since the validity of a model is to be judged by its predictive ability, the realism of its assumptions or the static nature of its structure become irrelevant issues. In a formal model, all assumptions are more or less abstract and unrealistic because a model cannot, by definition, capture or reproduce the whole of reality. Consequently, assumptions facilitate abstraction, which enables the economist to explain the underlying order.

Since standard economists place so much weight on the ability to predict as the means of verifying the truth of a theory, it is necessary to explore the success of such an endeavor in economics. Successful prediction of economic phenomena has been notably absent over past years. This failure is highlighted by the models' inability to deal with the nation's recent experience with unemployment, inflation, and the energy crisis. Insofar as positive economic theories are to be "judged solely by [their] predictive ability," why is it that, in practice, when economists' theories fail to fit the facts, they are not rejected?

Let us analyze the controversy over the causes of changes in output and the price level as an example to show that differences between Keynesians and the "monetarist" wing of the CEIs cannot be resolved on the basis of empirical results. We will find that since prediction is not sufficient, the reality of the theory's basic assumptions and propositions becomes important. In addition, we will attempt to show that underlying economic philosophies provide better guidance to understanding the differences between the two groups.

In a study for the Commission on Money and Credit,[2] Milton Friedman and David Meiselman set out to test empirically the predictive power of monetarist versus Keynesian theories of business fluctuations. They predicted consumption expenditures for each year between 1897 and 1958 using two different equations. They divided nominal income Y into autonomous expenditure A and induced expenditure B. The "Keynesian" equation used autonomous expenditure A as the independent variable and induced expenditure B as the dependent variable or the variable to be explained. The "monetarist" equation used the quantity of money M as the independent variable and induced expenditure B as the dependent variable. Autonomous expenditure A was defined as the sum of net private investment plus government deficit on income and product account plus net foreign balance. Quantity of money M was defined as currency plus demand deposits adjusted plus time deposits at all commercial banks.

Friedman and Meiselman claimed that their tests over the entire period 1897-1958 indicated that the quantity of money M was a better predictor of induced expenditure B than was autonomous expenditure A. Tests of various sub-periods confirmed these results. They also claimed that the *change* in nominal M was a better predictor of the *change* in nominal B than was the *change* in nominal A. finally, any correlation between autonomous expenditure A and induced expenditure B was claimed to reflect the effect of the quantity of money, M, on A and B simultaneously. Thus Friedman and Meiselman concluded that the CEI monetarist interpretation of business fluctuations was more accurate than Keynesian theory.

Keynesian rebuttals were quickly forthcoming. The *American Economic Review* printed two articles attacking the Friedman and Meiselman work, one by Albert Ando and Franco Modigliani and the other by Michael De Prano and Thomas Mayer.[3] Friedman and Meiselman wrote a reply in the same issue defending their procedures and results.[4] The following paragraphs briefly summarize the criticisms.[5]

One line of attack was to argue that the equations used in the test were so simplified that the results were relevant only to the abstract world represented by the models. Friedman and Meiselman gave no reasons why the results should be relevant to the actual economy. In addition, the two theories should be represented in equations that have been simplified to the same degree. However, Friedman and Meiselman presented no objective way of determining relative simplicity for two different models or equations.

The critics argued, further, that the test results need not hold for different, and particularly for more complex, specifications of the two theories, that is, the results were not statistically robust. Different definitions of the A and M variables could make the Keynesian autonomous expenditure A outperform the CEI monetarist quantity of money M.

Ando and Modigliani argued that Friedman and Meiselman's specification of autonomous expenditure A and, therefore, of induced expenditure B were incorrect in Keynesian terms. Friedman and Meiselman's simplification of Keynesian theory specified all investment, government spending, taxes, and imports as exogenously determined. At the same time, they assumed that all consumption was endogenously determined and that the balanced-budget multiplier was zero. Ando and Modigliani used a different specification of the Keynesian model and claimed that the Friedman-Meiselman definition was selected to maximize support for the CEI monetarist position. Friedman and Meiselman retorted that their definition was not *incorrect,* merely *selective.* De Prano and Mayer offered twenty different reasonable definitions of autonomous expenditure A and cast further doubt on the Friedman-Meiselman results, since the conclusions were sensitive to different definitions.

One implication of the above controversy is that the results of testing competing theories are dependent on the statistical testing procedures. Because there is no way to determine objectively the relative degree of simplicity or the proper definitions of the variables, it becomes impossible to settle disputes between rival theories by appeal to empirical testing. In fact, empirical testing has not been able to determine whether the predominant causation is the Keynesian A to Y to M, or the CEI monetarist M to Y to B. Consequently, there is no basis for deciding between the theories.

William Poole and Elinda Kornblith replicated the tests of all the previous contestants and, in addition, extended the tests to cover the 1959-70 period.[6] Their findings are worth quoting:

> Our findings emphasize the futility of the R^{2*} game. The F-M critics all came up with definitions of autonomous expenditures that produced regression R^2s rivaling or exceeding the R^2 for M_2. But beyond the period of estimation many of these relationships fall apart. Whatever one's biases in terms of the Keynesian and quantity theory approaches, these findings indicate that none of the single equation models predict the future very well. . . . In terms of verified empirical knowledge, economists have good reason to be modest.[7]

The first implication of the Keynesian-CEI monetarist debate is that, contrary to the logical positivist position of standard economics, empirical tests seldom will resolve theoretical disputes. This is true because there are insurmountable testing problems.

The testing process in economics is flawed in several serious ways. First, there are substantial problems in specifying the key variables. For example, what is the proper empirical definition of the theoretical concept quantity of money M? Should it be M_1 (currency plus demand deposits), M_{1a}, M_{1b}, or some other definition? Should large certificates of deposit be included and then excluded as their importance changes over time?[8] Should it be the size of M or its rate of change that is used? Monetarists cannot agree even among themselves. The same problems plague the empirical specification of the Keynesian theoretical concept of autonomous expenditure, A. There seems no objective way to decide these questions. Friedman has, of course, argued that the definitional

* A measure of statistical correlation.

issues can be settled empirically — use the definition that works. But this ultimately fails because different empirical approaches give different empirical results over different periods.

A second problem that plagues econometric testing is the question of the proper leads and lags. What is the proper time lag structure for testing the impact of M on Y? Problems of lag specification (we simply do not know what they are) make estimating the true lag structure next to impossible. The temptation is to select the structure that maximizes the R^2 between M and Y or A and B, as the case may be.

A third difficulty is the problem of distinguishing cause from effect in the test. For example, as mentioned earlier, does causation run M to Y to B as the CEI monetarists say, or A to Y to M as the Keynesians maintain? In other words, is M exogenously determined (by the Federal Reserve) or endogenously determined by other variables within the system, or some of both? While causality tests do exist and are used with increasing frequency they are not yet powerful enough to enable us to resolve the issue.

Finally, both the methods of collecting and the construction of empirical data are open to judgment, and such judgment can affect the final results.

Because of these econometric difficulties, the choice among alternative theories cannot be made solely on empirical grounds. In addition, the desirable qualities of a logical model — simplicity, generality, specificity, and aesthetic quality — must be used, and the relative evaluation of these qualities is largely determined by one's own vision of the economic process and attendant policy implications.

A second implication of the debate is that the basis for theory selection must be sought elsewhere than in empirical verification. Our claim is that the empirical controversy has always been secondary because the underlying issue is the difference in policy orientation. Theories are chosen because they yield policy implications that are compatible with one's vision of the economic process. An underlying and central issue, not touched by the debates, is over the degree of stability of a market economy.[9] Monetarist CEIs believe that the economy is basically stable and that active stabilization policy will actually result in destabilization. The Keynesians, who are also firm believers in the efficacy of the market system, believe that the economy has fundamental instabilities that require active intervention by government. No amount of empirical testing can finally mediate between these two views.

Where does this leave economy policy? It leaves it guided by a free-market ideology, whether CEI or Keynesian, whose "scientific" (in the sense of empirical proof) basis is questionable, at best. This is the inevitable outcome when economists delude themselves into believing that theoretical controversies can be resolved by appeal to statistical

testing. Since adverse results can always be explained away, the economist is left only with ideology as support. To make matters worse, this
situation is usually not recognized. Economists would do better to drop
these "scientific" pretensions and accept the fact that they are "story-
tellers."[10] In that case, statistical testing would become merely one more
piece of evidence contributing to the reality and coherence of the "story."
At the minimum, this methodological approach would generate caution
and humility. It might also direct the economist's attention to questions
of institutional structure that have been neglected by standard economists
because they have not been amenable to econometric investigation.

TOWARD A NEW POLITICAL ECONOMY: POST-KEYNESIAN INSTITUTIONALISM

There is an increasing number of economists, including ourselves,
who respond emphatically, "Yes, it is important that our theories have
a direct correspondence with observable economic reality." The essential characteristics of the economic world are not incorporated into
either CEI or Keynesian theory. Consequently neither approach will
adequately explain economic activity, predict economic results accurately, or propose decent public policies. The seventies are ample evidence for this claim, at least for the Keynesians. It is expected that
the 1980s will provide the same sort of incriminating evidence against
the CEIs.

In the remainder of the book we synthesize the work of these
economists, including our own, into a coherent "story" of the way the
economy operates, why it is malfunctioning, and what can be done to
make it perform better. This synthesis we call Post-Keynesian Institutionalism (PKI) to give it a label comparable to Keynesianism, Conservative Economic Individualism, and Marxism. We use this label
because its roots are in Keynes and in the American Institutionalists.[11]

The remainder of this chapter will present the pre-analytical world
view from which PKIs operate. Succeeding chapters will deal with
three other aspects of PKI thought: (1) the central features of PKI
theory; (2) the PKI explanation of the current stagflation; and (3) a set
of policy recommendations congruent with (1) and (2).

Methodology of Post-Keynesian Instutionalism: Look at the World, Then Theorize

We have intimated that Keynesians and CEIs profess to believe in
the existence of an ideal world defined by their theory of a market
economy. As it turns out, such economists frequently ignore important

knowledge about the real world. When, for example, it is suggested that much of the U.S. economy is not truly competitive, they do not accept this information as a new piece of useful data. Instead they either put forth monumental efforts to show that the suggestion is fatuous, or they ignore it altogether. CEIs and mainstream Keynesians frequently try to force the real economy into the mold of the ideal one they theorize about. Many of their policy prescriptions are consequently ill conceived and at odds with their supposed ends simply because they are founded on a theoretical economy and not the real one.

It is supposed, for instance, that policies which create a recession will reduce effective demand which is then supposed to force businesses to lower prices (or increase them more slowly) so they can sell more of their goods. Inflation will shrink quickly and when inflation falls, demand will increase again, workers will not expect inflationary wage gains, and all will be well. But what happens if businesses raise prices in the face of a recession instead of dropping them? In CEI and Keynesian eyes this certainly would be perverse behavior. And yet, anything more than a casual look at former recessions gives evidence that some businesses do indeed act in this fashion. Why would firms do this? There are several explanations, but few or none come from traditional economists. Instead of trying to explain such behavior they prefer to explain it away. Any business operating on such a basis, they would argue, is certainly not maximizing profits and therefore is not likely to remain in business long. In this way such evidence is ignored.

This is just one instance of the contradiction between the implications of the idealized economic system and the real world. Of course there are others and the implications for economic understanding are profound. If firms and individuals do not behave as they "should" according to the idealized system, then how do they act? Perhaps more importantly, why do they act that way? And finally, what is the significance of such behavior for the economic well-being of the public? The other theories cannot answer such questions and they do not even ask them. For PKIs, however, such problems are their bread and butter.

In general the PKI starts with a given situation and seeks to explain the dynamics of existing structures and institutions. What moves the economy? What makes it work? What kind of values does it support and instill? What motivates individuals to do anything? What is the nature of conflict and who has the power to get what they want and to influence structures and other people? By asking questions such as these the PKI economist hopes to come to an understanding of the way the economy actually functions.

PKIs believe that no two societies are alike. Each is the unique product of a unique set of historical events and the society's response to those events. Societies may be similar, but none are exactly the same. Nor are the people the same. Each social system is thus its own unique evolutionary system, one that changes over time in response to varying historical conditions.

Traditional economics, both CEI and Keynesianism, believes in the possibility of universal laws which transcend historical, cultural, and institutional differences between societies. Thus a market is a market is a market. Marxism has some similarity in that it holds that there are economic laws, but they are historically specific to a particular social system. Thus capitalism is capitalism is capitalism, no matter the country or time in which it operates.

On the other hand Post-Keynesian Institutionalists believe that so-called economic "laws" are nothing more than empirical generalizations that are historically specific and must be revised as culture and institutions change. Because of this belief PKIs concentrate on the particular circumstances of a system and their analysis is an important part of the overall analysis. Any evidence about actual behavior is accepted as a piece of information that must be fitted into the whole picture of the society.

But does all this have anything to do with the problems now faced by the U.S. economy? Certainly, because it implies that in order to understand the nature of the current crisis we must focus our attention on the current economic structure and not on the U.S. economic structure of the 19th century or on some concocted ideal of perfect competition. So while the CEIs and Keynesians focus on theoretical models of how the economy ought to work, the PKIs attempt to discover how the economy actually works. And not surprisingly they find that the root source of many of the ills facing the U.S. economy resides in the evolutionary developments of the structures or institutions that make up society — markets, corporations, labor-management relations, government.

The PKI approach to economic understanding, however, does have at least one serious drawback. Different economists may develop different explanations of the core causal factors in society. This cannot be avoided. While the CEI and Keynesian schools have developed a very formal, logically consistent and sophisticated (however unrealistic) body of theory from which most knowledgeable economists will derive the same results, no such corpus of theory exists among PKIs. As a result, different PKI economists see different factors as being the most crucial, and different PKI economists offer different solutions to economic problems.*

---

*In fact, some of the economists we would place in this category would be uncomfortable being classed in the same school of thought with some of the others.

But in spite of their differences PKIs still have much in common. At the methodological level, PKI economics can be characterized as holistic, systemic, and evolutionary. Social reality is seen as more than a specified set of relations; it is the process of change inherent in a set of social institutions which we call an economic system. The process of social change is not purely mechanical; it is the product of human action, but action which is definitely shaped and limited by the society in which it has its roots. Thus PKI is holistic because it focuses on the pattern of relations among parts and the whole. It is systemic because it believes that those parts make up a coherent whole and can be understood only in terms of the whole. It is evolutionary because changes in the pattern of relations are seen as the very essence of social reality.

At a more concrete level, PKI economics has an appreciation for the centrality of power and conflict in the economic process.

> The preoccupation with the role of conflict, power and coercion is an intellectual heritage which . . . early American institutionalists like Veblen and Commons have reformulated and integrated . . . into their analysis of "vested interests," absentee ownership, the economic role of the state, the legal foundations of capitalism, the importance of collective and political bargaining, public utility regulations and the analysis of collusion between financial, industrial and political power.[12]

This heritage is carried on today by John Kenneth Galbraith's work on the "planning system,"[13] Warren Samuels on law and economics,[14] Willard Mueller on antitrust,[15] Charles Craypo on the impact of conglomerate mergers on collective bargaining,[16] Michael Piore on dual labor markets,[17] and a host of scholars[18] — Joan Robinson, Alfred Eichner, John Cornwall, J. A. Kregel — on macrodynamics; the list could go on and on. They concentrate on the effect of changes in technology, social institutions, and distribution of power, treating them as an inherent part of the economic process.

PKIs emphasize the predominant role of *technology* in defining various power groups. Present technological levels that require mass production pit worker against management. Since technological developments have led to the growth of huge corporate enterprises, consumers are often pitted against producers, government bureaucrats square off against corporate planners, and so on. While given technologies do not in themselves absolutely determine the shape of society, it is changing technology that leads to conflict between different groups, realigns power, and initiates grand systemic change.

At the motivational level, PKI economics always has recognized the importance of "nonrational" human behavior in economic decision-making.[19] A thirst for power and adventure, a sense of independence, altruism, idle curiosity, custom, and habit may all be powerful motivations of economic behavior. Thus, PKIs have been particularly critical of the economic-man assumption: CEI or Keynesian rational, calculating individuals, harnessed to utility and profit maximization.[20]

These characteristics of PKI — holistic, systemic, evolutionary — combined with the appreciation for the centrality of power and conflict and the recognition of the importance of nonrational human behavior, differentiate PKI from standard economics. The CEI and Keynesian formal models simply cannot handle the range of variables, the specificity of institutions, and the nongenerality of behavior that are a part of PKI theory.

Beyond these characteristics of PKI thought, the central feature which links PKIs is their methodological predisposition, or simply put, the way they go about their work.[21] This link is found in the PKI propensity to explain their knowledge by "telling stories."[22] In other words, PKIs explain an economic or social system by means of a pattern model, a model which incorporates all relevant features of social action, gives them meaning and orders them into a coherent whole. The whole system is thus understood by linking these various parts (or subsystems) into a pattern of interaction which characterizes the essential nature of the larger system.

For the PKI, then, explanation of reality cannot be had through the application of universal laws, with successful predictions the only form of verification. Rather, an event or action is explained by identifying its place in a pattern that characterizes the ongoing processes of change in the whole system.

Thorstein Veblen, the recognized founder of the American Institutionalist tradition, brought this holistic philosophical orientation to the study of the U.S. economy. Veblen conceived of the economic order as an evolving scheme or a cultural process. His construction of a "systems economics" was to remain the point of reference from which later PKIs were to criticize the narrow "market economics of choice" espoused by standard economics. Samuels remarks: "The institutionalist paradigm focuses upon . . . an holistic and evolutionary view of the structure-behavior-performance of the economy . . . in a system of general interdependence or cumulative causation."[23] This could also serve as a summary of PKIs' methodology.

With such a starting point, that everything is affected by everything else, the PKI must develop a means to study given problems in the whole social system. Otherwise it would seem to be a hopelessly gigantic task. Obviously, though, if it is economic phenomena that are of most interest, then the PKI will begin looking at the particular structures, or subsystems, that seem to have the most pronounced impact on economic performance.

Alfred Eichner, a pioneering PKI, describes what a new political economy must do in a typically Western developed society:

> Under the systems approach, economics is no longer the study of how scarce resources are allocated. It is instead the study of how an economic system — defined as the set of social institutions responsible for meeting the material needs of society's members — is able to expand its output over time by producing and distributing a social surplus.[24]

Eichner takes it that the job of the economist is to study the system in all its different elements to understand how that system will function best to create and maintain a growing level of output. Eichner goes on to argue that the acid test for the validity of an economic theory in this sense of systems is whether or not certain actions (or policies) produce predicted results. If they do not, then the system has not been properly understood.[25] Whether PKIs will be given the chance to test their theory in this way is a question only time will answer.

One of the important implications of the systems approach and of the assumption that social systems are evolutionary is a different characterization of the economic process. The terminology used by PKIs includes historical time, dynamic behavior, and continuous change.

The concept of historical time was developed to counter the orthodox tendency to construct and refer to equilibrium models, a type of analysis which requires the use of what is known as logical time. Logical time takes no account of history and assumes that any point in the past can be reached again in the future, although past and future are terms not frequently used. The essence of the PKI claim is that individuals and society are travelling through time and can never return to previous states. When viewed in this way the concept of equilibrium rings resoundingly hollow, for who will know at what time, or in what situation, an equilibrium may be reached? The past is over and known with certainty, but the future is unknown and the road society travels is of uncertain destination.

The importance of the point is illustrated by a few relevant examples from the recent past. Who, for example, would have predicted the formation and apparent success of OPEC? Certainly not orthodox economists whose knowledge tells them that it is impossible for OPEC to exist. Milton Friedman predicted OPEC would survive less than six months. Few business analysts were able to foresee its advent either. Similarly, there seems to be no appropriate way of logically and rationally predicting what, where, and in what way corporate managers will choose to invest. Even the CEIs and Keynesians, who have developed wonderfully "precise" models, have a dismal record of predicting economic circumstances of the future over even relatively short time periods.

Consequent to an emphasis on historical time is the conception that the economy is in a continuous evolutionary pattern. Dynamic behavior is thus central to PKI theories. In orthodox theories the central analytical construct has traditionally been static equilibrium. So the theories ignore the fact that institutions and circumstances change (sometimes dramatically) over time.

This idea of continuous change is one of the areas where PKIs part company with their cousins, the Keynesians. For while the mainstream U.S. Keynesians invest their efforts in understanding the dynamics of change from one equilibrium position to another, PKIs argue that it is much better to forget about equilibrium altogether and think instead in terms of continuous transition, or constant disequilibrium. PKIs are thus led to explain circumstances in one period of time by analyzing the causes in the previous time period(s). Such an approach, focusing on the historical time-sequential links, leads into the PKI analysis of the historical determinants (or causes) of the price level, investment, and income distribution.

Eichner sums up the benefits of the systems approach in the following passage: "The advantage which it offers social scientists is that it can incorporate within its analytical structure (a) purposeful activity, (b) cumulative processes, and (c) the interaction of subsystems, both as part of a larger systems dynamic and in response to feedback from the environment."[26]

Once again, what makes this approach attractive is that it allows the analyst to examine the actual nature of an economic system without sifting everything through the framework of traditional economic theory. This gets one away from trying to fit everything into a preconceived framework which assumes that the basic nature of the system's activity is known already.

The Evolution of the Self-Regulating Market System: The PKI View

The PKI stance that economic analysis should be structured as holistic, systemic, and evolutionary, with an appreciation for the centrality of power and conflict, requires a historical view of the market economy. For the market is the key construct in all the theories. Whereas the CEI and Keynesian analyses take it as a datum, PKIs see it as an institution in constant evolution. The economy is an evolving system of self-regulating markets that had a beginning in historical time and has been in the process of transformation ever since. Let us develop this argument in some detail, building on the original work of Karl Polanyi.[27]

Most historians, whether their orientation is political, cultural or economic, clearly recognize that the eighteenth century was a turning point in the affairs of the Western world. It fell heir to momentous movements and events — intellectual, political, military, social, cultural, and economic. The enlightenment, with its emphasis on reason, natural law and progress, and its avant-garde — the philosophes and physiocrats — opened new vistas for humankind, although most of the population of Europe and the remainder of the world scarcely glimpsed those vistas. But the writings of the philosophes, Rousseau, Montesquieu and Voltaire in particular, infected the rising bourgeoisie of France and, together with the maladministrations of Louis XV and XVI, brought on the French Revolution, the second momentous event of the eighteenth century. The twilight of the divine-right monarchies had arrived on the Continent and would move to its inevitable end, despite the best efforts of the more enlightened despots.

In economic affairs, the eighteenth century began with François Quesnay's campaign against mercantilism and ended with the completion of Quesnay's campaign by Adam Smith. In the process, the classical school of economics, a new social science, came into being. Finally, in the course of the century, the agricultural and commercial revolutions of the previous two centuries led to the initiation of the industrial revolution in England in four key industries: mining, metallurgy, munitions, and textiles.

It was in this historical context that Polanyi pinpointed the emergence of the self-regulating market, a momentous event of the eighteenth century. He observed:

> Since the middle of the eighteenth century national markets had been developing; the price of grain was no longer local, but regional; this presupposed the almost general use of money and a wide marketability of goods. Market prices and incomes, including rents and wages, showed considerable stability. The Physiocrats were the first to note these regularities, which they could not even theoretically fit into a whole as feudal incomes were still prevalent in France, and labor was

often semiservile, so that neither rents nor wages were, as a rule, determined in the market. But the English countryside in Adam Smith's time had become part and parcel of a commercial society; the rent due to the landlord as well as the wages of the agricultural laborer showed a marked dependence on prices. Only exceptionally were wages or prices fixed by authorities. Malthus' population law and the law of diminishing returns as handled by Ricardo made the fertility of man and soil constitutive elements of the new realm the existence of which had been uncovered. Economic society had emerged as distinct from the political state.

The circumstances under which the existence of this human aggregate — a complex society — became apparent were of the utmost importance for the history of nineteenth century thought. Since the emerging society was no other than the market system, human society was now in danger of being shifted to foundations utterly foreign to the moral world of which the body politic hitherto had formed part.[28]

Significantly, however, it was England of the later eighteenth century which provided the fertile ground in which the self-regulating market could and initially did take root and mature. Not only had the industrial revolution begun in the four industries cited above; but, a fact of equal or greater importance, the initiation of the industrial revolution occurred at a period in English history when poverty and its tragic result, pauperism, showed an alarming increase. But even more to the point the poor laws were so modified as to throw a great mass of English paupers upon the mercy of the subsistence wage level propounded by Adam Smith.

Now that the self-regulated market had arrived at last, after several thousand years of experimentation, what were its characteristics? A market economy is an economy controlled, regulated, and directed by markets alone. Order in the production and distribution of goods is entrusted to this self-regulating mechanism. An economy of this kind derives from the expectation that human beings behave in such a way as to achieve money gains. It assumes markets in which the supply of goods, including services available at a definite price, will equal the demand at that price. A market economy assumes the presence of money, which functions as purchasing power in the hands of its owners. Production will then be controlled by prices, for the profits of those who direct production will depend upon them; the distribution of the goods also will depend upon prices, since prices form incomes and it is with the help of these incomes that the goods produced are distributed among the members of society. Thus, order in the production and distribution of goods is ensured by prices alone.

In contrast, during preceding historical periods, markets were never more than accessories of economic life. Generally, the economic system was embedded in the social system. In Babylonia and even Greece the local markets (trading centers) were compatible with the established social way of life; markets did not expand at the expense of the society. Even under the mercantile system of the previous two centuries, where markets had expanded to involve a large part of the nation, they were not free markets performing the functions mentioned above but rather were subjected to centralized administration.

In Karl Mannheim's words, the market was transformed from being a regulatory mechanism utilized by society into the very organizing principle of society itself.[29]

On the eve of the industrial revolution, the English economy could be characterized as follows: (1) although the new national markets were in some degree competitive, the overriding feature of these markets was regulation; (2) the self-sufficing household of the peasant remained the broad basis of the economic system and was being integrated into large national units through the formation of the internal market; and (3) agriculture was being supplemented by internal commerce although at the beginning of the eighteenth century the system of internal commerce was that of relatively isolated markets.

This new phenomenon, the self-regulating market, would include these additional ingredients: (1) self-regulation implied that all production was for sale on the market and that all incomes derived from such sales; (2) there were markets for all elements of industry including goods, labor, land and money, whose prices were respectively commodity prices, wages, rent and interest; (3) the state would do nothing to inhibit the formation of markets, and incomes would be formed only through sales; and (4) there would be no interference in adjustment of prices to changed market conditions.

The self-regulating market which came into existence during the latter part of the eighteenth century but which only became fully operative with the creation of a true labor market in 1834, with the repeal of the Speenhamland system,* could only have been an economic utopia somewhat along the lines envisaged by Adam Smith. The transition from regulated to self-regulating markets could only repre-

---

*During the most active period of the industrial revolution, that is, between 1795 and 1834, a true labor market did not come into being due to extensive poor relief, specifically the Speenhamland system which was not finally eliminated until 1834. Thus, in England, both land and money were mobilized before labor.

sent a complete transformation in the structure of society. A self-regulating market demanded nothing less than the institutional separation of society into an economic and a political sphere, a singular departure from previous societies where the economy was embedded in the social system and where "economic" decision-making was determined by larger needs and values.

Moreover, such an institutional pattern could not function unless society was subordinated to its requirements. A market economy could only exist in a market society. An examination of the institutional nature of a market economy will serve to illustrate this point.

In addition to commodities, labor, land and money are essential elements of industry and markets and form a vital part of the economic system. They are, in fact, just like commodities, to be bought and sold on the market. But labor, land, and money are obviously *not* commodities. Unlike commodities they are not "produced" primarily for sale. Labor is only another name for a human activity which is part of life itself, which is not "produced" for sale but for entirely different reasons. In addition, that human activity cannot be separated from the rest of life. Land is only another name for nature, which is not produced either. Actual money is merely a token of purchasing power that is not produced but comes into existence through the mechanism of banking or state finance. None of the three is produced for sale. The commodity description of labor, land, and money is purely fictitious. Never before in history had there been true self-regulating markets in labor, land, and money. As Polanyi notes, however:

> . . . it is with the help of this fiction that the actual markets for labor, land, and money are organized; they are being actually bought and sold on the market; their demand and supply are real magnitudes; and any measures or policies that would inhibit the formation of such markets would *ipso facto* endanger the self-regulation of the system. The commodity fiction, therefore, supplies a vital organizing principle in regard to the whole of society affecting almost all its institutions in the most varied way, namely, the principle according to which no arrangement or behavior should be allowed to exist that might prevent the actual functioning of the market mechanism on the lines of the commodity fiction.[30]

But this meant that the self-regulating market mechanism became, in fact, the sole director of the fate of human beings and of their natural environment. Polanyi observed that:

> . . . in regard to labor, land, and money such a postulate can be upheld. To allow the market mechanism to be sole director of the fate

of human beings and their natural environment, indeed, even of the amount and use of purchasing power, would result in the demolition of society. For the alleged commodity "labor power" cannot be shoved about, used indiscriminately, or even unused, without affecting also the human individual who happens to be the bearer of this peculiar commodity. In disposing of a man's labor power the system would, incidentally, dispose of the physical, psychological, and moral entity "man" attached to that tag. Robbed of the protective covering of cultural institutions, human beings would perish from the effects of social exposure; they would die as the victims of acute social dislocation through vice, perversion, crime, and starvation. Nature would be reduced to its elements, neighborhoods and landscapes defiled, rivers polluted, military safety jeopardized, the power to produce food and raw materials destroyed. Finally, the market administration of purchasing power would periodically liquidate business enterprise, for shortages and surfeits of money would prove as disastrous to business as floods and droughts in primitive society. Undoubtedly, labor, land, and money markets *are* essential to a market economy. But no society could stand the effects of such a system of crude fictions even for the shortest stretch of time unless its human and natural substance as well as its business organization was protected against the ravages of this satanic mill.[31]

This was indeed, a "self-destructive mechanism" which would have annihilated society but for protective countermoves.

Accordingly, no sooner had the utopia of the self-regulating market been established than it was challenged in order that society might itself survive. Polanyi observed:

Social history in the nineteenth century was thus the result of a double movement: the extension of the market organization in respect to genuine commodities was accompanied by its restriction in respect to fictitious ones. While on the one hand markets spread all over the face of the globe and the amont of goods involved grew to unbelievable proportions, on the other hand a network of measures and policies was integrated into powerful institutions designed to check the action of the market relative to labor, land and money. While the organization of world commodity markets, world capital markets and world currency markets under the aegis of the gold standard gave an unparalleled momentum to the mechanism of markets, a deep-seated movement sprang into being to resist the pernicious effects of a market-controlled economy. Society protected itself against the perils inherent in a self-regulating market system — this was the one comprehensive feature in the history of the age.[32]

It is appropriate to review, however briefly, the course of this market system both in its national and international context. Initially, therefore, Polanyi's basic premise regarding the market and society is worth repeating:

> Production is interaction of man and nature; if this process is to be organized through a self-regulating mechanism of barter and exchange, then man and nature must be brought into its orbit; they must be subject to supply and demand, that is, be dealt with as commodities, as goods for sale. . . . But, while production could theoretically be organized in this way, the commodity fiction disregarded the fact that leaving the fate of soil and people to the market would be tantamount to annihilating them. Accordingly, the countermove consisted in checking the action of the market in respect to the factors of production, labor and land. This was the main function of interventionism.[33]

Interventionism, of course, did not occur simultaneously both on the national scene and in international affairs. In England it did not really become a potent force until after mid-century while the international market system was not placed in jeopardy until the last quarter of the nineteenth century. The forces of intervention gathered only slowly but as their acceleration developed all were swept before them.

By 1820, in England at least, three tenets of classical laissez faire economics had been clearly identified: that commodities (including labor) find their price on the market; that the creation of money should be subject to an automatic mechanism; that goods should be free to flow from country to country without hindrance or preference. Thus policy called for a free labor market, the gold standard, and free international trade. Between 1820 and 1850 economic laissez faire was fully implemented in England, France, and the Low Countries.

In England, the Poor Law Amendment Bill terminating the Speenhamland system became effective in 1834 thereby ending the system of outdoor relief and creating a free labor market. By 1825, despite inflation and a business slump following the Napoleonic Wars, it was clear that Parliament intended to adhere to the classical principle of a sound currency and its method was to support and defend the gold standard. But the gold standard held forth the possibility of deflation and monetary stringency in the face of depression. The chief supporter of laissez faire and the self-regulated market, the manufacturer, had therefore to be protected. Wages had to fall at least in proportion to the general fall in prices, so as to allow the exploitation of an ever-expanding market. Thus, the repeal of the Corn Laws in 1846, a corollary of Peel's Bank Act of 1844, was undertaken to bring laissez faire to world trade, to allow the free flow of grain into Britain and to insure that wages and prices would tend to a free market equilibrium. By 1850 in England, therefore, it appeared that the self-regulating market was triumphant as these three elements, a true labor market, the gold standard, and free trade now formed a coherent whole. It might also be added that in France, Louis Philippe saw to it that the expectations of the rising middle classes were fulfilled.

The utilitarians, including Bentham, however, had long since reflected on the shortcomings and contradictions inherent in this classical utopia and were more than mildly distressed at the sacrifices such a system exacted from the people. The utilitarians specifically, and the excesses of the market system in general, sparked a revolt against these excesses among not only the working class but more significantly among the rising middle class. Polanyi termed this revolt the collectivist movement. In England the collectivists, led by the utilitarians, looked to the government for redress. On the Continent, after the unifications of Germany and Italy and the creation of the Third Republic in France the governments of these countries followed the utilitarian lead. *Scarcely more than a decade after the self-regulating market appeared to be triumphant, it was already in retreat, however grudgingly.*

There followed in England and on the Continent, particularly after the English Parliamentary Reform Act of 1867 which gave the working class the right to vote, a series of "protectionist" legislation. Factory laws, social insurance, municipal trading, health service and public utility laws were passed in close succession. Other developments also took place such as new tariffs, embargoes on immigration, national subsidies, formation of cartels and trusts, and curtailment of capital movements, all of which inhibited the self-regulating mechanism of the market. German, Japanese, and American growth in the late nineteenth and early twentieth centuries took place behind high tariff walls; and in the first two countries, government intervention was pervasive.

The countermove against economic liberalism and laissez faire possessed all the unmistakable characteristics of a spontaneous action. At innumerable disconnected points it set in without any traceable links between the interests directly affected or any ideological conformity between them. Even in the settlement of one and the same problem as in the case of workmen's compensation, solutions switched from individualist to collectivist merely as a result of the increasing realization of the nature of the problem in question. The change to collectivism, interestingly enough, took place in several countries at a similar stage in their industrial development. Finally, even free-market liberals were forced to support government intervention to prevent monopoly and so secure the preconditions of the self-regulating market. Indeed, such a market, in all of its manifestations, threatened society and eventually society took measures to protect itself.

Despite ample evidence that the self-regulating market, and with it nineteenth-century market society, had broken down, efforts were made during the post-World War I years to rehabilitate both. The root problems of market society, interventionism and currency, reappeared after Versailles and these issues became the center of politics in the twenties. The chief instigators of this effort, of course, were the laissez faire economists. Polanyi observed:

> Economic liberalism made a supreme bid to restore the self-regulation of the system by eliminating all interventionist policies which interfered with the freedom of markets for land, labor and money. It undertook no less than to solve, in an emergency, the secular problem involved in the three fundamental principles of free trade, a free labor market, and a freely functioning gold standard. It became, in effect, the spearhead of a heroic attempt to restore world trade, remove all avoidable hindrances to the mobility of labor, and reconstruct stable exchanges. This last aim had precedence over the rest. For unless confidence in the currencies was restored, the mechanism of the market could not function.[34]

A singular effort was made in Geneva during the twenties, particularly by Britain, France and the United States, to reestablish stable exchanges, i.e., a return to gold. But increasingly the responsibility for carrying this burden fell on the United States and when the depression struck in 1929, the effort dissolved with the stock market. The effort, however noble, to recreate free trade, a free labor market, and a freely functioning gold standard went the way of the inflated stock. The self-regulating market had succumbed to its own nemeses.

The response to this collapse was fascism in some countries and the expansion of the welfare state in others. The conclusion we draw from this look at history is that the free market economy in the sense of a self-regulating system is a utopian vision in the minds of economists that was a temporary aberration in the history of humankind. Individual markets may always have existed (at least for commodities) but an economy run by free markets required the actions of government to come into existence. The mercantilist controls over the economy that laissez faire economics fought against were merely that era's way of embedding the economy into the social system. The attempt to "free" markets (particularly for the fictitious commodities) from societal control was a failure. No one was willing to live with the results of a pure market system. No one, in practice, would accept the notion that everything and everyone's worth was measured by a market-determined price. Workers formed trade unions to eliminate competition in the labor market, business firms merged or sought government regulation to eliminate competition. Farmers sought government price supports. Consumers sought government protection from the free market in the form of pure food and drug acts, and on and on. Professionals convinced government that the public welfare demanded the licensing of lawyers and physicians.

Thus, if anything is "natural" it is the social control of the economy as a way of embedding it in the total social system; and, if anything is "unnatural" it is a laissez faire system of self-regulating markets. If we think government interferes with our private lives, an unregulated market system does it to an even greater degree. Therefore, we and most PKIs would argue that the burden of proof should lie with the free market devotees. History and common sense make the real issue: what type of policies should we use to obtain the economic results we want without allowing the economy to dictate our social and political values and needs?

8. Structure and Operation of the U.S. Economy: The PKI View

The PKIs' recognition that a pure free market economy was a historical aberration and that today's economy is the outcome of both private and public attempts to re-embed the economy into the social system provides a healthy skepticism about the actual functioning of our market economy and leads them to a close examination of contemporary institutions.

It is in the functioning of these institutions that PKIs find the explanations for contemporary economic problems, and of course the solutions will have to deal with this reality as well.

Polanyi's argument that the effort to escape the market is an inherent part of economic behavior leads PKIs to a division of the private economy into institutions that can insulate themselves from the market and those that cannot. Thus they divide the private economy into two sectors or markets, and we will add a third. In the first sector, economic power prevails; this is the oligopolistic, core, planning or fix-price sector of the large oligopolistic corporation. The second sector, the market sector, is made up of small competitive firms which are disciplined by the market. This sector is termed variously the competitive, periphery, market, or flex-price sector. The third sector which we add on is the underground or informal sector, a new extension of the market sector whose importance seems to be growing in recent years and whose functioning has somewhat different implications for the contemporary economy.

In addition, there is the public economy. Government operations at federal, state, and local levels now absorb about one-third of the national income. PKIs see government functioning as an actor in the economy and doing so with significant independence and substantial impact. We also note the importance of another component of the public economy, the not-for-profit sector.

167

After an initial analysis of the dual or tripartite nature of the institutions of the private economy and the interaction with the public economy, PKIs look more specifically at three key actors in the economy, the firm, the consumer, and the government, for it is their interaction that finally determines the course of the economy. We will follow this lead.

Thus we have a private economy divided into three sectors with two principal actors, and a public economy that while interwoven with the private economy functions independently with government as its major actor. Its not-for-profit component is also important in our present economy. It is their interaction which must be understood to begin to deal with our current problems; it is their reality which will affect any steps taken to deal with these problems.

STRUCTURE OF THE PRIVATE ECONOMY

The industrial world has been characterized as dualistic, with large oligopolistic (with only a few producers and/or sellers) international corporations on one side, and small competitive (many producers and/or sellers) local firms on the other. The division between these two sets of firms is that some belong to the "planning sector" and the others belong to the "market sector," to use Galbraith's terminology. Each sector is composed of qualitatively different types of firms which operate in substantially different economic environments. Each of these sectors may affect the other, but in large measure they act and respond to different sets of conditions. Let us analyze them before we deal with the underground economy and then the public economy.

The planning sector is composed of about one thousand of the largest corporations in the U.S. These firms produce nearly 60 percent of total national output.[1] They are typically highly capital-intensive in their production methods, so they provide jobs to less than 33 percent of the entire labor force. Their workers generally have strong unions and are well paid. Because these firms are large and oligopolistic, because it is very difficult for newcomers to enter the market, and because each producer substantially differentiates its product lines from those of others, corporations in the planning sector are able to obtain considerable control over the supply of particular goods and hence they can influence market price. In addition, they have substantial influence on the determination of government policy.

The market sector, on the other hand, is composed of the remaining 13.5 million firms. They are primarily engaged in the provision of services or in light manufacturing. Production in the market sector is typically labor intensive (especially and naturally in services), and about 67 percent of the private formal-sector labor force works in this sector. Virtually all of the new jobs created in the 1970s originated in the market sector (or in the public economy). Even so, less than half of the national product originates here. The market sector is characteristically competitive: it is easy for newcomers to set up a business, products are similar for all competitors, and firms are small and produce only a small fraction of the total output of that particular good. As a result, no single firm has enough power to affect either total supply or the price of the good. Nor does a firm have any more than marginal political impact.[2]

Galbraith sums up the most characteristic difference between the two sectors in these words: "The planning sector seeks to exercise control over its economic environment, and . . . it succeeds. The market system manifests the same desire, is much more visible in its effort and is much less successful. The one system dominates its environment; the other remains generally subordinated to it."[3] It is the market sector that conforms fairly closely to the economic vision of the CEIs. Firms here are competitive; they take prices as given by the market, and they have little or no control over the economic climate. They fit in or they die. They cannot "create" a demand for their products nor can they plan complicated stratagems to ward off the competitive advances of newly entering or old firms. The 1970s version of these firms was the franchise, but they did not change the reality of the sector.

The result is not idyllic. There is substantial inefficiency as four out of five new firms go bankrupt within five years of birth. Wage levels and security are far lower than in the planning sector, and many firms remain in business only because the owners "exploit" themselves with long hours and low profits.

The planning sector, however, is very different. The economic environment is consciously manipulated by the large corporations. Thanks to their almost bottomless pit of resources they can advertise widely, they can spend great sums on research and product innovation, and ordinarily they can "create" the demand they need to sell their products and make a profit. Together with their control over supply, under normal conditions planning sector corporations are able to plan, control and protect their prices, profit margins and other elements of their business environment. Planning sector firms do not take prices as a given, as is the case with competitive firms. To a great extent, the top one thousand firms are "price-makers," and not "price-takers." Thus even during 1981-82 when corporate bankruptcies reached their post-depression highs, few of the thousand were so threatened, and the Braniffs were the exception rather than the rule. Despite the depressed auto production, the Big Three were able to affect their market and operations so as to have several profitable quarters.

The third sector in the private economy is known by a variety of names — the irregular economy, the underground economy, the informal sector. In many ways it carries to its extreme the idea of the competitive firm: small, often only one person, easy entry, as all one needs is a street-corner to sell some goods on. In this sector we include those economic activities which go unreported in our present system of economic and tax measures — the exchange of services by craftsmen, illegal transactions, small unincorporated operations such as street vendors.

The inability of this sector to control prices is obvious, and in that sense it parallels the market sector. It has two implications of importance which differentiate it. First of all, it seems to be growing quite rapidly as a component of total economic activity. One estimate comparing its size to that of the official economy found it to be 19 percent in 1976, but 26.6 percent by 1978![4] Of course the estimates are difficult to make with any precision, but there is evidence that substantial growth has occurred. The second factor is the role of this sector in the labor market. There is evidence that the sector is playing the role of a shock absorber to disruptions in the labor market and increases in unemployment rates. It provides a means of support for those who cannot obtain formal-sector jobs, but at the same time it leads to an understating of unemployment figures and has very different implications for policy to affect unemployment. This is an area that will be dealt with later when we talk about the labor market.

With this division of the private economy into its three sectors, we can turn now to an analysis of how these sectors operate. PKIs place primary emphasis on the planning sector, because they believe it is the dominating force in the present day economy. Let us now look at the two major actors in the private economy, the firm in the planning sector and the consumer.

The Oligopolistic Firm

The crucial structure in the American economy is the firm, which in the present day is the modern corporation. Historical changes in the corporation are at the root of the economic problems we experience today. Through mergers, outright purchases of competitors or of firms in entirely different lines of business, expansion drives which push smaller firms out of the industry, or international expansion, companies in the U.S. have become continually larger ever since the first days of the country's industrialization in the mid- and late 1800s. The view of the firm in traditional economic theory — whether CEI or Keynesian — is of a smallish entity whose product is dictated by the consumer and whose method of production is dictated by competition. The reality is lightyears away for the typical firm in the planning sector. Table 8.1 gives a better view of economic reality — major corporations are larger than countries — by comparing the sales of corporations to the GNP of countries.

Table 8.1

Nations and Corporations: The Top 100 Economies

RANK	COUNTRY OR COMPANY	1978 GNP OR SALES ($ BILL.)	RANK	COUNTRY OR COMPANY	1978 GNP OR SALES ($ BILL.)
1	United States	2,106.9	32	Austria	41.3
2	Soviet Union	1,046.6	33	Venezuela	41.2
3	Japan	727.9	34	Nigeria	40.1
4	Germany (Federal Rep.)	513.1	35	Denmark	38.9
5	France	411.3	36	South Africa	37.7
6	China	324.0	37	Korea (Republic of)	35.4
7	United Kingdom	254.2	38	*Mobil*	34.7
8	Italy	210.7	39	Turkey	33.4
9	Canada	196.6	40	Norway	31.9
10	Brazil	148.9	41	Hungary	31.1
11	Poland	108.3	42	*Texaco*	28.6
12	India	105.1	43	*British Petroleum*	27.4
13	Australia	96.7	44	Bulgaria	24.8
14	Spain	95.0	45	Greece	24.2
15	Netherlands	88.1	46	Finland	23.8
16	Germany (Democratic Rep.)	81.0	47	*Standard Oil (Calif.)*	23.2
17	Iran	79.1	48	Taiwan	22.8
18	Mexico	76.2	49	*National Iranian Oil*	22.8
19	Sweden	73.7	50	Philippines	21.9
20	Czechoslovakia	70.7	51	Iraq	21.4
21	Belgium	69.7	52	*IBM*	21.1
22	Romania	67.4	53	Thailand	20.6
23	*General Motors*	63.2	54	*General Electric*	19.6
24	*Exxon*	60.3	55	Algeria	19.5
25	Yugoslavia	55.6	56	*Unilever*	18.9
26	Switzerland	54.6	57	Libya	18.6
27	Saudi Arabia	54.5	58	Columbia	18.4
28	Argentina	49.7	59	*Gulf Oil*	18.1
29	Indonesia	46.2	60	Chile	16.8
30	*Royal Dutch/Shell*	44.0	61	Pakistan	16.5
31	*Ford*	42.8	62	Peru	16.4

Table 8.1 (cont.)

Nations and Corporations: The Top 100 Economies

RANK	COUNTRY OR COMPANY	1978 GNP OR SALES ($ BILL.)	RANK	COUNTRY OR COMPANY	1978 GNP OR SALES ($ BILL.)
63	*Chrysler*	16.3	82	*Daimler-Benz*	12.1
64	Egypt	16.1	83	*Hoechst*	12.1
65	New Zealand	16.0	84	Cuba	11.4
66	Portugal	15.4	85	*Bayer*	11.4
67	*ITT*	15.3	86	*Shell Oil*	11.1
68	Kuwait	15.2	87	*U.S. Steel*	11.0
69	*Philips (N.V.)*	15.1	88	*Nestlé*	11.0
70	*Standard Oil (Ind.)*	14.9	89	Puerto Rico	10.8
71	Israel	14.8	90	*BASF (Germany)*	10.7
72	Malaysia	13.9	91	*Peugeot-Citroën*	10.6
73	*Siemens*	13.9	92	*du Pont*	10.6
74	Hong Kong	13.6	93	Morocco	10.4
75	*Volkswagen*	13.3	94	Ireland	10.3
76	*Toyota*	12.8	95	*Matsushita Electric*	10.0
77	*Renault*	12.7	96	*Nissan Motor*	9.8
78	*ENI (Italy)*	12.6	97	*Nippon Steel*	9.5
79	*Cie. Française des Pétroles*	12.5	98	*Western Electric*	9.5
80	Korea (Demo. People's Rep.)	12.4	99	*Continental Oil*	9.5
81	*Atlantic Richfield*	12.3	100	*Mitsubishi Heavy Industries*	9.2

Source: *Across the Board*, May, 1980, pp. 8-11.

Periodic government efforts at antitrust have been ineffectual, with the result that nothing has gotten in the way of the drive to grow ever bigger. Big conglomerate firms today are involved in so many activities that it is virtually impossible to keep track of them. A single conglomerate corporation may well be involved in such varied endeavors as dairy farming, tire production, insurance peddling, undergarment manufacture, cosmetics, etc. Or one firm may control a series of different operations which are a part of the same industry. Such a firm is "vertically integrated" because it is involved in owning and controlling all aspects of a given industry from the bottom to the top. The oil companies, for example, generally own the exploration, extraction, transportation, refining, and marketing operations of the various petroleum products.

All of this bigness results in substantial concentration of production in a few firms, a deviation from competitive conditions. Table 8.2 provides information on the concentration of economic power by industry; and this fails to capture the fact that the same firm may have subsidiaries in several industries.

Table 8.2

Percentage of Output* Produced by Firms in Selected High-Concentration Manufacturing Industries, 1970

INDUSTRY	PERCENT OF INDUSTRY OUTPUT PRODUCED BY LARGEST FOUR FIRMS
Primary aluminum	100
Locomotives and parts	97
Telephone and telegraph equipment	94
Electric lamps (bulbs)	92
Motor vehicles	91
Synthetic fibers	86
Cigarettes	84
Typewriters	81
Sewing machines	80
Gypsum products	79
Steam engines and turbines	77
Metal cans	72
Tires and inner tubes	72
Soap and detergents	70
Phonograph records	62
Distilled liquor	47

*As measured by value of shipment. Data are for 1970.

Source: Bureau of the Census, *Annual Survey of Manufacturers,* 1970.

The relentless tendency toward concentration has caught the eye of most PKIs, and for some this feature of the economy has become the central point of interest. They approach the study of the firm, the industry, and the economy by considering three areas: the *structure* of the firm in an industry, the *conduct* of the firm in its relevant affairs, and the subsequent *performance* in reference to the wider economic picture. Generally speaking the existing structure of the industry and the firms that comprise it generate a specific type of conduct in production and marketing activities, and both give rise to the performance of the industry with respect to the entire social and economic systems.

The structure of a particular industry is examined in terms of concentration, barriers to entry, product differentiation, internationality, and so on. The conduct of the firms in the industry is analyzed in areas such as acquisitions and mergers, pricing behavior, restrictive business practices, government lobbying, questionable payments, advertising, and forms of nonprice competition. Finally the performance of a firm and its industry are evaluated with respect to the impact on such economic indices as technological development, growth, employment, inflation, balance of payments, and so on.

In his look at certain critical industries (e.g., steel, oil, autos, drugs, rubber, chemicals, etc.), John Blair found conclusive evidence that the larger a firm is, the more likely it is to engage in pricing activities which are noncompetitive in nature.[5] That is, the prices set by large firms differ from those expected under competitive circumstances. He suggests that prices are set on the basis of target return pricing (a practice which seeks a certain level of profits no matter the quantity of goods sold), markup pricing (a system of pricing which automatically sets the price at, say, 40 percent over the cost of production), or perhaps just price followship (setting prices according to what the dominant firm in the industry decides to do).

Blair argues that the effects of such pricing behavior by highly concentrated firms are seen in performance in three areas. First, there is an income effect, i.e., such practices redistribute income from truly competitive firms in the market sector to those in the planning sector large enough not to be immediately threatened by lower prices of a competitor. Second, there is a potentially adverse effect on production. The presence of substantial market power may permit, especially over the period of the business cycle, a greater reduction or increase in output (and thus employment) and a different movement in prices than would occur under competition. And since government operates with an economic theory that predicts output and price movements in a competitive environment, policymakers may err monumentally in their estimates of potential effects of certain occurrences on the whole economy. The possibility of such egregious error is known as the policy effect because policymakers interpret and act upon these prices as if they were competitively determined. This effect is particularly critical if the pricing behavior of the firms in question is precisely the opposite of that predicted by government officials and economists. Indeed this appears to have occurred on more than one occasion as prices have been raised in the face of falling demand and lowered when demand picked up.

A classic example is that of the automobile companies who raised prices on 1976 models in the face of the most massive decline in demand experienced to that date. After the 1973 oil crisis, automobile sales and profits declined sharply during 1974 and 1975, and the industry's response was the markup pricing one of raising prices, not the competitive one of lowering prices. The same occurred in the 1980 recession,[6] and there were such examples with many models in the 1981-82 recession.

Clearly such behavior could cause the coincidence of high inflation and high unemployment. When aggregate demand is on the decline and unemployment is on the rise it is quite conceivable that some crucial industries will not reduce prices (or increase them less rapidly) to increase sales, but will hike prices faster in an attempt to maintain profit margins. And even if the large firms restrain the urge to raise prices and hold them steady (or raise them in accordance with the underlying rate of inflation), they will still be extremely reluctant, given their market power, to decrease prices.[7] So the conventional means of attacking inflation (i.e., by creating a recession) will in any case affect only minimally the part of the business world that is responsible for the inflationary tendencies.[8] More on this later.

There are, of course, many contributing factors to permit large firms to ignore competitive discipline. One is simply the absence of competitors or the ability to collude with the few that do exist. Another is the power to lobby politically for laws and resolutions favorable to big business. Still another is the growing ability to influence the economics that is taught in our universities. The comment made by William Simon, former treasury secretary under Nixon and Ford and once a likely candidate for a high cabinet post in the Reagan administration — that large corporations ought to refrain from donating funds to universities unless their curriculum was favorable to big business — has been followed to a greater extent than many of us would dare or care to believe.[9] The proliferation of endowed chairs in free-enterprise economics and the formation of free-enterprise institutes, e.g., at Texas A & M, are related trends.

But not all the blame of skirting competitive strictures falls on the corporations themselves. Labor unions also contribute to the stagflation tendencies of the present-day economy.[10] There is a high correlation between big and powerful unions and big and powerful corporations. Part of the reason for this is that since large corporations can pass the cost of higher wages and higher taxes along to the consumer in the form of higher prices, without themselves incurring any great pain, they have not been adamant in resisting union pressure. Thus, when labor unions demand wage settlements in excess of what they would

receive under competitive conditions, they too contribute to the inflationary bias by their insistence on inflationary wages. Thus the industrial structure which relates large corporations almost symbiotically
with large unions goes far to stimulate inflation and eventually to cause
stagflation as government responds to rising prices by restraining demand and therefore generates a reduction in output and a jump in
unemployment.

Most large corporations are conglomerates and transnational corporations (TNCs) which have their headquarters in one of the advanced market countries. The increasing transnationality of major corporations considerably weakens the ability of the government to control
the stability of the economy. The corporations can shift funds and production facilities in and out of the U.S. on a world-wide basis, which
undermines the nation's control over inflation, employment, growth,
taxation, and consistent national planning. This power of TNCs has
been made possible by technical revolutions in communications and
accounting and by the managerial revolution which allows central industrial planning on an international scale.

Such findings vitiate both CEI claims that government need not
intervene to ensure stability and the Keynesian contention that government, with proper policy, can promote a stable process of growth. The
CEI claims are relevant only to a world of perfect competition, a world
with little contemporary relevance. The Keynesian doctrine becomes
less tenable each year because TNCs are so powerful that domestic
governments have little ability to deal effectively with them. Each year
it is becoming more evident that legal and political institutions have not
kept pace with the changing techniques of accounting, finance, marketing and production utilized by the typical TNC. For example, new
accounting techniques allow corporations to shroud their operations
under a veil of secrecy. It is relatively easy, say, to show profits made
in the U.S. as earned in a nation where taxes on profits are lower than
they are in the U.S. This is called transfer pricing. And the state has
little ability to discover the truth or falsity of such actions, which greatly
diminishes its power to affect the operations of these corporations. The
state thus does not have sufficient information either to regulate the
TNCs or to make the crucial planning decisions on tax, monetary, or
employment policies for society. As a consequence, the corporate
managers of the planning sector have become, by default, the "planners" for the economy. The straightforward conclusion is that the
macromanagement policies of the government are fundamentally
weakened and thus the business cycle is less controllable.

The other major actor in the modern economy is the consumer.

Again PKIs see the consumer through eyes very different from those of CEIs or Keynesians.

The Consumer: Sovereign or Servant

Another cornerstone of the belief — whether CEI or Keynesian — in a free-market economy is the doctrine of consumer sovereignty. The strongest version has been stated by Ludwig von Mises:

> In the economic order based on private ownership in the means of production no special institutions, such as political democracy has created for itself, are needed to achieve corresponding success. All production must bend to the consumers' will. From the moment it fails to conform to the consumers' demands it becomes unprofitable. Thus free competition compels the obedience of the producer to the consumers' will and also, in case of need, the transfer of the means of production from the hands of those unwilling or unable to achieve what the consumer demands into the hands of those better able to direct production. The lord of production is the consumer. From this point of view the capitalist society is a democracy in which every penny represents a ballot paper. It is a democracy with an imperative and immediately revocable mandate to its deputies.[11]

Like many of the propositions of economics, the doctrine of consumers' sovereignty rests on a value-judgment and also on a factual assertion. The value-judgment is that it is desirable that consumers should control the economic system, and furthermore, that they should control it via their individual "dollar votes." This involves a further value-judgment that the distribution of wealth and income (which directly determines which consumers will have the most votes) is taken as given — that is, that it is acceptable or at least neutral. The factual assertion is that in the absence of governmental or other intervention, consumers do in fact so control the economic system through the price mechanism.

The PKI analysis of the actual U.S. economy casts grave doubt upon this doctrine. In fact, PKI analysis of the dual economy and of the dominance of the large corporation tends to support the opposite position — that is, producer sovereignty.

A number of qualifications to the doctrine of consumers' sovereignty are of course admitted by traditional economists. A certain degree of consumer ignorance is usually acknowledged and, because of this, organizations such as Consumers Union have found almost universal favor among economists. Labor organizations and sometimes farmers' organizations have often been exempted from the competitive norm. In accordance with liberal political philosophy, the theory does not advocate consumers' sovereignty for those unable to choose rationally, nor does it necessarily imply the desirability of allowing harmful choices to be reflected in the production pattern, e.g., dangerous drugs. CEIs and Keynesians do not believe that these limitations have undermined seriously the desirability of consumer control of the economic system through the operation of the price mechanism.

The main factual criticisms of the existing theory of consumers' behavior may be detailed in a limited number of categories.

The first criticism is against the assumption of precise, known, and ordered wants. The great majority of psychologists would hold that human behavior is considerably influenced by non-rational considerations. The motive for desiring a commodity may be subconscious, or different from the declared motive. Much of the practice of salesmanship has of course been based on this theory. As Rothenberg says, "What about the claim of psychologists that even most normal law-abiding adults do things they do not really want to? To be serious about sovereignty requires evaluating this claim and substituting corrected preferences in the criterion wherever it can be substantiated."[12]

A second criticism is against the assumption that consumers act autonomously. It is more likely that the preferences of different individuals are interdependent. This is the core of Veblen's theory of conspicuous consumption and emulation.

Closely connected with this is the criticism that acts of consumption do not merely affect the consumer but directly affect other individuals also. Rothenberg states that "there are three types of dependency. First, specific acts of consumption by others directly affect the individual; for example, the growing of roses by the neighbor of someone with a severe allergy. Second, the standard of living of specific other persons either elicits the individual's anger because of envy or pleasure because of empathy. Third, the person has strong opinions about what should be the general shape of the frequency distribution of income."[13] In another way this can be seen in the "consumption" of health, education, and the arts. Frequently the consumption of these goods by one individual makes possible a larger consumption of them by others. This has been recognized in economic theory under the title of "external economies of consumption." Acts of consumption may also give rise to external diseconomies, e.g., envy. Each act of consumption, like any other act, starts a train of consequences indefinitely long. Some of these will be statistically measurable; others will be not only unmeasurable, but unknowable. The concept of external economies and diseconomies of consumption easily leads to a recognition of the interdependence of consumers.

Fourth, it is known that consumers are in varying degrees open to persuasion by producers; to the extent this is true, the force of consumer sovereignty is reduced. The most obvious example is advertising. Over the past twenty years total expenditures on advertising and promotion each year have been greater than total expenditures on public elementary and secondary education. The magnitude of these expenditures coupled with the effort of the planning sector to control consumer preferences has led Galbraith to substitute for consumer sovereignty the "revised sequence," that is, producer sovereignty.

On a more fundamental sociological plane it can be argued, however, that the entire system of consumers' preferences is a consequence of the prevailing social and economic order. Paul Baran has ably stated this position and deserves to be quoted at length:

> . . . Statements that consumers like only what they care for and buy only what they wish to spend money on are obviously tautologies, but, being tautologies, they are equally obviously correct. From this to be sure, it does not follow . . . that the barrage of advertising and salesmanship to which the consumer is continually exposed has *no* influence on the formation of his wants. But neither is it true that these business practices constitute *the* decisive factor in making the consumer want what he wants. . . . Human wants are not *all* wholly "synthetic," created by Madison Avenue (or "purified" and "ennobled" by a Madison Avenue "in reverse": government regulatory boards and/or Distinguished Citizens Committee for the Promotion of Good Taste): that view reflects the spirit of limitless manipulability of man which is so characteristic of the "men in gray flannel suits" who dominate the executive offices of corporations and the important bureaus of the government. But neither do *all* wants stem from man's biotic urges or from a mythical eternally unchanging "human nature": that concept is metaphysical obscurantism which flies in the face of all historical knowledge and experience. The truth is that wants of people are complex historical phenomena reflecting the . . . interaction of their physiological requirements on the one hand, and the prevailing social and economic order on the other. The physiological requirements sometimes must be abstracted from for analytical purposes because they are *relatively constant.* And once this abstraction is explicitly made and firmly borne in mind, the make-up of human wants can (and must) be legitimately thought of as being "synthetic," i.e., determined by the nature of the economic and social order under which people live.[14]

If this is true then the "issue is *not* whether the prevailing social and economic order plays a prominent part in molding people's values, volitions, and preferences. The issue is rather *the kind of social and economic order* that does the molding, the kind of values, volitions, and preferences which it instills into the people under its sway."[15]

Even if one rejects this formulation, it is clear that consumers' preferences can only be satisfied within the limits of what producers decide to offer. Because a certain commodity is not marketed, we cannot conclude that it is not desired by consumers. Since there is no way of saying how customers would react to the presentation of (at present) nonexistent alternatives, such an argument would be circular. As Maurice Dobb has said, "It may well be the case that the majority of the prices registered on the market are in fact second best preferences compared with the choices which would have been made if the requisite alternatives had been available."[16]

Finally, the doctrine does not provide any mechanism for choosing between public and private goods, thereby making us in Galbraith's phrase, "privately affluent and publicly poor." Joan Robinson believes this situation is inherent in a free market system when she says:

> The foundation of a comfortable standard of life is a decent house. A family requires, above everything, a reliable health service and the best possible education, but a growing wealth always leaves us with a greater deficiency in just those things. It is not an accident that it should be so. Capitalist industry is dazzlingly efficient at producing goods to be sold in the shops, and directly and indirectly, profits are derived from selling. The services to meet basic human needs do not lend themselves to mass production and, especially as with our egalitarian democratic notions, they have to be offered irrespective of means to pay, they are not an easy field for making profits. Consequently they must be largely provided through taxation. To supply goods is a source of profit but to supply services is a "burden upon industry." It is for this reason that when, as a nation, we . . . "have never had it so good" we find that we "cannot afford" just what we most need.[17]

Scitovsky has made the same point, but from a slightly different angle. He says that the sovereignty of the consumer is not the same thing as the sovereignty of the individual or the citizen. The consumer is just one facet of the individual — the one that has to do with the consumption of goods bought and sold in the market place. Therefore, "choosing between market and collective goods, deciding whether a given service is better provided through the market or by public spending, determining the best allocation of public funds among their various uses—all these are economic choices no different and no less important than the consumer's choice between two market goods; and yet, our society has failed to develop adequate machinery through which the public could express its preferences on these issues."[18]

Most traditional economic analysis takes consumers' preferences as given, with no concern as to how they were developed. Once the starting point of economic discussion includes consumers' preferences as given data, it is easy to pass on to the assumption that the satisfaction of consumers' wants is an end which is "scientific" or nonnormative. Some writers have gone further and *defined* the efficiency of an economic system as the extent to which it satisfies given consumers' wants with given resources. The possibility then arises that policies dictated by economic efficiency (in this strictly limited sense) may come into conflict with policies desirable on ethical or political grounds, such as equity, which are not the concern of the economist as such. An example of this was given by Scitovsky: ". . . it is very important to realize that we defined economic efficiency as conformity to consumers' preferences and that economic efficiency is therefore a meaningful concept only as long as we accept the consumers' preferences as a datum. . . . We can make objective statements about efficiency whereas everyone makes his own judgments about equity according to his concience and ethical norms."[19]

The statement, "we can make objective statements about efficiency," is clearly untenable once consumers' sovereignty is recognized not as an "objective" criterion of efficiency but as an ethical norm itself. Moreover, the noncompetitive structure of much of the U.S. economy, the massive role of advertising, the importance of externalities, etc., all cast doubt upon the sovereignty of the consumer in directing the economy.

What finally emerges from this somewhat lengthy dissection of the doctrine of consumers' sovereignty? Simply that the reality of the U.S. economy indicates that if anyone has the power to be "sovereign"—that is, to direct the economy—it is the large corporate producer. To the extent this is true, the justification of market results as efficient and as the outcome of free choice is correspondingly undermined. Thus, one more foundation of the free market edifice appears flawed.

A few words regarding the relationship between the goals specified in chapter one and consumer sovereignty are in order at this point. The CEI would argue that the existence of consumer sovereignty is what guarantees efficiency, and thus life-sustenance, and is a major component of freedom itself.

Our analysis of both the firm in the planning sector and of the consumer indicates that the efficiency argument collapses and the freedom argument must be carefully qualified. Furthermore, the CEI claims ignore some important considerations.

The attempt to treat life-sustenance as a matter of providing consumers what they *want* (and are willing and able to pay for) ignores the differences among necessities, enhancement goods, and luxuries. Economic theory erases the differences by arguing that they all deliver satisfaction or utility to the purchaser. There are two problems with this stance. First, inequality of income allows some people to satisfy their wants for luxuries while other people are unable to obtain basic necessities. From the free market viewpoint both are equal in importance. "An economics that has no theoretical way of making a distinction between the importance of supplying water and the importance of supplying tobacco hardly seems relevant to a living organism, let alone to human development."[20]

Second, the power of modern advertising is continually used to provide commercial definitions for what satisfies various needs. Thus, luxury goods get pushed as necessities for any self-respecting person who wants the esteem of others. In addition, freedom gets defined as being able to *buy* what you want and to use it as you see fit.

THE PRIVATE ECONOMY AND POLICY

So far we have argued that the private economy in the U.S. is made up of two main sectors, one oligopolistic and one competitive, and is directed by large corporations, not consumers. In addition there is a growing irregular sector. The key question is how the existence of the oligopolistic, planning sector which dominates consumer sovereignty affects the operation of the economy. More particularly, how does it render ineffective stabilization policies which rely on market adjustment through prices? This can best be seen in two central markets, the labor market and the monetary sector. In the former, we will make the case that the structural reality makes usual CEI, price-oriented policy unable to affect the sector's performance on employment. In the monetary sector we will show that traditionally monetary policy has not been an independent actor, usable in fighting inflation. To change that situation would entail significant economic disruption, and it has. We will then look through PKI eyes at a key problem to the future of the U.S. economy, investment and the dynamics of the economy.

The Labor Market

A structural analysis of the labor market reveals little commensurability with the orthodox labor theory of wage and hours determination. Keynes himself was one of the first to notice that the demand for labor in dominant sectors of the economy is not greatly affected by changes in the real wage level. That is, when wages drop there probably will be no great increase in employment since a business's desire to hire labor is not very responsive to wage rates (within some reasonable range). Neither is the supply of labor determined exclusively, or even primarily, by levels of the real wage. What then does determine how many people will be hired and how many people will desire to work, and what determines how much they will be paid? This section will address the PKI response to this conundrum. The answer is not complete, but the broad outlines can easily be discerned.[21]

The PKI understanding of the labor market parallels the conception of the structure of American industry. Just as there is a dual industrial structure, so too is there a dual, or segmented, labor market. The primary market for labor is linked to the oligopolistic, or planning, sector of the economy. Workers in this sector typically receive high wages, are highly educated and/or skilled, enjoy substantial job security and opportunities for advancement, and enjoy the benefits garnered by their membership in a relatively strong union. The other sector of labor which corresponds to the market and the irregular sector is termed the "secondary market for labor." Here the job characteristics are exactly the reverse of those in the primary sector; low wages, low levels of education and/or skill, little job security or opportunity for advancement, and a typical lack of fruitful union activity. In general, the workers from the one sector do not openly compete for jobs with the workers employed in the other sector. And the irregular sector absorbs workers who cannot or will not work in the market sector.

Having divided up the scene into the primary and secondary labor markets, PKIs proceed to argue that the concepts of competitive supply and demand for labor are not relevant when the market is seen as it really is. Indeed, there is no wage level that will result in some stable equilibrium position where all have jobs who truly want them and all who employ workers are also satisfied. The reason is that the planning sector or primary labor market will not adjust as assumed. If we are correct on this point, then a reduction in wage levels will not, as some orthodox economists continue to profess, lead to a general reduction in unemployment. As we will see this has important ramifications for policy to deal with current problems.

When viewed from the PKI perspective it is seen that the demand for labor, the supply of labor, the level of real wages, and the employment level are all determined by distinctly different processes.

In the world of big business the demand for labor is the direct result of the decision on how much to produce and not a result of the going wage rate. In much of the oligopolistic core the degree of automation is extremely high, so the cost considerations of hiring or laying off workers are swamped by the need to make the best use of the extremely expensive capital stock. This is pushed to the extreme in the recent trend to using robots on assembly lines. Paying workers six dollars per hour or eight dollars per hour often does not play a large role in deciding how many workers to hire. During the late 1970s and early 1980s, large corporations have become more cost conscious because of the growth of international competition and the depressed state of the U.S. economy.

Conflict between management and labor unions is frequently over work rules and other areas of "management control" rather than wages. In addition, even if a firm desired to cut back or increase its usage of labor, oftentimes the inflexibility of the capital equipment will not allow for change in the short to medium term. If a given machine takes four persons to operate, then it makes no sense to try to run it with three. So in this sector wages have only a subsidiary influence on hiring practices; the level of product demand is the dominant influence. Most large firms maintain a certain level of excess capacity to accommodate short run shifts in demand. When demand is up they put more machines into action, or run a double shift, which will also raise their labor needs. Since much equipment is idle part of the time, since the cost of putting this equipment into operation is close to the average costs as a whole, and since the labor input is an increasingly smaller proportion of total cost, the product supply of the firm may vary over a certain range of output with very little effect on the price of the goods. It is finally the level of demand and the planned output of the firm, then, that determines how many workers will be hired, not primarily the level of wages.

Eileen Appelbaum ties together these various strands in the following succinct explanation of the determinants of the aggregate demand for labor:

> (Given) fixed technical coefficients in production (e.g., four workers to one machine) . . . the demand for production workers by firms in the core of the economy varies directly with the level of output the firm plans to produce, assuming there is excess capacity available so

that the firm is on the horizontal segment of its cost and supply curves (i.e., they will produce various levels of output at the same price) . . . The aggregate demand for labor by the business sector can be obtained by summing up the demand by all individual firms, and it depends in a systematic manner on the expected aggregate demand for output.[22]

It is not, therefore the real wage which determines the demand for labor, but rather the planning process of the firm. It projects and estimates the future strength or weakness of the economy and then decides how much to produce; it ultimately decides how many workers will be given jobs in the planning sector of the economy. One implication is that government efforts to *increase demand* will brighten the employment picture, while efforts to hold wages down will probably have minimal impact.

If the basic demand for labor is not determined by the real wage, market forces might still affect the supply of labor. Do people decide where to work and in what occupation according to different wage offers, or are there other considerations? Once again the PKIs find factors other than the real wage as dominant. Even Keynes observed in the twenties and thirties that the supply of labor is affected little by wage changes, for households are such that one member generally has to work a full time job, and often another member of the family does too. Changes in real wages generally affect consumption patterns more than hours worked. Also there have been many periods in recent history when it has been evident that wide variations in desired employment levels have occurred even when the real wage was not changing at all. There is some evidence that *declining* real wage rates since 1967 have increased the labor force participation rates of women and teenagers. In this case the effect is the opposite: *decreases* in real wages *increase* the household supply of labor, in an attempt to maintain the old (1967) level of consumption.[23]

Unlike mainstream economists who contend that workers decide to supply labor based on their optimization of the work-leisure tradeoff, PKIs argue that for the most part labor has little choice in the matter. Due to institutional constraints workers are expected to work a standard work week of forty hours and therefore marginal adjustments in an individual's supply of labor are both impractical and unrealistic.

The real issue, according to PKIs, is the process by which some workers come to supply labor to the planning sector which provides job security, higher wages and better working conditions, and why some workers must supply their labor to the market and informal sectors where turnover is high, wages are low and working conditions are poor. Since a fundamental prerequisite of continued profitability in the planning sector is uninterrupted production, personnel managers in this sector require a relatively stable work force. Moreover, due to the greater technological sophistication of production the work force must receive on-the-job training if productivity is to be maximized. Together with the imperative of uninterrupted production and the high costs of on-the-job training these personnel managers seek inexpensive screening devices by which to predetermine the potential job stability of prospective employees. The menu of screening devices typically includes discriminating against such groups as blacks, women, teenagers, and so on, which historically have had unstable work patterns; drawing on the firm's internal pool of labor to fill job slots through promotion up (or demotion down) the firm's internal career ladders; or requiring educational credentials which in effect certify the trainability and internalized self-discipline of the worker. Thus, workers are segmented primarily by differences in sex, ethnicity, class background and through unequal access to educational institutions. As a result, the supply of labor is determined largely by the demographic and sociocultural characteristics of the worker as determined by the requirements of the planning sector. This situation effectively limits equality of job opportunity and job mobility. Therefore, according to PKIs, the supply of labor has little if anything to do with the real wage or the leisure-income choice of the individual worker.

It is important to emphasize that the level of money wages is not determined by labor's supply and demand on the market. Rather, money wages are usually arrived at through a process of collective bargaining. The level of real wages (adjusted for inflation) is determined both by money wages and the rate of price level changes. Once a wage rate is arrived at in this way (many other factors possibly entering the negotiations) demand for labor is determined by the firm's planned outputs, and the supply of labor depends on the characteristics of the workers looking for work in the primary sector.

To stress the most important point in all this, it is not probable that a reduction in primary sector wage rates will lead to a drop in unemployment. The automatic and stable adjustment to full (natural) employment assumed by the CEIs is not likely in our oligopolistic economy. And in the secondary labor market there is not much possibility of the wage rate being lowered to reduce unemployment because, as Eileen Appelbaum says, "Unemployment is concentrated among secondary workers and is related to the characteristics of their jobs rather than to wage rates. (And therefore) . . . no further reduction in wage rates is likely to reduce unemployment rates for workers in the secondary sector."²⁴ So at the base of the problem are structural questions.* Market adjustment or simple government fine-tuning will not solve the problem of unemployment. Structural problems demand structural solutions. So the PKI explanation of unemployment and the direction they suggest as fruitful in dealing with it is very different from our earlier theories. As we will see later, however, there are policies which seem viable and can be effective in improving economic performance.

The Monetary Sector

The PKI analysis of the advanced monetary sector in the U.S. involves a complex weaving of three interrelated elements. First is a serious consideration of historical time and therefore recognition of an unchangeable past and a highly uncertain future. Second, PKIs argue that the overriding objective of the Federal Reserve Bank has historically been to respond to the liquidity needs of trade and commerce rather than independently to control the monetary environment in which the economic actors make decisions. The third element (which is a corollary of the second, but deserves separate emphasis) involves the "money wage/money supply nexus" which leads PKIs to conclude that the rate of growth in the money stock is generally endogenously determined.

The endogenous aspect of the money-creation process corresponds to the PKI claim that investment generates (causes) saving and not the reverse as classicals and their followers would have it. Together with the PKI theory of interest rates (an "administered" price set by the largest banks but conditioned by Fed actions), this result dissolves the old dichotomy between the so-called "real" (production) and "monetary" (financial) sectors.

The three characteristics outlined above also delineate the main points of contrast between PKI monetary analysis and the mainstream theories. Keynesians and CEI monetarists consider only logical time, view the money supply as exogenously determined by the direct action of the Federal Reserve, and many argue that the direction of causation runs from saving to investment. PKI's argue that their conception of the monetary sector provides a more realistic depiction of money flows and is therefore a more policy-relevant guide to the macroeconomic problems of our modern economy.

---

*An easily found piece of evidence that unemployment is related to job characteristics in the market sector is the help-wanted ads in the daily newspaper. There are many listings for skilled positions but few for unskilled.

Historical Time and Money. The key question for any monetary theory is why people would want to hold money when other assets pay a higher rate of return. In short, why do we need a special money asset? The answers abound.[25] PKIs answer the question by considering historical time.

Since the future is highly uncertain and risky, economic agents make use of contracts (loans, price and wage contracts) denominated in money units. These contracts permit some sharing of the burden of uncertainty in a world where production takes time. The need for some special asset to serve as a common denominator for these contracts is provided by the existence of money. Professor Moore explains, "It is the uncertainty inherent in historical time, rather than the lack of synchronization between expenses incurred and payments received, that is a necessary and sufficient condition for the existence of money. In a world of perfect certainty, in which the price of everything was known, all goods would be perfectly liquid, and there would be no need for a special money asset."[26] Therefore, individuals hold low-interest bearing liquidity (i.e., money) due to the fact that time moves unidirectionally into an essentially unknown future.

The Role and Behavior of the Fed. The PKI view of the objectives and behavior of the Federal Reserve Bank stands in sharp contrast to the views of both Keynesians and monetarists. While the latter emphasize the Fed's ability to *control* the rate of expansion of the stock of money and therefore control the monetary environment in which economic actors must make decisions, PKIs have emphasized the *accommodating* behavior of the Fed. In short, the central bank ends up *responding* to the decisions already made by the main economic agents — banks and corporations. The crucial implication of this view is that the rate of growth in the money stock is determined *endogenously* — that is, by the needs of the economy for liquidity. This result has obtained for primarily two reasons. First is the historical role of central banks and second is the relationship between changes in money wages and the money supply. Historically, the purpose of central banks has been to accommodate the stock of money to changes in the "needs of trade and commerce." That is, the Fed's historic function has been to respond to the growing credit (liquidity) requirements of an expanding economy. As Keynes insisted in his *Treatise on Money*,[27] money comes into existence along with debts, therefore firms will seek to increase debt-equity (leverage) ratios in order to finance increased production costs and additional investment in light of the expectation of rising future sales revenue. This increased demand for loans by the business sector signals the Fed to expand the availability of credit in the economy in order to finance continuing growth. Unless the Fed accommodates this increased demand for credit, firms must either draw upon existing liquid assets, raise prices or decide not to expand production. In any case, economic growth will be less than otherwise. We should note that in October, 1979, the Fed publicly changed this policy and has continued with its effort to set the growth rate of the money supply independently of economic conditions. The next chapter will argue that the results are a clear indication of why money has been endogenous before and will become so again.

A major implication of the usual accommodating behavior of the central bank is that it has permitted current investment expenditures to be carried out independently of current saving flows. That is, if businesses decided to invest more due to future expectations of increased sales growth by increasing their demand for credit *and* the bankers responded by increasing the supply of credit, *then investment determined saving* and not the reverse.

The other side of the PKI endogeneity result centers on the relationship between money wages and the money supply. Recall from the previous section (on labor markets) that PKIs view money wages as exogenously determined through the administered price process between employers and employees. In order to finance a higher level of money wages in the aggregate there must be a greater volume of money in circulation. Thus, in order to accommodate the payment of higher money wages the Fed must permit an increase in the money supply.

Still another aspect of the money wage/money supply nexus concerns the relationship among money wages, average labor productivity, and unit labor costs. Although these relationships will be taken up in more detail in the next chapter suffice it to say that if money wage increases exceed increases in average labor productivity, unit labor costs will rise. Since prices are in part cost-determined via the administered price process, prices will also rise. In order to finance the higher price level the Fed has generally accommodated by increasing the supply of money in circulation; otherwise the growth process would be choked off.

In summary, it follows that if one considers the historical role of the Fed and if money wages are exogenously determined, then prices must adjust to money wages. Prices can adjust in the context of continued growth only if the Fed accommodates the increase in money wages by expanding the money supply. Thus PKIs conclude that once money wages are determined (exogenously) and if the Fed is to support the needs of trade the money supply will respond endogenously to the administered wage-price process. This has been the case until recently, and we will see that the reason was to avoid the severe disruption a truly exogenously set money supply would cause.

PKI Dynamics: Investment and Pricing Behavior

Now that we have a clear picture of the structure of the economy according to PKI theory and how two of its key sectors function, let us turn to the behavior of the economy over time. This is the question of the dynamics of the American economy. In dealing with this issue, the most important variable is investment. If we can understand the various facets of both private and public investment—how much, what type, why and when it occurs, etc.—we will have gone far toward discovering why income is distributed as it is, why there is a particular price level, and how growth, inflation, and unemployment interact with each other and with investment itself.

Somewhat like the Keynesians, PKIs recognize the centrality of aggregate demand and how an initial increase in discretionary expenditures (of which investment is one) leads to a multiple increase in aggregate income. But PKIs also take notice of the role of investment in expanding productive capacity, following the lead of such economists as Harrod. It is important, therefore, to consider both sides of the dual nature of investment; how it affects short-term income, and how it adjusts productive capacity.

When both facets are considered, we return to the early idea of Keynes that the economy may be inherently unstable. John Cornwall states the problem in the form of a question: "Why," he asks, "should the growth of demand that results from a certain rate of growth of investment (the multiplier effect) be just equal to the rate of growth of capacity which results from this same growth of investment?"[28] Suppose, for example, that investment by corporations added proportionately more to productive capacity than to income (or aggregate demand). Firms would realize at some point that they were overcapitalized and their investment would fall. Such a reduction in investment would generate a fall in income and likewise a rise in unemployment. A recession would be upon us. Eventually investors would regain confidence, investment would rise, a general business expansion would occur, and one day the same difficulty as before would occur. We thus have a scenario of intermittent expansion and contraction, the essence of instability.

It seems then that if investment could be maintained at stable levels, the economy would remain fairly stable. But since investment decisions are usually based on what Keynes called "profit expectations," there is no reason to suppose that these expectations will be stable over time. Profit expectations are, in the final analysis, a firm's subjective judgment as to what future profits will be (say over the ten-year life of a new machine) if an investment is made now (in the new machine).

The expected future profits are then weighed against the cost, including interest charges, of the investment. If the future profits are greater than the costs the investment is worthwhile. The most important factor is the calculation of expected profits. The chief problem is *uncertainty* about the future. The greater the uncertainty, the greater the risk, and thus, the greater the probability that investments will be postponed. The causes of uncertainty are legion — rumors of war, inflation, political change, changing psychological moods — and, by the nature of the future, uncertainty can never be eliminated. But, as we will see later, a chief function of government is to reduce uncertainty. Cornwall thus says that "no matter what share of output is devoted to the production of investment goods, the unbalanced nature of the growth process that is taking place will inevitably lead to *fluctuations in the level of investment and thus in the rate* of expansion."[29]

Investment is the primary component in determining the level of economic activity, and thereby the rapidity of growth, the level of employment, the distribution of income, the rate of inflation, and so on. One area where this focus on investment as the prime mover is especially intriguing is that of the saving-investment nexus. It is generally thought by CEIs, Keynesians, and almost everybody else that the rate of saving determines how much is available for investment. Indeed, this may be partially true, and yet it obfuscates some important considerations at the same time. Consider the argument that the rate of investment plays a major role in determining aggregate output. Saving, as we know, is generally a certain percentage of output. So in some sense investment may be thought of as determining saving as well as the reverse. That investment and saving are interrelated in this way will become much clearer after a short foray into the PKI analysis of pricing behavior.

As we have seen the dominant firms in the planning sector have sufficient control to "administer" the prices of their output. If this is accurate (and there is evidence to support it) then the prices they select must be based on some predetermined objective. Most PKIs argue that this objective is typically to maximize the growth of sales revenue over time as a means to preserve or enlarge the firm's market share, subject to the requirement that a certain specified level of profits be maintained.[30] Firms will thus set prices at the levels which will most help them achieve this goal.

These considerations on the nature of price determination and behavioral goals of the large corporation in the planning sector have led PKIs to reconsider the microeconomic core of theory which underlies the standard macroeconomic policy proposals. In place of the orthodox economist's profit maximization rule, i.e., set output and price at levels which equate marginal revenue to marginal cost, PKIs argue that corporate managers set prices and output at levels which achieve a target level of profits. Therefore the strategic variable in the PKI schema is the *price markup over direct costs*.

In a markup pricing system direct costs are calculated, profit requirements are added on, and investment plans are thrown in on top of that. Thus there are now three components of price: (1) direct costs (labor, materials, rent, etc.), (2) a target level of profits to satisfy shareholders, and (3) funds to reinvest for further growth. This third component is the part tacked on to ensure an optimum growth of sales revenue. Its inclusion is defended on the grounds that the large oligopolistic firms in the U.S. rely primarily on internal sources of funds (i.e., retained earnings) to finance their fixed capital expenditures.[31] What then causes prices to shift? Basically two things: since target profits may remain more or less the same in normal circumstances, fluctuations in direct costs and changes in investment needs are the factors behind changes in the price levels of given products.

The process by which firms establish the size of the markup is as follows. First, the firm estimates the probable rate of growth of demand for its output. Then, it takes stock of its current rate of capacity utilization and its ability to meet the expected future product demand. With this information the firm can estimate its desired rate of capacity utilization. If current capacity is less than desired the firm will need to increase investment in order to preserve (or expand) its share of total industry output. Thus, the determination of future investment plans is based on the expected growth of demand.

The second step in this process is to choose the price markup which will generate the retained profits necessary to carry out the firm's investment plans. In other words, once future investment plans are determined the target level of profits necessary to finance the investment is fixed. Corporations then set prices at the level necessary to generate that target level of profits.

A major implication of this pricing behavior is that actual market prices do not reflect simply the current state of demand but also include planned investment which reflects expected future demand. Thus, prices cannot be viewed simply as short-run market clearing devices but, in addition, they signal shifts in the allocation of resources over time. The end result is that prices set by the large corporations in the planning sector reflect investment needs more than current market demand (within limits of course).

It has always been difficult to specify exactly how businesses determine how much and when to invest. We do know that investment decisions are based on the expected rate of return on an investment, but it is very difficult and perhaps futile to surmise how these expectations come into being. In some way, however, the firm looks to the future and anticipates the growth of demand for certain products. According to these expectations which are uncertain, investment needs are assessed, and once investment needs are ascertained, prices are set.

Now the second argument showing that investment determines saving is complete. Since retained earnings are counted as saving, and since it is investment planning which determines the need for retained earnings, so too we can argue that investment is the ultimate determinant of saving.

The implication of this result is quite important. CEIs see investment and growth as affected primarily by the prices which affect businesses. Keynesians place more emphasis on business investment but have a basic view that fiscal and monetary policy can offset the instability of investment and may even be able to stabilize it. However, PKIs see investment as virtually unaffected by prices. Thus the efforts of the supply-side economists to cut business taxes and so lower the price of investment are seen as irrelevant to the investment process. And without a change in the structures that affect business decision-making, orthodox policy will not be able to control the destabilizing effects of investment.

A Summing Up

The labor market and the monetary sector are crucial to the functioning of the planning sector, and economic policy to deal with macroeconomic problems has been formulated to affect this key sector. But when looked at through the PKI analysis, the price-oriented policies of the CEIs and the Keynesians can be expected to have little impact on the employment decisions in the sector. So it should come as little surprise that unemployment persists and appears insensitive to domestic policy.

Similarly, traditional reliance on the control of the money supply to control inflation has been unrealistic because of a faulty understanding of the functioning of the Central Bank (the Fed) whose role was to avoid domestic disruption by accommodating wage agreements and the currency requirements of ordinary trade. This has changed to some degree since 1979 with consequent major disruption of the economy, an indication of the implications of overlooking the structural realities of the economy.

The treatment of the two sectors brings home forcefully the PKI stance: simple price policies or fine-tuning of the economy cannot succeed in dealing with our current problems. Only an understanding of and willingness to deal with the structures of our economy provide any likelihood of success.

This is emphasized in PKI dynamics where the importance of ordinary policy efforts is emphasized against the backdrop of instability generated in the investment process. Without efforts to deal with the structures of the economy, the possibility of improving economic performance is slight.

THE PUBLIC ECONOMY

The U.S. political economy is composed of both a private economy and a public economy. The private economy can be divided into a planning sector, a market sector, and an informal sector. The public economy can be divided into the governmental sector and the not-for-profit sector. The latter generally is classified as part of the private economy but we prefer to treat it as part of the public economy because of the similarity of goals and motivations of the not-for-profit institutions — private universities, hospitals, foundations, pension funds, credit unions, labor unions, churches.

The following figures provide an idea of how important the public economy is in terms of size. The governmental sector, as measured by taxes at all levels as a percentage of gross national product (GNP), accounts for about one-third of the total economy. Unfortunately we do not collect statistics separately for the not-for-profit sector. An estimate for 1973, made by Burton Weisbrod from a survey of 432 organizations, indicates that the total revenue for the not-for-profit sector was $530.9 billion.[32] Were this figure directly comparable to GNP, the not-for-profit sector would have accounted for 41 percent of GNP in 1973. Unfortunately, it is not; these total revenue figures contain an unknown amount of double counting. For example, the premium paid to Blue Cross/Blue Shield by the individual and the subsequent payment to the physician are both counted in Weisbrod's revenue estimate. However, it is clear that the not-for-profit sector is large and it is growing.

The Governmental Sector: Views of the State

Let us focus first on the role of the governmental sector — or to use the more common term, the state — in a capitalist market economy. This involves the double problem of *what is* the role of the state and *what should be* the role of the state. Let us review the positions of the Conservative Economic Individualists, the Keynesians, and the Marxists before detailing our own Post-Keynesian Institutionalist view.

The different views of the role of the state depend upon the different theories' evaluations of the market economy—whether they believe it capable of meeting peoples' many needs and desires (life-sustenance); whether they believe it inherently equitable and fair, thus encouraging self-esteem; and whether they believe that it promotes human freedom.

The CEI and Keynesian Views. Not surprisingly, CEIs give the market system high praise for its efficiency in producing those goods and services people desire. Moreover, this is accomplished without coercion or centralized direction by a conscious body. This point cannot be overstated for the CEIs who, in the words of one famous member, "take freedom of the individual, or perhaps the family, as our ultimate goal in judging social arrangements."[33] They contend that individuals striving to maximize their own self-interest will unwittingly maximize society's self-interest; indeed, society fares *better* than if individuals, or the state, attempted to promote its interests. In contrast, the state can be, and generally has been, controlled by a small group to serve their own interest and thwart the desire of the individuals of the society.

Within the institutional framework of competitive capitalism, economic freedom is maximized. The market coordinates the voluntary activities and decisions of vast numbers of individuals and enterprises, all pursuing their own interests, without any individual, group, or authority directing. This explains the "miracle" of the market. Moreover, CEIs assert, the foundations of economic freedom established by competitive capitalism are the necessary prerequisite for a society of free individuals. In accord with Marxists and PKIs, they believe that human freedom is linked intimately to the institutional framework under which production and consumption is carried out. As Milton Friedman says, "Viewed as a means to the end of political freedom, economic arrangements are important because of their effect on the concentration or dispersion of power. The kind of economic organization that provides economic freedom directly, namely, competitive capitalism, also promotes political freedom because it separates economic power from political power and in this way enables the one to offset the other."[34] CEI theorists obviously believe that old dictum "Power corrupts and absolute power corrupts absolutely." Thus, to ensure that society's goals are met, they rely on a market system which, to their way of thinking, disperses power in such a way that no one individual, firm, or government can dictate to another. Indeed government is seen as the most likely nexus for power concentration and so its size and role must be minimized.

CEIs, crediting the decentralized market mechanism with optimal efficiency, insist upon relying on it to as great an extent as possible. Only as a last resort should one turn to the state for economic decision-making, and its scope should be limited and its power likewise dispersed. Thus by relying primarily on the market system, which generates freedom, and on a limited, decentralized political system, human freedom is maximized. Now, let us examine more specifically what "to as great an extent as possible" and "only as a last resort" actually mean in practice.

There are important roles for the government in the CEI schema which the market cannot perform itself. A principal one is the protection of property rights. This is the key to successful operation of the free market system; otherwise, contracts, copyrights, patents, and the like, would carry little meaning. Then, of course, there are the obvious functions which few, except perhaps anarchists, would argue with. These functions include: maintaining law and order, providing for national and civil defense, constructing public works that the private sector is unable to construct and providing a monetary framework.

CEIs contend that the government can *intervene* legitimately in the economy only in the case of market failure. The main reasons for market failure arise either from externalities, that is, when an action of an individual or firm has a negative or positive effect on other individuals for which it is not possible or feasible to charge or recompense them; or from monopolies and oligopolies which diverge from the assumed small, independent, powerless price-takers.

The scope and spectrum for state activity varies widely between the most conservative CEIs and the most liberal Keynesians. CEIs, like Milton Friedman, see basic stability in the economy and very few imperfections in the market and, thus, little justification for government intervention. They see many of our present economic problems being exacerbated by the growing power of the state. For example, the use of Keynesian fiscal and monetary policy merely generates greater instability. Moreover, they suggest that many current government activities and legislation hinder the smooth functioning of the market. For instance, minimum wage laws, social security, tariffs on imports and restrictions of exports, most regulation of industry, and national parks do not meet their criteria for government intervention. These and most other government programs reduce the efficient working of the market and, equally important, they represent a significant encroachment on personal freedom, according to the CEIs.

On the other hand, liberal Keynesians, like Paul Samuelson, see more pervasive market failure, ranging over a wide spectrum and including extensive imperfections in the market mechanism. The central task of our affluent capitalism, by liberal standards, is to strike an appropriate balance between the market and the polity, taking account of the strengths and weaknesses of both. Liberal Keynesians have more faith in stabilization policies than do the CEIs, pointing to the 1960s as a measure of its success. Thus they encourage and support the use of fiscal and monetary policy to stabilize the macroeconomy.

They also view government programs to alleviate poverty as the primary reason that the number of people living below the poverty line has been reduced. Liberals find the degree of monopolization, the extent of externalities, unemployment, the poor, the disadvantaged of society evidence of market failure, and they claim these reasons call for, even require, substantial government intervention. Only then will the proper working of the market be assured and, thereby, our life-sustenance, self-esteem, and personal freedom enhanced. For the Keynesian, the government in our democracy is an authentic reflection of the interplay of pluralistic interests of the modern, complex society. It must be relied upon to balance competing interests since market imperfections have led to concentrated economic power, and reliance on markets would simply allow the economically powerful to rule the society.

One very important part the government plays in Keynesian eyes is its effect on the goal of equity, thus far ignored in our discussion. A perfectly functioning competitive market guarantees an efficient allocation of resources, but it in no way assures society of an acceptable distribution of those goods and services. In other words, even if an economy had the extreme situation of only 2 percent of the population having 98 percent of a nation's income, the market mechanism would be unaffected, generating an optimal or efficient allocation of the economy's resources; for market theory takes as a given the initial distribution of income. Society may deem that initial income distribution unjust. Such a belief leads many liberal Keynesian economists to claim that government must address the question of redistribution of income.

Among liberals and conservatives alike, however, there is a strong, deep conviction in the fundamental value of the competitive market system. They believe it is, unquestionably, the most efficient economic system, assuring the optimal allocation of resources and, even more importantly, guaranteeing that our individual freedom is preserved and strengthened. The role for the state, in their schema, is limited: the state may be needed by the market on occasion to further the system's smooth functioning, but the state should not supplant the market.

The result is that the CEIs and Keynesians see the government sector as exogenous to the economic system. In the CEI view the state enforces the rules of the game or it intervenes to the detriment of all. In the Keynesian view the state intervenes when the rules of the game yield widely unacceptable results and it intervenes as a societal representative in stabilizing the economy. In either case the real action is in the private market economy. As a result both CEI and Keynesian theories have had difficulty in incorporating the government sector in their models. Their best attempt has been an unconvincing use of competitive equilibrium theory to explain behavior in the public economy as an instance of "public choice" akin to consumer choice.

The Marxist View. In the economic system, Marxists assert, workers lose control over their own lives: they only find work when the capitalist finds it profitable. Thus human needs may go unmet, factories may lie idle, workers may be seeking employment, but unless capitalists see a profit-making opportunity, the market mechanism is not set in motion. This lack of coordination and cooperation is seen as totally irrational by Marxists.

Irrational or not, the system is maintained because those who have economic power ascend to positions of political power or are able to exert their power over those who do. Marxists thus scoff at the idea of the capitalist system maintaining a democracy: if it is a democracy, they claim, it is a perverted one—primarily for the rich and powerful. From their positions and through their connections, capitalists are able to use the state to further their own ends. They set up the educational system, thereby transmitting capitalist ideology to the country's youth. They set up the courts and appoint the judges, thereby assuring the sanction of private property. They run the newspapers, radio stations, magazines, and television stations. The notion of the efficacy and equity of the capitalist system permeates the entire social system, argue the Marxists, through this subtle propagandizing of the capitalists.

The state is seen as a manifestation of concentrated economic power. To deny that the monopolists and oligopolists possess vast power is folly; the point is to discover how they wield it through the political system. First and foremost, the state protects private property, that is, the interests of capitalists. As the Marxist theorist Ralph Miliband put it, "the state in these class societies is primarily and inevitably the guardian and protector of the economic interests which are dominant in them. Its *real* purpose and mission is to ensure their continued predominance, not to prevent it."[35]

Thus far we have seen that Marxists view the state as essentially the mistress of the capitalist. Now we must turn to their view of the specific favors the mistress performs, to James O'Connor's analysis of the state[36] which we discussed earlier in the chapter on Marxism.

O'Connor begins with the premise that the state must fulfill two functions: accumulation and legitimation. The former, an offensive function, is to provide "social capital." Of this function there are two sub-categories: "social investment," i.e., infrastructure which increases the productivity of labor; and "social consumption," e.g., disability insurance which lowers the wage capitalists must pay workers. The legitimation function, a defensive one, is to delude the workers into believing the system is an equitable one and, thus, to quell social unrest. These are called "social expenses" and would include items like food stamps, Medicare, and Medicaid. They must be extracted by government out of business profits, though according to Marxists the state only provides these services to maintain a congenial atmosphere for the capitalists. These two functions — accumulation and legitimation — are the dual and contradictory goals of the capitalist state and in attempting to fulfill both the result is economic, political, and social crisis. The crisis results because the state must grow (through the accumulation process) to maintain and further monopoly capital; but as a result of the ensuing growth of monopoly, there is increased unemployment, inflation, stagflation, and poverty calling for an even larger state (through the legitimization process). In other words, as O'Connor states, "the growth of the state is both a cause and effect of the expansion of monopoly capital."[37] The ever-increasing growth of the state translates into ever-increasing expenditures for legitimation and accumulation, but the profits these expenditures generate are entirely appropriated by monopoly capital. The ensuing crisis is a result of the growing demands upon the state's shrinking purse.

The only practical solution to the fiscal and social crisis which will enable capitalism as a system to survive is for the state to cooperate more fully with monopoly capital to encourage production (that is, lower costs) in both the state and private sectors. In other words, the answer is a social-industrial complex (SIC) which will retain profits in the private sphere while relieving the fiscal pressure. For the SIC to emerge, three political changes are required. First, the "ties between monopoly capital and the state will have to become even closer." Second, "the influence of competitive capital, particularly its influence and power in local and state government and in Congress, would have to be weakened." And, third, "stronger bonds between monopoly capital and organized labor would be necessary."[38]

O'Connor and other Marxists do not gladly greet the emerging SIC. They envision it as redistributing income from labor to the owners of capital through taxation by the state. In other words, all tax-payers will fund the activities of the SIC, but the benefits will accrue to capitalists. Simply put, Marxists believe the only survival path open to capitalism is through the means of "friendly fascism."

Marxists, like CEIs, see an intimate relation between the political apparatus that governs society and the economic sector which guides production. There, obviously, the similarity ends: CEIs view capital-ism as a liberating economic system transmitting its non-coercive basis to the polity. Marxists believe the oppressive nature of the capitalist system is pervasive in the structure of the state. In effect the state is seen as the dictatorship of the ruling class over the remainder of society.

Marxist economic theory displays the effects of this view of the state. First, in terms of analysis the focus is on the capital accumulation process in the private sector. The state is brought into the analysis only for its role of aiding the accumulation process. Second, in terms of policy the Marxist position leaves no room for an independent role for the state.

The PKI View. PKIs believe that in limiting economics to a study of maximizing behavior, traditional economists engage in a level of theo-retical abstraction that is too high and a scope too narrow to deal ade-quately with current social problems, let alone understand the com-plicated world around us. The most glaring examples are illustrated by traditional theorists ignoring, or relegating to unimportance, the crucial issues of technological change and the exercise of power in the economy and the polity. Matters such as these are of vital importance in explaining inflation, unemployment, stagflation, inadequate health care and housing, corporate flight, rural and urban poverty, to men-tion a few of the major problems facing our society today.

In addition, several areas of contention exist between CEIs and Keynesians on the one side and PKIs on the other, and these will serve to highlight the different roles of the state each favors. Traditional economists maintain that society is simply a collection of individuals, while PKIs see society as an organic whole greater than the sum of its individual parts. In addition, their views vary greatly on the nature of human behavior. Whereas traditional economists believe human be-havior is fundamentally rationalistic, atomistic, and hedonistic, PKIs conceive of a broader human nature, including habit, custom, sense of adventure, even perversity, in addition to acquisitiveness. PKIs also utilize a broader conception of the economic system. Specifically, whereas traditional economists downplay the existence or importance of power in the hands of any individual economic agent, PKIs place at the center of their analysis an explicit consideration of certain powerful institutions: large corporations, unions, the state. Finally, while PKIs value freedom no less than CEIs, they contend that in some ways the market system restricts rather than promotes freedom. Basic freedom includes adequate food, shelter, health care, and education which, PKIs assert, are necessary for the exercise of freedom and which the private market system seldom provides for all. Thus, intervention by the state is frequently necessary to make freedom real for the poor.

CEIs see the growth of the government sector as an aberration caused by misguided political philosophy. Keynesians see the growth as a response to the need to provide macrostabilization, correct market failures, and care for the losers in the economic game. They admit that the growth has gotten out of hand and that government programs should be redesigned to use rather than override the market. Marxists see the growth of the state as a result of the accumulation and legitimation needs of the capitalist class.

PKIs see the growth of government as a natural phenomenon required to re-embed the economy into the social system. As the various groups in the economy have sought to thwart the workings of the free market system they have called on government for help: pure food and drug legislation for consumers, price supports for farmers, minimum wage and maximum hour laws for workers, licensing for attorneys and physicians, tariffs for business, and on and on. In addition, government was needed to facilitate private arrangements to circumvent the market: endorsing collective bargaining as a national policy, allowing the elimination of competition through corporate mergers, and allowing professional organizations to set standards for their members.

In fact, no one (except CEIs) wants the free market system to be the organizing principle of society itself. At most, people want it to be the primary regulatory mechanism utilized by society to achieve its goals.

As a result of the need to oversee this re-embedding process government has become a primary economic agent along with business firms, labor unions, and consumers. Government, as the key actor in the public economy, operates with a degree of independence unthinkable to the Marxist, but bounded by constraints ignored by CEIs and Keynesians. The historical evidence is overwhelming that government is not merely the servant of the capitalist class. On the other hand, it is clear that the government *must,* if it is to survive, support the private economy by performing the accumulation and legitimation functions described by O'Connor.

PKIs argue that any relevant economic theory must provide a central role for government as an *actor* not just a referee or umpire. PKI theory attempts to do this by focusing on the distribution of power as the key to understanding the economy.

The Not-for-Profit Sector

What do the Ford Foundation, University of Notre Dame, United Way, First United Methodist Church, the local Elks Club, the Teamster's Pension Fund, the volunteer fire department, Blue Cross/Blue Shield, United Automobile Workers, and the South Side Credit Union have in common? As Weisbrod says, they are ". . . like the government sector—much involved in the provision of collective-consumption goods."[39] That is not all they do, but for our purposes it is the most important.

Collective goods are those that can be enjoyed simultaneously by more than one person without limiting access to anyone. These range from pure public goods to simply goods with externalities. Once a pure public good, a lighthouse for example, is provided, it is impossible to limit access. Any passing ship can use the services of the lighthouse. As a result no profit-seeking firm has an incentive to produce public goods since there is no way to charge for their use.

Some privately produced goods generate externalities both positive (social benefits) and negative (social costs) which affect people who were not involved in the transaction. Pollution is a social cost inflicted on others by those who produce and those who use automobiles. Since the pollution cost is not borne by the producer or individual consumer, too much pollution is produced (and too many automobiles). When one neighbor maintains his or her house, it raises the value of all the houses in the neighborhood. This is an example of a social benefit reaped by all the neighbors. Since not all the benefits are captured by the one maintaining his or her house there is less incentive to do so and thus less "maintenance" is produced.

The existence of pure public goods and externalities results in market failure. That is, the market system underproduces public goods and those private goods with social benefits, and it overproduces private goods with social costs. Government, having the power to compel payment or compliance, has been seen traditionally by economists as the institutional mechanism to correct these market failures. However, historically we have turned not only to government but also to voluntary, not-for-profit organizations. Weisbrod says:

> . . . before a political majority comes to demand governmental provision, the minority that demands governmental provision of a good will be undersatisfied and will turn to voluntary organizations . . . .
> It is noteworthy, therefore, that in sixteenth-century England, where governmental provision of any civilian goods or services was very modest, private "philanthropies" (voluntary organizations) were providing funds for such wide-ranging collective activities as schools, hospitals, nontoll roads, fire fighting apparatus, public parks, bridges, dikes and causeways, digging of drainage canals, waterworks, wharves and docks, harbor cleaning, libraries, care of prisoners in jails, and charity to the poor—in short, for the gamut of nonmilitary goods that we identify today as governmental responsibilities.[40]

It is clear that voluntary not-for-profit organizations are thriving today. There are several reasons for this. Not only are there significant market failures in producing collective consumption goods but government has proven that its capability for correcting them is limited. Government is faced with limited and frequently biased information regarding peoples' needs and wants for collective consumption. Also the incentive structure within which government officials operate frequently does not coincide with that necessary to correct market failures. Another reason for the importance of the not-for-profit sector is the fact that many collective goods and services are desired by only some of the population. Thus it is natural that sub-groups band together to fulfill their needs.

For many people these voluntary not-for-profit organizations do much more than provide a needed collective consumption good as a part of life-sustenance. They are also vital in helping people achieve self-esteem and freedom. Churches, neighborhood associations, legal aid societies, civil rights organizations all aid people in this way. In addition, voluntary not-for-profit organizations often function as "mediating institutions" between the individual family and the huge mega-institutions of society—large corporations in the planning sector and government agencies. We will pursue this issue in the last chapter when discussing alternative solutions for the current economic crisis.

With this brief sketch of PKI theory, we can now develop an explanation for the current crisis, for at the heart of stagflation, or "double trouble," lie the interrelationships among investment, pricing behavior, and a third factor, income distribution. These private-sector factors, combined with public sector operations that affect uncertainty, are the key to understanding what is wrong in the U.S. economy.

In the next chapter we will look more specifically at the contemporary problems of the economy and will see how PKIs explain them. One important aspect of this treatment will be to look at the programs implemented by the Fed and the Reagan Administration to see how the PKI analysis can explain the obvious difficulties they are having.

9. Stagflation and Economic Crisis

The "golden age" of American capitalism was 1961-67. Per capita income and consumption expanded dramatically. Keynesian economics seemed to meet its test, for full employment and stable prices were achieved. In the euphoria of the moment, "fine-tuning" was expected to banish forever the twin evils of inflation and unemployment. In addition to successful macromanagement the period saw the launching of the Peace Corps and the War on Poverty. The civil rights movement made spectacular gains. It was the era of the New Frontier and the Great Society. The "mixed economy" appeared on the verge of making possible the fulfillment of our three goals—life-sustenance, self-esteem, and freedom.

But then trouble began. First came the war in Vietnam, then the revolt of the young, inflation, pollution, food and oil shortages, and recession. And as if this were not enough, the whole Keynesian consensus was shattered by the simultaneous appearance of massive unemployment and double-digit inflation—the paradigmatic manifestation of the economic crisis. Since 1975 the crisis has changed from acute to chronic. Economists and politicians now talk hopefully of achieving 6 percent inflation and 6 percent unemployment over the next decade. Many seem willing to abandon the fulfillment of our goals, at least for the poor, in the process.

Since the problem of stagflation has pushed from the public agenda all other problems, we will concentrate on analyzing this "crisis" in this chapter. At the same time we must remember that solving stagflation will not, in itself, achieve our three goals.

The starting point of the PKI analysis of stagflation is that cyclical fluctuations in employment, prices, and income are inherent in the nature of a market economy. Decentralized decision-making means that full capacity production is only one possible outcome of an indefinite number, an insight that elevates Marx and Keynes above their peers and which must form the basis of any adequate analysis of the contemporary economy. CEIs ignore or deny this position, but the evidence is against them. The history of the American economy indicates that full employment with stable prices is an aberration that occurred only during 1961-67.

Why did the Keynesian solution of government fiscal and monetary stabilization work only during that short-lived "golden age"? Several factors helped destroy that momentary triumph and guarantee that our contemporary problems will afflict the economy for the foreseeable future.

Structure of the economy. The price-setting process in the planning sector has become increasingly insensitive to market or to policy influence, and as a result there is an inherent tendency to inflation in the economy. Markets no longer discipline price setting because of the growth in concentration and the tendency of firms to use "markup" pricing for their products. Government can affect prices by imposing demand restraint, but the requisite decline in demand for a given impact on prices has become so large that the mix of unemployment and inflation which can be obtained is itself unacceptable.

Also as a result of the need to provide minimum economic security for the unsuccessful participants in the modern consumer society and of the growth of a domestic and international war capability, a relatively autonomous bureaucratic and military sector has grown up. This results in the creation of another competitor for the output of society, a competitor whose very operation can often interfere with productivity in the private sector. Thus there is a dual impact which sums to added inflationary pressures in the economy.

Emphasis on economic growth. The attempt to build a mass-consumption society since World War II has contributed to undermining the stability of the system. The highly resource-using nature of the economy has led to the beginnings of severe shortages in energy supplies and a variety of raw materials. These shortages have and will continue to drive up costs and prices, making the maintenance of the consumer society ever more difficult. Yet the "growth psychology" which expects ever-increasing income and consumption will be greatly threatened by any slackening in growth; and in that event there will result a sharply increased struggle over income shares.

Loss of U.S. hegemony over the international economy. A crucial problem with the earlier approach is the stark fact that much of the prosperity of the 1960s was based on U.S. hegemonic control of the international market system. Our goods were the most esteemed in the world; our power could, for a small price, ensure stability and continued harmony with a friend or bring to heel a country which challenged U.S. supremacy. Perhaps most tangibly, the U.S. could run persistent balance-of-payments deficits which allowed higher levels of goods consumption through the goodwill of foreign central banks. OPEC, competition from Japan, South Korea and others, the loss of the ability to control world events, all of these factors changed the economic environment to such an extent that both the Keynesian and the CEI approaches are simply inadequate to deal with current realities.

Let us now analyze in some detail these reasons for the stagflation crisis in the U.S. economy.

THE STRUCTURAL ROOTS OF THE PROBLEMS

The key to understanding and analyzing our current economic problems is the sectorization of the economy which we made in chapter 8. There we divided the economy into a private economy with three sub-sectors — planning, market and irregular — and a public economy with two sub-sectors — government and non-profit. Let us examine each of them in turn to see how they play out their role in the continuing difficulties of the economy.

The Private Economy: Planning Sector

The principal reason economists and government administrators since the late sixties have been ineffectual in their attempts to correct the nation's economic ills is simply that they have failed to acknowledge the existence, let alone the predominance, of the planning sector. Both CEI and Keynesian theories are based on the presumption that the entire U.S. economy is competitive, not just the market sector. Retention of this presumption, and the formulation of policy based on it, has resulted very directly in the crisis proportions of unemployment, inflation, and unstable growth which began in the late sixties and have been gradually but consistently worsening ever since.

The dynamics of our explanation of the crisis are found in the nature of the planning sector itself and in the interaction between the planning sector, the market sector, and the public sector.

The planning sector dominates the economy and conditions the functioning of the other sectors. As such it must be at the center of any explanation of the current malaise. Several qualifications of this claim could be made. First of all it is difficult to specify precisely the firms and industries of the planning sector. One approach would be to follow

Galbraith and suggest that the top one thousand industrial firms are in the planning sector.[1] Another approach would be an industry-by-industry study to find the concentrated industries and the dominant firms in them. These would be predominantly industrial firms, but would include firms in other sectors that can control their environment for any of a variety of reasons. Portions of the transportation sector, of finance, of services, etc. would be part of the planning sector. But for our purposes the key conclusion is that there are significant and important segments of the U.S. economy that are not market-dominated, that in a significant sense can control their immediate environment under ordinary circumstances.

The second qualification is that many indicators of economic performance would show that the planning sector is becoming less important in the economy. For example, the Fortune 500 largest industrial firms account for 15 million jobs; this quantity has increased very little during the 1970s and since 1950 has only doubled, while their sales were increasing thirteenfold.[2] Although we would add many additional firms to get to our planning sector, in an economy with 100 million persons employed the planning sector will not dominate the labor market in terms of jobs. Its dominance is of another variety. Patterns for wage agreements and trends in overall employment are set in that sector simply because of its linkages with the rest of the economy. What occurs there in terms of wages and jobs affects everything else as it affects the amount of income that the workers have and therefore their expenditures on other goods, which in turn affects sales of these goods, and so on. So although writers such as Emma Rothschild[3] quite correctly point out the growing importance of services and retail sales (which are part of the market sector), the key to the functioning of the economy remains the planning sector, and policy must deal with its reality to be successful. This is the major failure of present-day policy.

Let us turn now to the functioning of the planning sector and how it has engendered the current intransigent problems. There are two questions to be dealt with. The first is how the planning sector contributes to inflation, unemployment, and instability. The second is why current economic policies of a Keynesian or CEI variety cannot stabilize the economy without exacerbating the already difficult situation.

Since planning-sector firms are generally protected from the discipline of the market, their price-setting behavior will have an implicit inflationary bias. Let us see how that operates.

A long-running debate in economics is whether inflation is "demand-pull" or "cost-push." But actually it is neither; it is a result of the social conflict over who will receive the income generated in the society. In this sector, this is a battle between owners and workers over who will receive the income from production, based upon some concept of a fair distribution of income. But workers have a very different estimate than owners do of what is fair.

The planning sector has been the core of the economy in the twentieth century, and the conflict over income shares has been negotiated in the realization of the oligopolistic power possessed by the firms in the planning sector. Thus workers in those industries have benefitted as well, enjoying higher average wages and much better working conditions in general than workers in other sectors of the economy. Fringe benefits are the envy of other workers as well. This is the "primary" labor market.

Similar relations exist in the negotiations between the firms and their suppliers of raw materials, working capital, etc. The decisions on input prices, including wages, which are made in this sector have traditionally set a pattern for the entire economy. And since planning-sector firms can generally set the price of their product using markup pricing, their incentive for hard bargaining on labor contracts or supplier contracts is lessened. Thus there is a tendency for costs to rise above what they might otherwise be, and as a result for prices of products to be higher as well, especially in the planning sector. The ability to bargain in this sector, with the effect of raising the overall wage structure in the economy, is one factor which has offset Marx's claim that wages would be pushed to the subsistence minimum.

What has made this inflationary pressure acute and has led to the current problems is a decline in the performance of the planning sector firms. This is generally described as the "falling productivity of American industry." If firms become more efficient and get more output from their operations, higher input costs need not result in actual price increases. But such increases in efficiency have not been forthcoming during the 1970s, for a series of complex reasons. Workers are most often blamed, with little justification; government is another favorite culprit. Part of it is the effect of technology—the dearth of productivity-increasing technology recently, the exhaustion of benefits from large-scale production—and part of it is the change in the mix of the economy from products open to productivity increases to other types of products. But another part which is certainly important and which underlies many of the debacles we have recently seen is the U.S. corporation itself and the type of manager that reaches its upper echelons.[4]

To summarize an extensive debate, it is the financial analyst seeking short-run goals rather than the production specialist concentrating on long-run growth who reaches the top; and this leads to an inability to compete in technological terms with the Germans, Japanese and others. Technology is where the dynamism of our economy is generated. R & D expenditures have fallen over the past fifteen years as managers improve this year's—and even this quarter's—"bottom line" through mergers, short-run product redesign, and other cosmetic changes.[5] There is some awareness of this problem. For example, General Electric's new president, John Welch, has radically altered management practices.

> Mr. Welch blames the foreign threat to GE and other American companies on many of the management principles that GE itself helped shape in the 1960s and 1970s—a time, he says, when companies were "managed, not led." He fears that managing assets as if they were investment portfolios, seeking short-term profits at the sacrifice of longterm gains, and stressing conservatism over innovation may have permanently crippled many of America's major industries.[6]

It is significant that Welch is a chemical engineer who started in production at GE in 1960.

The large corporation is becoming ever more bureaucratized, resulting in greater inefficiency and lowered productivity. Lester Thurow has said, "American government may be bureaucratic and inefficient, but American industry is just as bureaucratic and inefficient."[7] Between 1977 and 1980, blue-collar employment increased six hundred thousand while white-collar employment increased 5.5 million. And this increase was overwhelmingly in the private sector.

Lowered productivity increases slow down the growth of aggregate supply and, given some growth in aggregate demand, contribute to stagflation.

As noted in the last chapter, the operation of the planning sector can finally generate economy-wide inflation only if government does not undertake policies to fight this inflation. The government validates this wage-price structure when the Federal Reserve allows the supply of money to grow in accordance with the new demand for money. And by doing so they ensure the continuation of an inflationary cycle. This allows economic activity to continue at its normal level while accommodating the demand for inflationary money. Importantly, it also masks the owner-worker struggle for greater shares of the national output. If the increased money supply were not forthcoming to validate increased money wages, the struggle over income shares would become clearer and thus more dangerous. In addition the functioning of the planning sector would be severely disrupted.

But if inflation is the result of a social conflict over income shares, what then determines unemployment, and why are the two not necessarily related?

Whereas orthodox theory suggests that firms adjust prices to equate output and demand, our treatment indicates that in the planning sector adjustment comes about through changes in employment and thereby in the level of output.

Demand for workers in the planning sector is determined by the corporate manager's "best guess" concerning the quantity of output which that firm can expect to sell in the future. The supply of workers depends on demographic and other sociocultural factors. The aggregate level of employment in the current period is therefore determined by the expected level of aggregate demand in the next period, and anything affecting that expectation will affect employment. But the impact of wages will be small. Likewise, the rate of unemployment will depend on how fast the labor force is growing relative to how optimistic corporations are about the pace of economic growth in the future.

The role of demand finally brings us to the investment process in the planning sector, for it has a substantial impact on the level of employment. Investment has traditionally been the source of instability in the economy, and the recent recessions have seen it play a major role though an export drop was also important in 1981-82. Investment decisions in the planning sector are made on two bases. The first is an estimate of the future prospects of the economy, expectations about economic performance. Such views are unstable and can swing to extremes quite rapidly, engendering instability in investment. Such swings also affect demand and employment since investment is a component of demand.

The second factor which plays a role is the availability of funds for the investment program. It is on this side that much of the supply-side program hopes to operate. But it should be realized that large portions of the investment program of the planning firms are internally financed by retained earnings. To gain an idea of the magnitude of this source of funding it should be noted that retained earnings of corporations were $333 billion in 1980 while personal saving amounted to a much smaller $104 billion.[8]

The amount of these funds is directly tied to the pricing decisions of firms. For the markup price is determined based upon some goal for profits and implicitly upon some goal for investment. Thus a given investment program can be financed by manipulating the price of output. But we can see that a major source of instability in demand and therefore in output of the planning sector is an imbalance between these retained earnings and the investment program. For if the firms' expectations lead them to reduce their investment program, their retained earnings are not necessarily linked and so demand may fall substantially, with definite consequences for employment. Let us amplify this point. Retained earnings are considered savings because they are funds temporarily withdrawn from the spending stream. If a few giant firms retained earnings in significant amounts, but (for whatever caprice) decided to postpone their investment programs, then aggregate demand would fall and eventually output and employment would fall in response to the diminished demand. Thus, a downward cycle would have been generated.

So we can see that the planning sector has a major influence on inflation, unemployment, and instability in the economy, and that this influence has increased along with concentration as noted in the last chapter. The question as to why policy cannot offset the consequences of planning sector behavior is our next concern.

Keynesian fiscal and monetary policy seemed effective as long as inflation was not a problem, as long as productivity increases in the planning sector were able to offset the higher input costs. Once this was no longer the case and inflation had become a serious problem, Keynesian prescriptions became unacceptable. Government efforts to offset reductions in aggregate demand due to declines in investment merely exacerbated inflation. And to stop inflation, a major decrease in aggregate demand and employment was necessary. Thus the advent of inflation is really the demise of the North American version of Keynesianism.

The "new" CEI policies which have been implemented under the Reagan administration, to the great detriment of the economy, require somewhat more expansive treatment.

The statements and policies now issuing forth from economists and politicians in Washington are based on a hodge-podge of essentially CEI-oriented ideas. To deal with inflation, reduction of federal spending, and reduction of the budget deficit is one mandatory item; and lowering money-supply growth is another.

The first idea is based on a belief that inflation is a demand phenomenon, and a reduction in aggregate demand will stop inflation. We have seen, however, that in the planning sector such an effect is not likely, or certainly the required demand reduction is substantial. What is more likely is that the planning sector firms will adjust their markups and in fact may raise prices in an attempt to maintain profits.

In addition to the conceptual flaw with the program its operationalization is proving quite difficult. We have been treated to the spectacle of the fiscally conservative Ronald Reagan addressing a "balanced budget" rally to push a program that would make his own deficit budgets illegal! Indeed his administration is assured of being the deficit champion of U.S. history. What went wrong? Part of it was the cut in taxes designed to increase saving, an unlikely and irrelevant policy as we shall see later. But even more fundamentally the deflationary effects of monetary policy have had a dramatic impact on tax revenues, and the programmed increases in defense spending have more than offset expenditure cuts in other government programs. In addition to skewing expenditures into a sector which is part of the planning sector par excellence, and therefore likely to be more prone to inflation, the stark contrast of rhetoric and reality can only worsen expectations of inflation. Thus this first portion of the program is a complete muddle which should have some impact on inflation but may affect stability and employment substantially. Indeed the preoccupation with cutting government expenditures in the face of 10 percent unemployment shows the sense of unreality in policy-making. We can only be thankful that the internal logic of the program was flawed or we would be moving toward far higher unemployment rates.

The other main line of attack is to curtail the growth of the money supply. Again the results have been and will be disastrous. We will see the effect on the market sector later. But the effect on the planning sector will be of two varieties. Some firms which are financed mostly through internal channels will be affected very little. Indeed they may even be forced to raise their prices as higher interest rates force their direct costs of working capital upward — and along with it the markup. So inflation will not be stopped here. But some firms will be pushed to the wall as they may not be able to cover their costs. Thus the International Harvesters of the economy will have to close plants and lay off workers, exacerbating the unemployment problem but making little impact on output price levels.

Thus the effect of monetary policy on inflation will be attenuated. To be sure a stringent monetary policy maintained over a long enough period of time can bring down the inflation rate. But its implicit inflationary effect through costs of production mean that this will take a long period of time. And the firms which are forced into bankruptcy and the jobs which are lost will come quickly. Our CEIs have an implicit and generally unexpressed view that there is employment for all who wish it. As unemployment reaches toward 10 percent, only the gullible are likely to believe that.

So what can be done to deal with stagflation, if both the CEI and Keynesian approaches are not going to be successful in the planning sector? As we will see in the next chapter there are structural changes which can be undertaken to improve the tradeoff and to bring the economy's performance back within an acceptable range.[9]

But the new component of the Reagan program, supply-side economics, is designed to deal with the stagflation problem by increasing saving and investment, thereby increasing output and jobs and lowering inflation. But the tax incentives offered as the central part of the new supply-side economics and designed to spur investment and thereby growth are also misplaced.[10] Shareholders certainly have an appetite for such incentives and for that reason preach the traditional line that such policies will improve investment opportunities. But it is apparent that these incentives will only go to swell profit margins while the investment decisions of the planning sector will remain a function of expectations of future economic activity. Supply-side economics may prompt a sizeable redistribution from the poor to the rich, but the effect on other vital economic indicators will be minimal unless future expectations are substantially improved—and that is a matter of faith. The only effective manner to increase and stabilize investment in the planning sector is through planning that will provide for a more stable set of expectations.[11] But that is a matter for our last chapter.

To sum up this section it will be useful to quote Alfred Eichner once more:

> If there is perhaps one point on which economists with a post-Keynesian perspective are likely to agree, it is that inflation cannot be controlled through conventional instruments of fiscal and monetary policy. This is because they regard inflation as resulting, not necessarily from any "excess demand" for goods, but rather from a more fundamental conflict over the distribution of available income and output. The conventional policy instruments, by curtailing the level of economic activity simply reduce the amount of income and output available for distribution, thereby heightening the social conflict underlying the inflationary process.[12]

The Private Economy: The Market Sector

This is the competitive economy that CEIs and Keynesians would like to consider *the* economy. It has grown rapidly, more rapidly than the planning sector; and its role in job creation during the 1970s was central. It is also the realm of the "secondary labor market," that of low-paying jobs, fewer hours of work per week, little possibility for advancement, etc. But it is a sector with low value added in production and with little possibility of technical change or increase in productivity.[13]

For the most part, inflationary pressures do not originate in this sector, for firms face many competitors and thus have less leeway in setting their prices. They are "price-takers" rather than "price-makers." Given the central role the sector played in generating employment during the 1970s, the problem of policy becomes one of avoiding damage to the sector or slowing its contribution to employment. One of the implications of the Fed's willingness to validate wage contracts during the 1970s was low interest rates and buoyant demand by the planning sector's labor force. These were the prerequisites for expansion of the market sector.

But the current stabilization efforts are reversing both of these factors. Planning sector firms have reduced employment and this lowers demand for the products of the market sector. Even more importantly, however, the relatively easy credit which provided for the expansion of these businesses is no longer to be had at rates which allow a profit. Consequently, the growth of the market sector is hampered and there are cutbacks in employment. The rate of bankruptcy has reached depression heights, and for the most part these are market-sector firms. Thus we are seeing a reversal of the growth of the 1970s as a result of the stabilization efforts of the Reagan administration. Ironically, one of the chief victims of CEI policies is the small business firm of the market sector.

Again there are structural policies which could be undertaken to facilitate the functioning of this sector, and they will be treated in the next chapter.

The Private Economy: Irregular Sector

This is the economy's final shock absorber. As primary or secondary labor force jobs are unavailable, persons are forced to enter the irregular sector. Thus we find former teachers painting houses, former sales representatives doing delivery work, and apparently increasing numbers of persons entering illegal occupations. For example, it has been estimated that the fourth largest cash agriculture crop in the U.S. is now marijuana.

It appears that under present programs this sector may be the only growth sector of the 1980s. Since in general these firms require very little capital, stringent monetary policy cannot affect them. Similarly, since the transactions often take the form of a barter of skilled services, unemployment rates will not affect them. Yet we have to ask if this is the best our economy can do to provide life-sustenance, self-esteem, and freedom. To be sure there are those who choose to enter this sector for the esteem gained from the personal relations and the freedom an unrestricted and uncontrolled environment provides. But we have only to think of the street-corner apple-sellers during the Depression to realize that the sector has its less cheery side. Restrictions on eligibility for welfare and on payments for unemployment are removing some of the options for maintaining a decent life for many Americans. Rather than pushing them into the irregular sector we would hope to be able to provide a more stable and buoyant destination for their talents.

The Public Economy: Government

Much of the economic impact of the government sector was discussed in the last chapter. Besides fiscal and monetary policy, government affects stagflation in two additional ways. First of all, there is the impact on productivity of government regulations. There is little doubt that the regulations on emissions, on safety in mines, on re-processing of nuclear fuels, on licensing of nuclear power plants, increase the costs to the firms involved. This shows up in higher prices for given levels of output. At one level it is obvious that such regulations simply represent the protection of the public from market failure. One only has to think of the costs of a major nuclear disaster which would exhaust the net worth of the firm and would still leave substantial claims outstanding. At some level even the industries seem to realize this; for example, General Public Utilities sued the Nuclear Regulatory Commission after the Three Mile Island disaster for exerting *too little* regulatory control!

But there are examples of regulation and regulatory processes that could be done more efficiently and with less cost. This is not to say that the headlong rush in Washington to deregulation that began with the Carter administration and has accelerated with the Reagan administration is effectively dealing with these questions. What is more likely is that there will be substantial costs to deregulation which only gradually will be realized. As outlined in the next chapter, an effective government policy must lead to a more rational process of re-regulation.

The other impact is the direct provision of employment. While government does compete with the private sector for resources in some areas, its employment impact was quite important in the 1970s not so much for its size as for who benefitted from it. As Lester Thurow has noted, a high percentage of the professional jobs that were gained by minorities and by women since 1960 were in the 18 percent of the labor force in the government sector.[14] This was true for lower-level jobs also. So government employment had an important impact on lessening the effects of discrimination, an effect which is being reversed as employment is cut. So while reduction in the size of government may aid in lowering inflation to some degree, the adverse employment effects will be more dramatic, and the tradeoff will become more difficult. Add to this the inflationary impact of shifting government expenditures into the military area, and the effects of the changes in the government sector are unlikely to be beneficial in solving stagflation.

The Public Economy: Not-for-Profit Sector

Few generalizations can be made about this sector. For the most part it has little market power, though potentially it has significant power as we will see in the next chapter. Its structure has not been a factor in stagflation but its expansion holds out hope of providing new ways of achieving our economic goals.

Summary

So we find the impact of our sectors on inflation, unemployment and instability to differ substantially. And we find that the types of policies used to fight stagflation have substantially different effects across sectors. For the most part, the policies of the Keynesians seem unlikely to solve stagflation when viewed across sectors, and the policies of the CEIs even less so.

At this point it is necessary to turn to the second factor which has played a role in generating stagflation, the "growth" syndrome of the postwar economy.

EMPHASIS ON ECONOMIC GROWTH

They key to much of the past success of the U.S. economic system has been economic growth. As a consequence, the American economy, particularly the planning sector and its financial component, operates on the premise of continuous economic growth. But for reasons of physical and social limits and growing limits on U.S. hegemony, that premise is ever more untenable and indeed dangerous. The interruption of the pattern of continual growth in the 1970s has contributed to stagflation.

The present and future reality is such that optimism on growth is unlikely to be warranted. This does not mean an era of zero growth, but rather implies that growth will not cover mistakes as has been the case in the past, that productivity increases will become increasingly difficult, and that there will be new types of difficulties for ordinary ways of doing business which will challenge the creativity of all sectors of the economy.

Let us see the factors which will put limits on the growth of the U.S. economy.

Physical Limits

The first limit which must be faced is physical, based on natural resource availability. We are not adopting the Club of Rome stance where the whole world system collapses at a certain point, but we are saying that growth will come harder as production costs escalate, that continued growth in the U.S. economy will be more difficult. A major reason is that previous growth was based on a profligate use of natural resources. This was so for four reasons.

First, exhaustible energy and natural resource prices have not reflected their true scarcity because the market system has not costed them out properly. The market price reflects today's cost of obtaining the resources and ignores the fact they may be exhausted tomorrow. The implicit assumption has always been that technology will provide a substitute and the result is an economy based on cheap energy and natural resources. As the demand increases around the world the resultant scarcity will limit a continuation of this resource-using style of growth.

Second, corporations in the planning sector have compounded the problem by competing through product innovation and differentiation resulting in an emphasis on stylistic and physical obsolescence. When goods are designed to be thrown away after use, or to be used less than their physical capacity because of style changes, or constructed to fall apart sooner than necessary, the result is increased wastage of energy and natural resources. Physical limits and consumer resistance to the maintenance of this style of competition pose serious challenges to the viability of the planning sector.

Third, economic growth has been based on the ideology of individual consumption. The awesome power of modern advertising has spread the free-market gospel — the good life comes from increases in consumption of individually marketable goods and services. People are urged to believe they *must* have individual washers and dryers instead of laundromats, and private automobiles instead of public transportation. Individually owned consumer durables that sit idle most of the time use up more resources than if they had been provided on a collective basis — in laundromats and community centers, for example. This phenomenon is particularly important when viewed in a worldwide context. The earth's resources simply could not sustain the world's adoption of this style of individualist-oriented consumption growth.

Fourth, pollution abatement poses physical limits to continued reliance on traditional economic growth. Corporations attempt to minimize private costs of production. Since the cost of polluted air and water have been borne by the public, production processes have tended to ignore social costs—e.g., pollution. As public awareness forces firms to internalize these costs, thus driving up the costs of production, further limits will be imposed on continued growth.

These physical limits to growth pose difficulties and challenges to the planning sector and to the economy as a whole. "Business-as-usual" will become impossible. Increasing scarcity of energy and natural resources will result in worsened inflation that will undermine the corporate emphasis upon product competition and individual consumption—unless there are major adjustments in our economic behavior.

Social Limits

A second set of limits to growth—social limits—poses even greater challenges because they strike to the heart of a market economy. The current style of growth not only exacerbates physical limits but it also engenders social limits that further undermine the viability of the economy as it presently operates. These social limits are of two types. First, growth has been based on the production of "positional goods" which is self-defeating. Second, growth has relied on self-interest as its motor force. This in turn has undermined the general "moral base" necessary for the economic system to remain viable. Let us take up each of these in turn.

First, in a growth period, "positional" goods become an ever larger portion of total production. These are goods whose consumption is available only to those who have reached a certain economic position. Present-day Washington continually provides us with examples: one-thousand-dollar suits, limousines, etc. But the pursuit of positional goods is self-defeating because by definition they can be enjoyed only if you have them and others do not. Growth allows others to obtain them, undermining your satisfaction while adding little to theirs since the goods become less positional. There are two types of positional goods. One kind—large diamonds, a one-of-a-kind designer dress—are those enjoyed solely for snob appeal. They set their owner apart from the crowd. The now famous Nancy Reagan formal gowns are a good illustration. But if everyone has access to them they lose their ability to reflect supposed status.

A second kind are those goods—quiet beaches, uncongested roads, servants—which are unavailable if many have access to them. If we all can afford to take a vacation, the beaches no longer will be quiet. If we all can afford cars, the roads become congested. And as we all gain more income from growth, no one has to be a servant. We now allow people to immigrate temporarily to provide this service.

The result is that peoples' expectations from growth are constantly disappointed. But this drives them to seek new goods to capture "positional" advantages, leaving the majority constantly frustrated and reinforcing the resource-using nature of the economy. Furthermore, this constant frustration of peoples' dreams increases disharmony and conflict between social groups. One form this takes is an ever more fierce struggle among social classes and occupational groups for larger shares of per capita GNP. As noted above, this struggle is a key factor in the present inflationary situation and may require controls that undermine the "free" market system. But in terms of the goals of an economic system, this struggle obviously undermines fellowship and certainly forces a reconsideration of the meaning of free choice in consumption.

The second social limit points out that traditional economics has forgotten one of Adam Smith's key insights. It is true he claimed that self-interest will lead to the common good if there is sufficient competition; but also, and more importantly, he claimed that this is true *only* if most people in society accepted a general moral law as a guide for their behavior, i.e., if there were a moral base for the society.[15]

The assumption that self-interest in a competitive environment is sufficient to yield the common good is an illusion. Policies and programs such as the CEIs which are based on "unleashing" our competitive instincts are similarly illusory. An economy, capitalist or socialist, where everyone—buyers, sellers, workers, managers, consumers, firms—constantly lied, stole, committed fraud and violence, etc., would neither yield the common good nor would it be stable. Yet pushed to its logical extreme, individual self-interest suggests that it would usually be in the interest of an individual to evade the rules by which other players are guided. Similarly, the "free-rider" concept suggests that it is in an individual's interest not to cooperate in a situation of social interdependence if others do cooperate, for he/she will obtain the same benefits without any sacrifice. Therefore, why do not individuals in societies always operate in this fashion? The answer is not fear of the police power of the state, but rather that our selfishness or tendency to maximize our material welfare at the expense of others is inhibited by a deeply ingrained moral sense, one often based on religious convictions.

Peter Berger reminds us that "No society, modern or otherwise, can survive without what Durkheim called a 'collective conscience,' that is without moral values that have general authority."[16] Fred Hirsch reintroduces the idea of moral law into economic analysis: "truth, trust, acceptance, restraint, obligation—these are among the social virtues grounded in religious belief which . . . play a central role in the functioning of an individualistic, contractual economy. . . . The point is that conventional, mutual standards of honesty and trust are public goods that are necessary inputs for much of economic output."[17]

The major source of this social morality has been the religious heritage of the precapitalist and preindustrial past. However, this legacy of religious values has diminished over time because of a twofold change: the repudiation of the social character and responsibility of religion has meant its banishment to a purely private matter,[18] and the elevation of self-interest as a praiseworthy virtue in turn has undermined that privatized religious ethic.

In our present-day market economies, the erosion of this preindustrial, precapitalist moral legacy has proceeded slowly for two reasons: (1) economic growth has been spread over a very long time period, and (2) that growth relied on decentralized decision-making for the most part. This slow and seemingly natural process allowed popular acceptance and permitted adjustment in the moral base of the society, so that there seemed to be consistency between that base and economic behavior. However, the limits to this process are now being reached in the United States, and the present fervor for individualistic competition — market-place magic — is a last-gasp effort to reverse history. This must of necessity produce conflict.

Capitalist development was far from conflict-free in the past. But one of its advantages was the absence of an identifiable villain behind the disruptions which occurred. Such changes resulted from the independent decisions of thousands of persons acting independently and rationally. None could rig the rules to his or her benefit, so inequalities appeared legitimate and the undermining of religious values had no identifiable cause. The rise of the large corporation and centrality of government in most countries today, however, provide a target for dissatisfaction. In such circumstances the legitimacy of inequalities and deterioration of values are open to question and to challenge. The gradual disappearance of the moral base of society forces government to attempt to act as a substitute and to provide a context which will encourage principled action among the elite in the planning sector while at the same time ensuring acceptance of the outcome by the majority.

Let us summarize the argument thus far. The erosion of the inherited moral base under the onslaught of continuous growth and spread of individualism creates the following situation: economic actors, especially the entrepreneurial elite, have been freed of the old religious and moral values; but the individualistic growth process does not provide any ready substitute social morality. Thus the previously effective inhibitions on lying, cheating, and stealing have lost their effectiveness and the functioning of both the public and private economy is likely to be poorer than in the past. The growth of the illegal components of the irregular sector is the logical outcome of the process.

The central role played by the state in managing the economy is a second factor which generates social limits to growth. There is a central flaw in the current Keynesian approach which calls for the pursuit of self-interest by individuals in the private sector, but forbids it in the public sector. The expectation that public servants will not promote their private interests at the expense of the public interest reinforces the argument that the economy rests as importantly on moral behavior as on self-interested behavior. "The more a market economy is subjected to state intervention and correction, the more dependent its functioning becomes on restriction of the individualistic calculus in certain spheres, as well as on certain elemental moral standards among both the controllers and the controlled. The most important of these are standards of truth, honesty, physical restraint, and respect for law."[19] But the more that self-interest progresses and the more that the original moral base of the society is undercut, the less likely are these conditions to be met.

Attempts to rely solely on material incentives in the private sector and more particularly in the public sector suffer from two defects. In the first place, stationing a policeman on every corner to prevent cheating simply does not work. Regulators are at a disadvantage because they have less information than those whose behavior they are trying to regulate. In addition, who regulates the regulators? Thus, there is no substitute for an internalized moral law that directs persons to seek their self-interest only in "fair" ways.[20] Secondly, reliance on external sanctions further undermines the remaining aspects of an internalized moral law.

In summary, the erosion of society's moral base under the onslaught of self-interest has important practical results. As Hirsch says:

> Religious obligation performed a secular function that, with the development of modern society, became more rather than less important. It helped to reconcile the conflict between private and social needs at the individual level and did it by internalizing norms of behavior. It thereby provided the necessary social binding for an individualistic, *non*altruistic market economy. This was the non-Marxist social function of religion. Without it, the claims on altruistic feelings, or on explicit social cooperation, would greatly increase, as was foreseen, and to some extent welcomed, by a long line of humanists and secular moralists. Less love of God necessitates more love of Man.[21]

So only if we begin to deal creatively with the physical limits on growth and more importantly with the social limits to growth will we be able to begin to solve our current economic problems. Our suggestions in the next chapter are attempts to start us on this path.

LOSS OF U.S. HEGEMONY IN THE INTERNATIONAL ECONOMY

There is one other factor in the current crisis which deserves separate treatment because of its importance. This is the position of the U.S. in the world economy. Perhaps the most important change of the 1970s was the alteration or ratification of the existing reality, from a Western system characterized by U.S. hegemony and independence to one in which the U.S. is interdependent or even dependent on other countries. The effect of this change has been profound. As we will see it has exacerbated the economic problems that were originating in other areas and has further interfered with the effectiveness of orthodox policy in dealing with them.

We will use a shorthand term for this, "Latinamericanization," both because we are now facing many of the same problems that have been characteristic of Latin America over the last decades and because the term is becoming more common in the literature.[22]

Some of the evidence of this change is well known and indeed obvious. The best example is the ability of OPEC to effect two massive increases in the price of oil. Even if oil prices weaken, the real change from the pre-1974 level will remain impressive. Similar in nature though of a shorter duration was the Arab countries' embargo on oil shipments to the U.S., which did not bring the country to its knees but was successful in causing major economic disruption.

At one point it appeared that the United States would face such cartels in products from bauxite to bananas and now in tin. Efforts in bauxite failed because of availability of new sources, and the banana cartel was broken by a well-designed payment of $1.25 million to the President of Honduras. In any case the experience has shown the U.S. to be vulnerable to outside pressures from raw material producers, upon whom we are ever more dependent for supplies. And when market conditions are favorable, we can expect them to press their advantage to the limit, unafraid of U.S. power.

But the 1970s revealed many other areas in which the workings of the international economy had an independent effect on the U.S. A case can be made that the major policy developments of the 1970s were not taken autonomously by the U.S. but were forced on policymakers by external pressures. Two incidents stand out in this regard. The first was the August 15, 1971 bombshell of Richard Nixon in which he effectively removed the U.S. from any gold standard and at the same time adopted a rigid program of wage and price controls, contrary to all of his pronouncements to that point. Of course Nixon was looking ahead to 1972, but the key factors in these decisions were international. The U.S. for the first time had begun to run deficits on its merchandise trade, which called into question the country's ability to redeem the massive amount of dollars that had been cycled through the international financial markets. And the Bank of England made it quite clear that it was no longer willing to absorb additional dollars to support their fixed value. Thus adjustment had to be made by the United States. This new reality forced the radical decisions which were taken and led finally to a reformulation of the manner in which the U.S. enters international capital markets.

This in turn had a major effect on the international economic system. International financial and commerical order is difficult to achieve among equals, and since the erosion of the United States' economic power after 1965, no single nation has been sufficiently powerful to impose order unilaterally. The breakdown of the Bretton Woods system in August, 1971, resulted in floating exchange rates which, when coupled with recession in several major nations, poses a constant threat of an international commercial disintegration which, in turn, would reinforce the domestic recession forces.[23]

The second case of an internationally induced domestic policy change was the revolution in interest rates which took place in 1979 when the Federal Reserve Board decided to deemphasize interest rate targets and to concentrate instead on the growth of the money supply. A key factor here was the discontinuity between the U.S. structure of interest rates and the international structure, and the concomitant growth rates of the money supply and rates of inflation. In these areas the United States was quite out of line with European countries. Paul Volker went to Europe for consultations, and either because of pressure from his counterparts or their support, upon his return called a Saturday meeting of the Board of Governors and adopted the new strategy which has completely changed the role of interest rates in the economy.[24]

So in both cases of fundamental reformulation of domestic economic policy, the proximate cause was the vulnerability of the U.S. economy to foreign economic pressure and influence. This is a far cry from the hegemonic days of the 1950s and 1960s where U.S. desires became reality, despite resistance by statesmen such as de Gaulle.

Other examples could be offered and there is an ample literature which deals with components of this question.

Returning to the topic at hand, the claim which rests on this reading of the 1970s is that there was a significant change in the external conditioning factors vis-à-vis the U.S. economy, that for the first time in the postwar period, our economy became open to external pressures and influences. Let us now look at three indicators of this loss of independence which have led the U.S. to resemble more closely the Latin American economies.

Inflation

Comparing the inflation experience of the U.S. in the 1970s with the Latin American experience prior to that time shows that the U.S. rate is quite close to the average for Latin America, and of course it is much higher than the U.S. historical average.

We would contend that this significant change in U.S. performance is partly a direct result of its openness to conditioning influences from without, that one major factor in this upsurge of inflation is the inability of the U.S. to control and set the prices for major goods which are traded internationally. Of course the most obvious example of this is oil where the actions of OPEC directly raised the domestic rate of inflation through their effect on the price of oil and its derivatives. But we would go further and claim that it is likely that the U.S. inflation rate will remain higher than its historical level, close to some international rate, because of two other factors.[25] Given its new international vulnerability and the particular structure of its industrial sector, there will be structural inflation as we have noted above. A second factor which will serve to keep the rate of inflation high is inflationary expectations. One puzzling aspect of the economy is the continuing high rate of interest (monetary and real), but our claim is that these rates correctly reflect expectations about inflation, expectations which are based on an awareness of the vulnerability of the U.S. economy. These expectations in turn serve to lower the effectiveness of downward price pressures and thus to maintain the rates of inflation at their higher level.

Of course this claim flies in the face of the reigning orthodoxy in the U.S., i.e., that the Federal Reserve Board can determine the rate of inflation by determining the rate of growth of the money supply. It should suffice to note that the modest success of the Fed in controlling the money supply has been greater than its success in controlling inflation; and this is a situation that we feel is likely to continue unless there are structural adjustments.

Unemployment

During the 1970s the U.S. economy was quite successful in providing jobs, as participation rates rose, especially among married women. As noted earlier, most of these jobs, in fact practically all of them, were in service sectors. The industrial and farm sectors produced almost no new jobs. Yet the increase in service jobs didn't keep pace with the labor force, and unemployment has risen over the whole period. Even prior to the recession of 1981-82, there was a substantial increase in part-time work and in discouraged workers who left the labor market. The stagnation of the industrial or primary labor market is again partly attributable to the external conditioning of the U.S. which saw the traditional industries under attack internationally, and many of the new industries rapidly moving overseas.

This performance is likely to continue as even with massive wage reductions, the U.S. will have a hard time competing internationally. So in the absence of new policies we are likely to have chronically higher unemployment rates as a result of the change in external conditioning factors.

Another important aspect of Latinamericanization is the kind of institutional and structural change that goes on in the domestic sphere in the face of this industrial stagnation. We have noted the creation of the irregular economy, or what in the Latin American literature would be called the "informal sector." These are the sidewalk sellers of goods, or the service providers who swap services. It is difficult to estimate the size of this economy, but it seems to be growing and to be an important factor in allowing the survival of persons who cannot find formal jobs. As unemployment compensation and welfare are cut, it will become increasingly important as a manner to allow people to survive at all.

So again, in response to changed international conditions, we find a deterioration in the performance of the U.S. economy, one that is structured into the economy and which is spawning international change as a response.

Balance-of-Payments Performance

We noted above the effect of international pressures on domestic economic policy. This has long been the reality of Latin America. Many Latin American economic strategies have grown up as a response to the situation of the balance of payments. For example, underlying their import substitution strategy adopted during the 1950s was the view that reliance on traditional primary exports would always leave the countries in a vulnerable situation with precarious terms of trade, and that industrial diversification and development were the mechanisms to escape this situation.

But as should be well known, this strategy did not remove the difficulties faced by the countries. Over time, it became quite common for countries to be forced to resort to the International Monetary Fund for stabilization help in balancing their international payments. And one visit to the Fund did not usually suffice, as the rate of recidivism was high. Prime examples are Peru, Guyana, Bolivia, and Chile.

Technical adjustments have been made to avoid such problems; for example, many Latin American countries adopted crawling-peg exchange rates to avoid such imbalances. But it is still common for major readjustments to be necessary, as was the case in Argentina in 1980-81 and in Mexico in 1982. Other more exotic measures have also failed as curatives: e.g., the Chilean-University of Chicago open-economy model with fixed exchange rates and a passive monetary policy resulted in a substantially overvalued peso by 1982, despite the major depression the economy had undergone. The policy was abandoned. Only Brazil has been able to continue on its desired path despite its balance-of-payments difficulties, a direct result of its continued access to international capital markets for the foreign development of major mineral finds.

Obviously the United States in no way has reached the situation of the Latin American countries. Major currencies are still expressed in terms of dollars and the price of that crucial product, oil, is also quoted in dollars. The dollar recently reached a twelve-year high against other countries. However, there are significant changes that have come about as part of the new U.S. situation. The dollar floats rather than being fixed against a fictional gold quantity, psychologically a major change; and changes in the value of the dollar will have important domestic impacts. Much of its strength in recent years seems to be a result of the rapid and now sustained rise in the interest-rate structure in the economy. This has lowered inflationary pressures; but if interest rates fall rapidly, inflation will be stimulated through exchange-rate adjustments, and the fall will be attenuated.

But the changed situation of the U.S., its "Latinamericanization," becomes more clear when we look at a series of more specific indicators. The first is the continued inability of the U.S. economy to attain any degree of trade balance with Japan. In 1981 the deficit was $13 billion. This has led to a series of efforts to control imports from Japan, the most notable being the voluntary quota on automobiles and the 25 percent tariff on imports of small trucks. There had been similar steps taken in earlier years, such as the voluntary quota program on textiles or steel trigger prices. But it is clear that in many key industries — autos, steel, much of electronics — currency adjustments are unlikely to result in competitiveness, and the U.S. has the choice of seeing the industry wither or protecting it in some fashion to allow an orderly adjustment. Of course there were similar examples earlier, but never in so many U.S. industries nor with such a potentially great impact on the economy.[26]

The situation again differs from that of the Latin American countries, but it differs even more substantially from the historical U.S. experience. There are pressures from the balance-of-payments side which have affected U.S. economic policy as noted above and which will continue the "Latinamericanization" process.

Lessons from Latin America

As U.S. international hegemony continues to erode and Latinamericanization advances, what lessons can be gleaned from earlier Latin American experience with inflation, unemployment, and balance-of-payments difficulties?

Certainly the most important lesson is that economies can function rather well in the presence of significant rates of inflation and that there are a variety of ways in which economies can adjust to inflation. Thus it is shortsighted to decimate the economy by causing major recessions in order to have some small impact on inflation.

Of course there may be added difficulties as an economy moves from low to higher inflation rates. But this is likely to be even more the case as it moves from low to higher unemployment rates. In most cases entry into the informal sector was voluntary, the best option available. But for U.S. workers being displaced from jobs, the irregular sector may not be sufficient as a source of income or meaning. It is likely that the irregular economy can play some role as a shock absorber, but as unemployment rises along with a redistribution of income to the wealthy, this may become a volatile issue. The negative effect on employment of such redistribution and the resentment aroused by changes in relative incomes, a powerful factor in people's sense of well-being, may heighten the level of social conflict. One clear implication is that steps should be taken to reverse the Reagan policies that redistribute income from the poor to the wealthy.

In the case of balance of payments, the implication is that the independence of domestic fiscal and monetary policy has been damaged beyond recovery. When domestic problems or international disruptions call for a policy response, it can now be taken only in full awareness of the linkage between that policy and the international economy. This will often have the effect of limiting the policy options and of exacerbating the domestic problems. We are still far from having our stabilization policy set by the IMF; but in more subtle ways, limits on our policy options exist. Except in the case of a highly stable world economy, one which does not seem to be in the offing, these limits are likely to cause a further deterioration in our economic performance.

Beyond these lessons, any suggestions become much more speculative. It may be that the greatest problem in Latin America, and perhaps also in the U.S., is the political tension generated by the high unemployment and substantially skewed distribution of income. In such circumstances, individual or group gains depend heavily on political power and mobilization among competing claims, with the "free market" of Chile being the prime example. In the waning days of the Nixon administration we had a military president, Alexander Haig, who "was in charge" in the White House. One can only hope that was an aberration and that the process of Latinamericanization does not carry us to that point.

CONCLUSION

In this chapter we have attempted to weave together a variety of factors into a coherent explanation of stagflation and the general economic crisis facing the U.S. today. However, we need more than explanations of the crisis; we also need solutions. In our final chapter we will develop the policy implications of the analysis presented in this and earlier chapters.

10. Toward a New Social Contract

The first part of this book set the main competing theories of the economy into historical context, in order to show that the CEI and Keynesian approaches to economic problems presume an economy completely different from our present one. Their policies, as we have shown, would have been more appropriate in earlier times when the actual economy more nearly resembled the one assumed in the theories. The second part examined two frameworks which have their roots in history, but which differ in implying that nothing can be done to confront our contemporary problems: the long-swing theorists would have us hope we were on the upswing, while the Marxists would have us wait until the economy fell about us. The last part has laid a new basis for confronting our contemporary problems in the hopes of better attaining our three goals for the economy: life-sustenance, esteem (or fellowship), and freedom. In doing so we provided the historical context for PKI thinking and its emphasis on the structures of the economy and on power. We then looked at three key factors which have generated our present problems — structural changes in the economy, the problems in maintaining economic growth, and the loss of international hegemony.

In this final chapter we will examine a set of proposals, from a PKI perspective, which provide a more meaningful approach to dealing with the economy's problems. Contrary to the supply-side approach which was so successfully sold to the voting public, they cannot be reduced to a simple diagram drawn on a napkin. The U.S. economy is complex, and constructing a workable policy is a delicate task indeed. A more detailed and pragmatic set of policies would avoid the severe disruption the economy has suffered on the supply-side altar, especially if those policies are based on a clearer understanding of the economy.

Similarly, the full employment, low inflation, and continuous economic growth of the Keynesian theory achieved by manipulating monetary and fiscal policy is not the promise of the PKI policies we advocate. That day is gone. Rather we point to a new direction in the economy whose success will be based on a realistic appraisal of the economy, rather than on some simple analogue to an imaginary nineteenth-century economy. It is also a direction which will be consistent with the goals we have specified and which we think that most Americans share. It tries to deal realistically with social limits to growth and it tries to confront the conflict over income shares without setting up a Trojan horse to mislead citizens about the impact of policies.

The first section attempts to specify the general context in which the three goals of the economy can be pursued. All too often the choice is framed as either the market or bureaucratic control. Our earlier treatment should have shown that both of these approaches carry with them problems which hamper the functioning of the economy. Both approaches must have some role, but there must be a carefully developed and maintained relation between them. There will be a tension, but this can be productive and creative.

The second section turns to the specific policies and programs that we advocate. We group them under three guiding principles—stewardship, jubilee, and subsidiarity,—which if maintained can allow policy to walk the tightrope between the unproductive extremes. As we define each of these principles, we will note a number of policies consistent with that principle and which will contribute to the pursuit of the goals of the economy.

Such policies cannot, will not, and should not be adopted over night. But they can be the basis for an approach to economic policy that will unite large segments of society. And as these policies are adopted, the deteriorating performance of the U.S. economy and our disillusionment with it can be reversed.

NEITHER FREE MARKETS NOR BUREAUCRATIC CONTROL

At the most basic level economics concerns itself with the question of how an economy allocates its resources—its raw materials, capital, and labor—among competing uses. Often economists can be divided by the mechanism that they would rely on to determine this allocation. There are three possible mechanisms: markets, bureaucratic administration, and love. Under a system of allocation by markets, people cooperate with each other conditionally: A will do something for B, if B does something in return. In a bureaucratic control system, people cooperate because they are told to do so and fear the consequences if they do not, or they simply accept the command because it is traditional. In a system of allocation by love or altruism, people cooperate and do things for each other with no strings attached.

CEIs would place almost complete reliance on markets, except in an area like defense where bureaucratic control is unavoidable. Efforts to use love would be seen as self-defeating. Keynesians would also give a central role to markets, but there would be numerous areas in which bureaucratic control would be needed to improve the functioning of markets. They would not see love as very useful either.

Sole reliance on any one of these mechanisms is misguided, as each has implicit in it flaws which prevent it from being a successful mechanism for solving our economic problems.

Markets *appear* to be highly efficient because their attendant social costs are unmeasured. We have of course normal externalities which are increasingly important in our modern economy. But there are other more fundamental problems as well.

The ordinary day-to-day operation of the economy creates winners and losers; for example, new technology wipes out some peoples' jobs, increasing land values result in capital gains for some and higher rents for others, new highways destroy some neighborhoods and appreciate others. The problem of economic losers has been magnified by changes in the political structure. When economic and political power was distributed so that economic losses could be imposed on one part of the population — usually the least powerful — by another part or by government acting as the latter's agent, the change appeared efficient. Now, however, two changes have taken place. That part of our population who used to be voiceless are no longer willing to accept losses quietly, and are able to increase substantially the costs for those who wish to impose losses upon them. The second change is the natural increase in the role of government in the economy.

An aware public resists economic changes, whether triggered by markets or government, because of these attendant social costs. As a result the process of change is slowed down. This is particularly true when government is involved because it is more sensitive to public opinion than the private sector. Government involvement merely brings into the open social costs that were always there, and which the market served to hide. The unemployed textile worker paid the cost of our getting shirts 10 percent cheaper. Trade adjustment assistance spreads that cost to the taxpayers. And reliance on markets would only hide that cost, not remove it.

Bureaucratic allocation raises several problems: massive amounts of information must somehow be made available to the central decision-making body; free choice must be surrendered, either democratically or dictatorally, to that same body, and the totalitarian tendencies resulting from uniting political and economic power in the same hands have to be dealt with.

Marxists and radical socialists of various hues have failed to deal with this fundamental insight when they talk about replacing production for profit with production for use.[1] It is not as easy as it sounds. The only radical alternative that has undergone the test of experience is the bureaucratic central planning of the Soviet Union and the Eastern European countries. Their record on our three goals is not very impressive. They have made great strides toward providing life-sustenance, particularly for the poorest, but freedom and esteem (fellowship) are in little evidence and dictatorship and sycophancy are the rule.[2]

The mechanism of "love" has problems as well. In Cuba and China the regimes have tried to create a "new man," cleansed from self-interest and motivated by service to others. That is, love has been the guide to allocation of resources. A job should be chosen not for self-advancement but rather because it is of use to others. While the results are not all in yet, because the experience has been so short, the results so far are not reassuring. Again, while great achievements have been made in overcoming scarcity the record is poor on freedom and ambiguous on esteem (fellowship). An indication of this is China's recent and definitive move to a more market-based system of material incentives to motivate production.

The difficulties of using love to allocate resources are inherent in the idea. For me to allocate my time and income for others' welfare I have to know what will increase other peoples' welfare. Not only is this amount of information impossible to obtain for more than a small group, but inevitably there will be conflicts between peoples' perceived interests. The only solution is a central body which somehow processes the information and tells me what should be done. Again, the problem of centralized power rears its head. Also the tendency toward self-interest cannot be written off simply as a manifestation of the class-nature of people under capitalism, to be changed in a new society. Marxist historian Eugene Genovese recognized this problem when he wrote:

> The nationalization of property and its attendant centralization of political power create powerful tendencies toward dictatorship and totalitarianism. Accordingly, they must be checked by the establishment of autonomous institutions — unions, newspapers, universities, etc. — with an adequate property base of their own. No faith can be

placed in the supposed goodness of man; on the contrary, the essential doctrines of Christian theology and Freudian psychology concerning human frailty and potential aggression must be taken with deadly seriousness. To 'liberate' the good in people requires severe institutional and social restraints on what is and will remain the evil.[3]

Given that no one allocative system is without severe problems, what does that imply for our choice of a mechanism to aid in attaining the three goals of our economy?

Toward Life-Sustenance

Some mix of the three allocation systems must be utilized to improve our economy's economic performance. To ascertain how that mix should be developed, let us examine the goal of life-sustenance.

The key area in which the market fails to perform is that of investment. As we saw earlier, uncertainty and expectations play a vital role in investment decisions, and the market has no way of dealing with them. Indeed, if anything, as a society moves toward greater use of the market, it appears to increase uncertainty and therefore instability in investment.[4] Thus purely market-based allocation must be circumscribed and new mechanisms developed. The second area in which the market fails is in its inability to resist the tendencies to concentration and monopoly. Thus there must be new mechanisms developed to deal with these problems.

Bureaucratic control fails most in its tendency to engender inefficiency. There can be little doubt about the expansion of bureaucracy since the Second World War, and many aspects of what the government does impinge upon the economy. But the actual policies undertaken have been developed piecemeal and through a process of political bargaining. What results is a crazy-quilt with little or no internal coherence and a number of areas where there are obvious inefficiencies as a result. What is needed is a rationalization of these policies, and a reevaluation in light of their impact on efficiency — as well as on other social goals. This is not to say that a meat-cleaver should be taken to them on the presupposition that all regulations are bad. Rather they should be examined and improved.

Love as an allocative mechanism probably plays less of a role in attaining life-sustenance because of its impact on efficiency. Nonetheless, love demands at least that the basic needs of all members of society should be met. We are a wealthy society, despite our current difficulties, and the needs of the elderly, the poor, the physically or mentally impaired should not be sacrificed to some vision of a perfectly competitive world. Again this is not to say that current policies are perfect, but they should not simply be dismantled.

So any policies will have to be clear about what kinds of goals are acceptable for our society, and they will have to take into account the limitations of each of the mechanisms for resource allocation.

Esteem and Fellowship

The esteem issue also is a complicated one. An unregulated market system places a premium on competition among people and results by its nature in substantial inequalities. Indeed such inequalities are extolled by the proponents of market systems.[5] Esteem and fellowship thrive where people are led to cooperate in social endeavors and where there is time and opportunity to relate to each other as loving, sharing human beings.[6] Fellowship is encouraged where there is a minimum of social forces that erect barriers among people. Thus, extreme income inequality makes individual esteem and fellowship next to impossible. Emphasis on individual self-advancement makes solidarity difficult to maintain. Race and class discrimination generate hostility which makes right relationships among people difficult.

On the other hand, the charge that the growth of the public sector reduces each person to a number is not pure demagoguery. The impersonal relationship between public institutions and individuals is built into the system. In a reference to Sweden which also fits the problem in the United States, Arne Ruth wrote:

> This gives rise to an irrational and, in my opinion, insoluble conflict. We all insist that public agencies treat us fairly, that is, that they follow the relevant rules and regulations to the letter and apply them uniformly to everyone. If they do not, we call it corruption. But this sort of impartiality is at the same time experienced as an outrage to our self-esteem, since it means that all human qualities — indeed, everything that makes us unique individuals — are regarded as irrelevant.[7]

So we approach civil servants with a double message: be fair, but realize that my case is different from everyone else's.

Anyone who has corresponded with the tax authorities knows how insoluble this dilemma is and what aggressions it can let loose. The only way civil servants can protect themselves is to elevate their work routines to law. In this way they sweep out, of necessity, any remnants of humanity in the bureaucratic system. The public sector has its own code of ethics, different from that which otherwise guides the relations of people with each other.

CEIs speak openly of these dangers but their only answer is the market. When people buy services in the market they can make demands. But the people who have little income will be worth less than ever.

Another problem is the decline of personal responsibility toward others that has accompanied the rise of the welfare state. The French Marxist André Gorz has addressed this issue:

> Fatigue, crowded conditions, lack of time, and the severance of contacts with one's neighbors mean that many people stop helping each other on their own initiative. This social disintegration always leads to the development and strengthening of the State's institutional activities. Individuals, cut off from each other, demand that the State become actively involved, that it step in more and more to assist them when they have lost the ability to care for themselves, to help each other, and to look after their children. The trend of having institutions take over these functions leads to increased professionalization, specialization, and separation of responsibilities. This in its turn contributes to the further disintegration of the society.[8]

Thus, both the free market and government intervention in the market pose problems for improving the quality of self-esteem or fellowship in society.

Therefore, policies must be based on a mix of the market and bureaucracy, but always in a context of fellowship and esteem. They must respect and nurture the humanity of the citizens, they must have a major element of love. This of course becomes especially difficult in times of economic crisis, but there are policies which can operate consistent with this goal.

Freedom and Equality of Opportunity

The same ambiguity about mechanisms exists over the issue of freedom. Despite the usual assumption, it is not true that markets necessarily enhance freedom and government intervention reduces it. The issue is much more complex. Complete freedom is not definable once two human wills exist in the same interdependent universe. In a political democracy a majority make a decision and the state then enforces the decision, by force if necessary. If a tax increase is voted the state forces dissenting individuals to comply. Thus *explicit coercion* is used to restrict individual freedom.

What is often overlooked is the fact that markets do the same thing. The *implicit coercion* of the market mechanism forces labor to move from rural to urban areas, limits the ability to choose by income level, and imposes discipline through the threat of unemployment. In a market system the degree of freedom varies with income, especially in the case of consumer sovereignty. As a result, the market restricts freedom just as surely as does the state.

In an earlier chapter, we attempted to create a more realistic understanding of consumer sovereignty. We showed how firms manipulate preferences with some success in creating "producer sovereignty." In a similar fashion, the operation of the labor market is far from the paragon of freedom assumed by CEIs. We noted earlier that a better characterization of the labor market is as a dual market where in the secondary market workers are forced into an insecure situation and their possibilities for any type of advancement are few. So they are at the whim of the market, and this is most true when we have periods of high unemployment. They *must* hold on to whatever job they may have, despite any distaste they may feel, for the simple reason that there may not be another job.

In point of fact, factors such as discrimination based on race and sex continue to have a substantial effect on what people can attain. Women continue to receive less than men for the same work, racial minorities continue to lag behind whites in their overall labor market experience.[9]

And it is in this latter area that we can see government's positive effects on freedom and equality of opportunity. For as noted earlier, many of the gains that were made by blacks and women came about because government employment was opened to them, much more than in the private sector. This provided an avenue of advancement in accord with abilities. One of the implications of current CEI policies is to reverse this, to take away this freedom and equality of opportunity.

Let us hasten to add that this does not mean that government is immune to criticism. We have already noted the difficulty of dealing with bureaucracies. And there are ample individual cases which President Reagan seems to thrive on bringing up in which there are apparently capricious uses of power and regulation to severely and detrimentally affect someone's life. So while government is not the ogre that CEIs would have us believe, it is also not always the white knight of hope either.

Building some mechanism to counter the detrimental impact of government on freedom is important, and to the extent that it can limit the market's negative impact as well, it would be quite useful. This is why in the next section we advocate the continuation and fostering of mediating institutions.

Thus, again, the argument against government intervention in the economy is more complicated than free market devotees claim.

So we conclude that no one allocative mechanism can successfully enable our economy to attain the three goals of life-sustenance, esteem, and freedom. The market, bureaucratic control, and love all have their drawbacks as mechanisms for directing society's resources toward those ends. So some combination of them must be incorporated in any policies that are undertaken to deal with the current economic crisis. This conclusion will guide us in the next section as we examine specific policy suggestions and attempt to sketch out an ethical framework for those policies.

THE SOCIAL CONTRACT

Any attempt to develop a new social consensus must recognize the clear lessons of history: a laissez faire system of self-regulating markets is a utopian dream existing only in the minds of economists. The reality is that all peoples have always embedded the economy into the total social system. The market economy is no exception. Since its inception, every group in society — business, labor, farmers, consumers — has struggled to abort the workings of the market. Any realistic policy must accept this fact and design a policy which utilizes and subordinates markets to the attainment of individual's and society's moral values and goals.

At the most fundamental level, the economic problems of the current day originate in a moral crisis and in an inability to control the resulting social conflict. The moral crisis has occurred because of the erosion of the moral base of the society that economists have simply assumed was there, an assumption which is less and less viable. Social conflict has grown out of this erosion and out of the inability to bring about widespread agreement on the distribution of the fruits of production.

In dealing with the current crisis one must take these two facts as a basis. To deal with the social conflict a new social consensus must be created. For only if a new social contract can be negotiated and agreed upon by the different classes of society can the economy and the society be revitalized.

This can take place only within a moral context, one in which the too-easy separation of moral values and economic behavior is realized for what it is—impossible and destructive. So another key starting point is a moral stance consistent with our underlying value structure but which can guide us in making our economic decisions, both individually and as a society.

We suggest there are three such central moral values: stewardship, jubilee, and subsidiarity, which must be brought to the fore. In suggesting them, we find they relate directly to the three economic goals of life-sustenance, esteem, and freedom. Under each of them, we will delineate the national economic policies that can build upon that moral base and can operate technically on the economy to improve its economic performance.

We should note the contrast with the manner in which the current economic program was conceived and developed. There was indeed an effort to provide a moral base, but it was the base of the competitive individual whose selfish behavior would be made socially beneficial by the invisible hand. Current performance should be evidence enough of the program's wrongheadedness. And secondly, the program did not deal openly with the social contract. It has attempted to enforce a redistribution of income, but by hiding it behind the rhetoric and illusions of "supply-side economics." Any program must be open about its impact, and admit that some adjustment needs to be made in income shares. Its success will come when the social contract is accepted and the moral underpinnings are found consistent with the belief structure of the society. This may make it politically less salable, but it will ultimately make the policies adopted more successful; indeed it is the basis for any successful confrontation with the reality of current economic problems. We offer these policies for thought, reflection, and action.

Stewardship—Life Sustenance

The initial moral value which runs deeply in the moral tradition of most Americans is stewardship.[10]

A steward or trustee conception of property differs from that which underlies the theory of the market economy. John Locke argued that private property was a necessary part of a good society. He based his argument on a labor theory of property. Private property is justified by and derived from the labor of its owner. This labor theory of property came to be one of the crucial elements of the classical economic doctrine. Because persons had wrested the soil from the state of nature and had cut the trees, that land should be theirs and they should be entitled to use it for whatever purpose they saw fit — and so should their children and grandchildren. The modern economy, with its dominant planning sector of huge corporations, is far removed from property creation in the sense of Locke. So in contrast to the Lockean theory of property the stewardship conception states that private individuals may own *and use* property for their own interests *but* only as long as it does not result in harm to the common good. For example, the need of a community for employment must be weighed against a firm's property right to relocate a plant to a different community.

The specific implication of this moral canon is that society has a responsibility for the resources which are at its disposal, and they must be used well. More specifically, if the system of automatic adjustment through the invisible hand cannot deal meaningfully with the current problems, there should be no difficulty with interfering to ensure that economic performance improves; indeed, there is a mandate to do so. In contrast with the current administration, property is not an absolute right and never has been. We do not suggest that property rights be interfered with capriciously, but where the evidence shows that some interference or change can improve the overall functioning of the economy, that should be done to remain consistent with the demands of stewardship.

We can use stewardship as a point of departure in seeking policies which can be more successful in attaining life-sustenance. New policies are suggested in four areas. The first is a program of national economic planning whose purpose will be to bring some degree of certainty to the investment climate so that the up- and down-swings of the 1970s are not so pronounced and there can be a stable increase in our productive capacity and productivity. The second problem that must be addressed is the social conflict over income shares. In dealing with it we suggest the adoption of a specific incomes policy, rather than the present practice of slight-of-hand incomes policies. The functioning of large corporations in the U.S. economy is the third policy area addressed, and we propose that their detrimental impact on the current situation be dealt with by working toward more worker self-management and by giving serious consideration to changing the ownership structure of the major corporations. The final area again stems from the concept of stewardship which implies that the whole earth is held under stewardship and thus policies must take on an international perspective. We argue the necessity of Third World development and the centrality of coordinating economic policy with the other major industrial countries.

Before we move to specifics, it is important again to emphasize the inadequacy of reliance on one allocation mechanism alone. Thus when we advocate a type of national economic planning and an incomes policy, this must be seen in the context of market allocation in most areas of the economy, along with decentralized, love-based organizational structures such as worker ownership and subsidiarity that can act as a check on the pretensions of bureaucracy.

National Economic Planning. We recommend that the United States begin a process that will lead to democratic national economic planning. North Americans cringe at talk of national planning because the term smacks too much of dictatorship or even communism. It must be recognized that national planning does not necessarily mean total governmental control. Under "indicative" planning government creates incentives and perhaps controls prices, but only so that private corporations will choose to operate in such a way that their actions are beneficial instead of destructive to social goals like stability, full employment, steady prices, a reduction in poverty, and so on. By democratic it is meant that those in charge of planning are responsible to the people of the nation. If they plan in ways unacceptable to the people, the planners can be removed from office. Strengthening smaller decentralized organizations can facilitate this.

It is difficult to say what precise form a national planning body would take and exactly what its duties and offices would be, as the specifics would emerge from the process of its formation. But certainly wage and price controls on the planning sector would have to be a central feature of the planning process. Since it is the price-making behavior of the large firms that has both inflationary and destabilizing tendencies, such controls would be essential in the effort to restrain large corporations and unions from behaving in socially harmful ways. With the breakdown of the stabilizing mechanisms of the private market, economic policy must be formulated to deal specifically with the large corporations where power is the disciplinary agent and not the market. Similarly, growth goals and projections would have to be incorporated to remove some of the uncertainty which leads to instability in investment. What is necessary, to paraphrase Gunnar Mydral, is to make the private profit-making system a servant and not the master of the general public. A number of authors have tried to sketch out the specifics of planning in the U.S. and we base the following on the work of two prominent PKIs, the late Gerhard Colm[11] and John Kenneth Galbraith,[12] in addition to the experience of the Western European countries (particularly Scandinavia).[13]

A system of national economic planning must posit "performance" and "priority" goals. Performance goals include full employment, economic growth, and price stability. Priority goals concern the question of resource allocation among competing goals — national defense, education, health care, and so on. In "national economic councils" (that would need to be established), representatives of various groups would discuss the relative merits of competing goals and call upon scientific and technical experts for advice in determining priorities. A "national economic budget" would be used to quantify national priority goals and make them consistent with the nation's private goals and the available supply of resources.

The heart of such a system of national economic planning is the national economic budget (NEB). The conceptual framework of the NEB is a two-part — real flows and financial flows — model of the economic system. The total real flow consists of the goods and services produced in the economy during a specified period of time as measured by the adjusted national product accounts. The total financial flow can be seen as national income earned or spent. The basic macroeconomic problem is to maintain coordination between the real and the financial flows so that what is annually produced is purchased or consumed. According to CEI theory the real and financial flows are automatically coordinated by the workings of the free market system. In the contemporary U.S. economy, markets fail in this task which is one reason why national economic planning is necessary.

An NEB is a projection of the national economic accounts into a future period — one year, five years, and so on. With assumptions about productivity, labor force and other input requirements projections can be made of full-employment-level production. These are the real flows. Then a projection is made of the private consumption, business investment, and government expenditures needed to purchase this output and thus ensure that full employment is achieved. These are the financial flows.

The NEB is a projection of society's economic goals as expressed in national product and expenditure terms. As Colm says of the NEBs: "Their main feature is that they reflect [national] objectives and state policy goals."[14] In effect, the NEB expresses the country's economic priorities in quantitative terms and thus provides a basis for policy decisions. Allan Gruchy summarizes the potential usefulness of NEBs as follows:

> The government's fiscal, monetary, spending, price and other policies can be related to the quantified objectives set forth in the annual and long term national economic budgets. Since output and expenditure goals are quantified, policy discussions are made more concrete. The effect of any proposed policy or program on the nation's real and financial flows can be expressed in quantitative form. This facilitates discussion and agreement among various major private economic interest groups and the government.

The meshing or coordination of the real and financial flows observed in a national economic budget is a managed or planned harmonization of these two flows. It is quite unlike the harmonization that would automatically develop in a perfectly competitive economy. The equilibrium projected in the national economic budget is a planned equilibrium that the government hopes to achieve by supplementing the private market mechanism.[15]

Information and consultation are crucial to the process. The Employment Act of 1946 called for close cooperation and frequent consultation among industry, agriculture, labor, and all levels of government in implementing the goals of the act. Committees of these groups should be established and meet regularly with the Council of Economic Advisers and other appropriate government offices.

Using guidelines provided by the President, the Council of Economic Advisers could prepare, as part of the *Economic Report of the President,* an NEB for the coming year and for each of the following four years. In the annual *Budget Message of the President,* the President could present a four-year fiscal budget outlook with, in addition, a ten-year fiscal budget projection. These and other measures would provide the Congress and the public with the required information for public and private economic decision-making.

The economic plan would consist of the following: (1) an analysis of recent economic trends and the outlook for the plan period; (2) the economic objectives or goals to be achieved which would involve the construction of an NEB to show the projected increase in GNP and its planned disposal among private and public consumption, investment, change in inventories, and the export or import surplus; (3) a discussion of production, consumption, investment, and foreign trade over the plan period and the associated resource problems; (4) a discussion of other goals — worker self-management, decentralization, greater equality, cleaner environment, etc. — and their interrelationship with the quantitatively expressed goals of employment, growth, and inflation; and (5) a presentation of the various financial and other policies and measures needed to achieve both the performance and priority goals.

Other approaches to planning are possible. But any one chosen should operate so as to reduce uncertainty in business expectations and thus to stabilize investment. Similarly it must limit the ability of the planning sector to set prices free of constraints. These are the keys to better economic performance. In addition, the market must be preserved, not everywhere as CEIs would have it, but where appropriate. And the bureaucratic tendencies of such efforts must be countered by a vibrant and alive set of organizations and associations at a "people" level.

Incomes Policy. Clearly an "incomes policy" is necessary to manage the conflict over income shares in the planning sector, since this conflict is a root cause of inflation. In the long run an effective incomes policy requires an agreement about the fairness of income distribution — that is, a new social contract based on the stewardship mandate. However, in the short run, such a policy to control on an economy-wide basis the rate of increase of all forms of money incomes could be effective. This is particularly the case if people believe it is a necessary first step toward implementing a whole new economic program that embodies a new social contract.

Again there are many different approaches which could be used. The most prominent of these incomes policies is the tax-based incomes policy (or TIP) developed by Sidney Weintraub and Henry Wallich.[16] The crux of TIP is to utilize taxes as a means of tying increases in money incomes to increases in productivity. Suppose, for example, that productivity were rising at an annual rate of 3 percent (the rule until recently). Weintraub would then prescribe a limit on wage and salary increases of, say, 5 to 6 percent per annum. This 2 to 3 percent over productivity gains would allow some leeway to firms with greater or lesser productivity improvements, but it would also cap inflation at some low level. If the norm were violated a stiff tax would be charged to the offending firm, thus providing strong incentive to stay within the limit. Weintraub believes that if this policy were applied to the one thousand or two thousand largest firms in the U.S. it would be a major contributor to lowering inflation.

There are several variants of this policy, but they all deal with limiting income increases to some present level.

All versions of incomes policies share the common objective of limiting inflationary increases in wages, salaries, and profit income. This common goal is consistent with the PKI explanation of stagflation which centers on the inherent social conflict over income distribution and the need to limit wage and salary increases to the increase in average productivity, and to avoid major shifts toward profits as a result of greater bargaining power. And once the inflation side of stagflation is under control, the government is free to use its policy instruments (taxes, spending, and money supply control) to stabilize demand and thereby generate the proper level of investment to ensure optimum growth and full employment.

Worker Self-Management. The problems of productivity and of social strife over income distribution can also be dealt with by encouraging new alternatives to our traditional corporate organization.

As a starting point, new forms of ownership and control of the major corporations in the planning sector should be encouraged. Private ownership is still important for the 13.5 million small businesses in the U.S. However, for the two thousand large corporations that produce 70 percent of all material output, the link between ownership and incentive has been greatly reduced, if not severed. Executives now operate these corporations with minimal interference from owners. One way of dealing with this would be to make the social context of the corporation more central and to begin to move them under joint public-private management control. Townships, states, workers, or similar collective bodies could become partners.

The most likely such approach would be the encouragement of workers' self-management and worker ownership. This is because of the link to productivity which would come from worker ownership and management. Such self-management would also foster esteem and fellowship. Of course, most firms and their managers do not want to see democracy expanded in the workplace. They tend to believe that efficiency and discipline require one absolute center of control over work — their control. Nevertheless, in a number of cases, managers are exploring ways to change the organization of production to increase their workers' job satisfaction. The reason for these new management initiatives is clear — under the old system, many workers expressed their boredom, anger and despair by working as slowly as possible, by appearing at work irregularly, by doing poor quality work, by occasional acts of sabotage, by frequent job changes. The "efficient" system of authoritarian discipline and minute division of labor is a contributing factor to declining productivity in the U.S. economy. General Motors, finally heeding the fifteen-year-old advice of the UAW, and taking the cue from Japanese experience, has begun a major experiment in worker self-management (but not ownership). Clearly workplace democracy and worker self-management are important ingredients not only to esteem and fellowship but also to productive efficiency. Federal legislation should require corporations to establish factory councils or possibly reserve seats on boards of directors for worker representatives in workplaces where employees want them. A 1977 Swedish law requires corporations to include workplace participation as an issue in contract negotiations with unions. Federal chartering of corporations could become another way of forcing companies to discuss workplace democracy with their employees.

How can worker self-management be extended without waiting for government or employer initiatives? Only workers can decide on the changes they want. Thus, there is no set formula. It is useful, however, to look at some ways workers have tried to gain control over their work situations. It is worthwhile to cite at length from a report by the DSOC Industrial Democracy Task Force:[17]

> *Autonomous Groups*: The workers in a shop can take over the organization of their own work, deciding how to do it and who will do what and when. For example, workers in a Kentucky coal mine are now managing themselves successfully; one of their achievements has been a record level of safety. Or an assembly line can be broken into sub-assembly teams, each responsible for an identifiable task — welding a bus fender onto a bus, for example. Then the workers themselves can decide how they will do the job.
>
> *Job Rotation*: Workers can trade off jobs within autonomous teams. By changing positions several times a day, they can make their jobs less repetitious. They can move from job to job within their office or workshop if they prefer. Utility men already perform several jobs a day in the auto plants: working utility is considered a more interesting assignment. To be able to rotate jobs, a worker would need to learn several different tasks. Rotating jobs doesn't eliminate the repetitiveness within each assignment, so many workers may not feel it's worth the trouble; but it can help break up the day and can be part of a package of changes.
>
> *Job Enrichment*: Time-and-motion studies break jobs down into their smallest, most repetitive motions. Workers can reverse that direction by adding tasks so that they do a complete operation or make a whole product. For instance, each worker can inspect her or his own work, taking responsibility for quality control. Or workers can repair their machines; maintenance need not always be a separate task.
>
> *Redesign the Machines and the Shops*: There is nothing sacred about the way workplaces are presently set up. In fact, machines and processes are always being redesigned and replaced. Workers can play a leading part in redesign, by suggesting changes in existing machinery, equipment, layout and methods of work. They can object to changes that make their work lives less comfortable, more boring, more dangerous. They can require companies to plan for changing existing machinery and for designing new technology so that in time the technology serves people instead of the other way around.
>
> *Health and Safety Councils and Factory Councils*: A committee that investigates health and safety conditions in the workplace is useful, and may lead to other forms of worker participation. In Sweden, legisla-

tion has given worker representatives the power to shut down operations when they judge conditions to be unsafe. On a broader scale,
factory councils can be places where workers express their ideas
about the way work is organized, discipline and changes in machines.
But such bodies must not replace grievance procedures and undermine collective bargaining.

Worker Directors and Codetermination: In West Germany, unions
nominate up to half of the members of boards of directors. Having
worker directors allows unions to get more information and a voice
in determining corporate policies. For example, the German auto
workers prevented Volkswagen from building an assembly plant in
the United States until an agreement was reached to protect the
rights of German workers.

Collective Bargaining: Collective bargaining has already given the
workers a share of the power in the workplace. It may be used to extend the workers' power in any of the directions listed above, to protect jobs, and to obtain a fair share of the benefits of "experiments"
in industrial democracy and job redesign.

More Knowledge and Training: All of the possibilities in this list mean
that workers will need more information and more opportunity to
develop their abilities. They will need to learn more skills and will
need a sense of how their jobs fit into the production process. The
higher the level of democracy, the greater the need for workers and
their unions to know more about the company's finances, organization and policies. Moreover, workers often enjoy getting more involved in solving problems on the job. Recognizing these aspirations,
the UAW has created joint programs that train workers in problem-
solving techniques that enable them to improve their own jobs.

Workers can make progress toward self-management in their
workplace but systemic changes are needed to obtain full industrial
democracy. Certainly full-employment policies and national economic
planning are among them.

International Economic Policy. Every problem in the U.S. economy — from
the price of sugar to unemployment in Youngstown — is in part a reflection of what is occurring internationally. We must develop an "international consciousness and conscience" as a first step toward dealing with
problems in the international economy. The keystone of our efforts
must be that the dispossessed of the U.S. and rest of the world should
not be made even worse off by attempts to solve these problems.

Instability in the international economy, particularly in finance, makes it difficult for the U.S. to control its domestic economic policy. A system of national economic planning will require greater stability and certainty from the international economy. Since no one country can impose its will on the international economy, the U.S. must lead the other concerned countries in setting up, through the United Nations, an institutional equivalent of a world public sector with the authority to bring about a coordination of national economic policies. This would enable stability to be attained in exchange rates and international liquidity which, in turn, would be necessary for national economic planning. The initial gropings in this direction are the economic "summits" of the industrial countries, but much more must be done.

Let us look at two specific problems to understand better the need for an international consciousness and a coordination of economic policies among nations. Nowhere is the international linkage among problems more tangible than in the case of the foreign undocumented workers who have come to the United States seeking work. Many have come from Mexico so let us concentrate on them. Such migrations are not new, and public policy has alternated between acceptance and repression because their presence in the U.S. has both benefits and costs. The economic gains from undocumented workers are many. One beneficiary is the U.S. consumer of agricultural or service products who obtains them for a lower price because of the low wages received by undocumented workers. Mexico also gains from the outmigration from its rural areas, for it would otherwise have to undertake an economically and politically costly program of agricultural development. And of course U.S. politicians have in the migrants a convenient scapegoat for domestic problems.

But the costs are substantial as well. The grey area in which the undocumented workers operate exposes them to a series of abuses and makes their very existence precarious. The wages of U.S. workers in the agriculture or service sectors are depressed by the ready availability of low-price labor, and Mexican agriculture continues to deteriorate with land concentration increasing, much of the production exported, and food imports becoming increasingly important.

The meetings between presidents of the United States and Mexico have dealt with this issue as well as with oil, tourism, gas, manufactured exports, etc. Yet this source of friction and potential instability has not been dealt with. The decisions taken have not given primary consideration to the needs of the undocumented workers nor of the low-wage earners in the U.S. Any true solution must contain the following elements: guarantees against deportation or legal harassment for undocumented workers in the U.S. as a way of protecting them from exploitation and of providing opportunities to organize and to ensure decent treatment; enforcement of minimum wage legislation; a program of agricultural development in Mexico to provide jobs and a decent living for the many rural poor of the country; protection of U.S. workers from the use of undocumented workers to break strikes; reformulation of immigration policy and a full employment program in the U.S. which can prevent the use of undocumented workers as scapegoats for our own economic problems. Unless these elements are present, U.S. and foreign workers can be played off against each other to the detriment of all.

A second issue of importance is the recent and ongoing attempt to negotiate a "New International Economic Order." There are many issues involved, most of which deal with getting more resources to Third World countries to help in meeting their basic needs. One key program which shows the importance of an international perspective is "commodity stabilization." Sugar will serve as an excellent example.

Sugar is produced in many countries in the world, including the U.S., and in some countries its production provides a major source of income for poor rural workers. After being sold during the 1960s at about 11¢ per pound, in the 1970s the price of sugar began to rise. It was 12¢ at the start of 1972, rose to 13¢ by 1973 and to 14¢ by 1974. It then skyrocketed, reaching 60¢ per pound at wholesale by the end of 1974. The rapid rise in price was followed by an equally rapid decline in the world price to 21¢ by 1976 and to 7¢ presently. This mercuric behavior had a number of negative effects: Third World economies were thrown into disarray by the rapid increase in income and its equally sudden disappearance; consumers' plans were upset by the rapid changes; the sugar industry could not plan for orderly growth and development given the instability of prices; and the changes have resulted in a U.S. domestic price of 22.5¢ which is over double the initial price, largely because of government response to industry demands for help in face of falling prices.

These problems and the subsequent disappearance of jobs in the cane sugar fields of Louisiana could have been avoided if a meaningful world stabilization program had been in effect. The same case can be made with other commodities as well.

It is important to realize that on this issue there is an obvious unity of interest among the people in the U.S. and those in Third World countries. They would like their earnings to stabilize, our workers and consumers would benefit from similar stability.

These two examples show that many of the solutions to economic problems must cut across national boundaries, and must be based on a sense of solidarity with the citizens of other countries. Similar examples could be given on coordination of economic policy with Europe.

But the case is made. All of our policies must have an international dimension, and there must be coordination and policy development in the context of stewardship. Only in this way — not through letting the market run rampant — can there be meaningful progress toward improving performance of life-sustenance.

Jubilee — Self-Esteem and Fellowship

Esteem and fellowship do not thrive in the context of extreme competition, where esteem comes from one's position relative to others. An alternative approach to such hierarchial patterns is the biblical concept of jubilee. It grows out of the institution described in Leviticus which saw every fifty years a time of celebration but also a time of restitution, remission and release, where slaves were released and land and houses that had been sold reverted to the original owners or their heirs. In this fashion, the society had a mechanism which allowed inequality (competition) but also redressed its detrimental tendencies in the interest of maintaining the society intact.

Our economy does not function any better because of the substantial inequalities which we have built into it, contrary to what the present CEI administration would have us believe. Are our workers' energies stimulated by the possibility of buying $10,000 designer revolvers or $95,000 chinchilla bedspreads that continued in popularity even during the worst of the 1981-82 recession?[18] Would corporate chief executives quit to the quiet of their homes if their incomes were lower than the 1977 median of $471,000? Hardly, as they would still be rewarded well in monetary terms and in psychic income — pride, challenge, power, status.

A more successful approach economically and in terms of the goal of esteem and fellowship would be to have an ethic of jubilee. By this we do not mean an immediate and massive redistribution of income, but rather the adoption of policies that provide, with dignity, an income guarantee and a full employment policy for all who want to work. In addition, basic goods, and especially housing, should be ensured to all.

These policies would not only increase the absolute level of income of the lower income population but would reduce de facto the relative income differences. A jubilee ethic would provide the conditions necessary for esteem and fellowship. Let us turn now to some specific policies.

Full-Employment Policy. Unemployment is more than a statistic. Lurking behind the statistics are real people whose human dignity has proven to be inseparable from their employment.

Dr. Harvey Brenner of Johns Hopkins Medical School has been studying the unemployed for a number of years.[19] He has found that as unemployment increases, there are corresponding increases in the suicide rate among middle-aged males, incarcerations in state prisons, new admissions to mental hospitals, and infant mortality rates in urban areas. One of the somber effects of the 1981-82 recession was a dramatic increase in child abuse cases in areas hard hit by unemployment.[20]

Dr. Sidney Cobb of Brown University and Dr. Stanislav Kasl of Yale have done extensive research on the health and behavior effects of unemployment caused by plant closings.[21] Over the thirteen-year period of their study they found a suicide rate among unemployed workers which was thirty times the national average. They also found a higher incidence of a whole series of diseases (e.g., heart disease, hypertension, diabetes, peptic ulcer) among the unemployed than among employed workers. They found that job losses had serious psychological effects such as extreme depression, tension, anxiety, insecurity and loss of self-esteem. This result is not surprising because in a market economy employment (or lots of money) is necessary to one's identity as a human being. We don't ask someone, "Who are you?" but rather "What do you do?" I am a professor or a carpenter. I work for General Motors or the University of Notre Dame. We have imbibed the individualist tradition with its emphasis on achievement and attribution of responsibility to individuals. At its most extreme the argument assumes that workers are unemployed because they are lazy, lack skills, or demand wages that are too high.

These psychological effects are compounded by the real material problems unemployment causes. Employment is the only source of income for most people and income is necessary to lead a life of dignity. Food, clothing, housing, education, recreation all cost money.

A fifty-two-year-old newly unemployed worker summed up his feelings after fruitlessly trying to find a new job. "Things you've always taken for granted fall apart. It is to feel the disintegration of your confidence as a man, and your ability to protect your family from economic disaster. It is to see the doubt on the faces of your children."

The lack of employment is one of the main structural problems of a market economy. CEIs assume unemployment is a natural phenomenon that is the price of a free economy. Keynesians argue that it is the unfortunate but perhaps unavoidable by-product of controlling inflation. But in reality unemployment exists because in our economy a majority own no land, tools or capital but have only their labor to sell. A minority own all of the land, tools and capital and then hire labor to work with the capital. The owners hire when it appears profitable and do not hire when profit expectations are low. Thus the economy is organized in such a way that employment is a by-product of profit-making; and there is no reason to believe that this will result in full employment. Except during wartime the U.S. economy rarely has had unemployment rates below 4 percent.

Since private economic institutions cannot provide full employment the responsibility rests with society. The national planning mentioned above can aid in stabilizing employment. But so far we have been unwilling to guarantee useful employment for everyone able and willing to work (the Humphrey-Hawkins Act of 1978 is a full-employment bill, but it is toothless). Rather we put people on welfare which further lowers their self-esteem and assaults their dignity. The real immorality of unemployment is our unwillingness to modify defective economic institutions and to pay the price necessary to eliminate the cause of the sufferings. The unemployed and millions of others, including all those urban youth who never had a job, bear the costs of technological change, plant relocations, and government cutbacks in spending. We as consumers benefit in lower prices, and the owners of corporations benefit in higher profits. But what of those unemployed who "lie sleepless in bed waiting for the dawn of a new day and realize that something is terribly wrong with America"?

A way must be found, whether through a public employment program or job tax credits to the private sector, to guarantee a job to everyone willing and able to work. This need has been recognized for a long time but never implemented. President Truman's last *Economic Report* in January, 1953, stated:[22]

> It means full utilization of our natural resources, our technology and science, our farms and factories, our business brains, and our labor skills. The concept of full employment values ends as well as means; it values leisure as well as work; it values self-development as well as dedication to a common cooperation. Full employment means maximum opportunity under the American system of responsible freedom.

> And it is a concept which must grow as our capabilities grow. Full employment tomorrow is something different from full employment today. The growth of opportunity, with a growing population and an expanding technology, requires a constantly expanding economy. This is needed to abolish poverty and to remove insecurity from substantial portions of our population. It offers the prospects of transforming class or group conflict into cooperation and mutual trust, because the achievement of more for all reduces the struggle of some to get more at the expense of others.

> Although our dedication to full employment has made great strides within recent memory, we cannot afford to be complacent. We can-

not assume that henceforth what needs to be done to promote the maintenance of full employment will be done. None of us—regardless of party—should let the idea of full employment degenerate into a slogan bandied for narrow political advantage. Like freedom, it needs to be guarded zealously and translated into action on a continuing basis. Moreover, if we fail in this, our very freedom may be placed in jeopardy.

A full-employment guarantee is sometimes opposed on the ground that it would hinder labor productivity. However, countries with much greater employment security—Japan and Germany—have had more rapidly increasing productivity for decades and now have surpassed us in labor productivity. If fear of unemployment causes restrictive work rules, the job security created by guaranteed full employment may enhance rather than retard productivity.

Certainly national economic planning is essential to guarantee full employment. But more is necessary. In addition to running the economy at a "full-employment" level of national product and expenditure, two other policies are necessary. First, a national employment service needs to be established. Second, *community* full employment needs to be made the goal, not simple aggregate full employment.

A national employment service should be established. It would have two primary purposes—job search-placement and retraining. Even with a full-employment level of national expenditure, frequently the people and the jobs are in different locations and the skills available and the skills needed do not match. One task, therefore, is to aid the unemployed to search out jobs in other areas and help them relocate. Alternatively, jobs could be moved to where the unemployed are locaed, and that is discussed next as part of a community full-employment program. Sweden has an employment service that could serve as a model. It is computerized and all employers, wherever located, list job openings with the service; people looking for jobs file applications which are then matched up with the vacancies. Employment counselors work with individual workers in deciding which openings to apply for. The worker's dossier is then sent to the appropriate firms. When and if the worker is hired, the employment service advances relocation expenses and two month's salary. The worker pays this back over several years. In Sweden this system has worked to maintain unemployment rates typically below two percent.

In a rapidly changing economy the demand for work skills is changing constantly also. As a result there is frequently a mismatch between the skills demanded by employers and the skills possessed by the unemployed. This requires that appropriate retraining be provided.

The employment service, in conjunction with employers, unions, and state employment agencies, should be charged with this task. This would be a cost-effective program. The reduction in unemployment and the higher productivity levels of workers would add up to substantial gains in output.

In addition to increasing the mobility and marketability of individual workers, policies must be developed that have community full employment as their objective. That is, instead of merely setting an aggregate goal — say, four percent unemployment — policies should target that level of unemployment at the community level.* This will require economic planning, both at the national and community levels, to be effective. A number of policies are necessary.

First, *social* cost-benefit studies must be done of ailing industries and of plant relocations. These are the two major sources of local unemployment once a full employment level of expenditures is achieved at the national level. Care must be taken not to subsidize firms that should go out of business. On the other hand many small firms which are very efficient fail because they cannot obtain loans in competition with planning-sector firms. This is where a policy of *credit rationing* can be useful. In a market economy, credit is rationed to the highest bidder. This rigs the game in favor of the largest and most powerful firms. A specific policy of allocating some percentage of total credit to small firms would be a step toward revitalizing local communities.

Plant relocations from one community to another are a much more serious problem. Most relocations are done by planning-sector firms. From their *private* cost-benefit analysis it is efficient to close operations in South Bend, Indiana and move them to North Carolina. A *social* cost-benefit analysis might indicate that the move is inefficient. The social costs include the idled factory buildings, schools, sewer systems, and other social infrastructure left behind in the old community (typically in the Northeast or Midwest) and the increasing costs of providing all these services in the new community (frequently in the Sunbelt). The result is a deterioration in the elements of the old infrastructure and a failure to build adequate new ones. Thus Toledo's roads and sewers fall apart and Phoenix does not build enough. In addition, there is the unemployment-insurance and welfare-benefits cost of those left behind. And this leaves out the human suffering of those unemployed or forced to sever their roots and migrate to seek work.

---

*The definition of community will have to be flexible. For example, the Ohio Valley region might be defined as a community because of its economic integration and geographic proximity. In other cases Standard Metropolitan Statistical Areas — basically a city with its suburbs — might be used.

Second, community-targeted full employment policies require the capacity to anticipate plant shutdowns in given industries. This in turn requires the development of early-warning systems and forecasting models that yield predictions about the private sector. In addition, it requires that the national economic budget provide accurate forecasts of ongoing and new areas of public investment such as mass transit. For both the private and public sectors there will be needed projections of skill requirements if retraining programs are to be successful.

Third, community revitalization requires that the national economic plan include incentive policies that allocate capital among specific industries and geographic regions.

Fourth, public investment and direct purchases from the private sector must be part of the overall plan to obtain community full employment. Thus one important consideration in the letting of government contracts should be community need.

Ironically, this type of public planning for community revitalization and full employment may be the only way small-scale, local business firms survive in the face of competition from the large corporations. In one of his novels, Charles Dickens said, "Every man for himself said the elephant as he danced among the chickens." Government planning might help the chickens to survive.

Job creation in the private sector must be supplemented by public service jobs (on a state and local basis) so that all who are capable of working can have the opportunity to work. This requires expenditures, again on a decentralized basis, for child-care centers so that parents without partners can leave the home to work. Job creation must be supplemented with *training* programs to upgrade skills so these jobs do not become dead-end dumping grounds for the poor. An added advantage of an employment program is that people *earn* their incomes and thus preserve their dignity as human beings, therefore easing the pursuit of self-esteem and fellowship. And from society's standpoint we do not waste our most precious asset, our citizens.

A Guaranteed Annual Income. For those unable to work—the handicapped, the sick, women with small children—a fair and efficient income transfer payment system is needed. A national graduated income supplement could raise everyone above the poverty level for much less cost and bureaucracy than under the present system of state-run welfare programs.[23]

An income-maintenance program must avoid the bureaucracy, high cost, and demeaning quality of a means test. It would be more efficient to give everyone an income supplement that is subject to progressive taxation. Such a program must be a replacement for the present welfare system not an add-on; it must include work incentives; it must promote the integrity of the family; and it must be easy to administer by being integrated into the tax system. Leonard Greene explains how such a program would work.

> Every adult and, at a different level, every child is to receive a taxable income supplement. The dollar value of that supplement will be reflected on the income tax return as a reduction of taxes owed. If the amount of taxes owed is less than the supplement, a cash refund will be made. A family with no income will receive the full amount of the supplement in cash payments. Because the supplement is taxable income, its net value is progressive in accordance with the graduated income tax.

> The Graduated Income Supplement will not call for a determination of the assets or the need of recipients. Its basic payments will be unrelated to any financial standard. However, thanks to taxation, it will operate as an income-related program.[24]

If the amount of the supplement were $1,500 for adults and $800 for children (yielding $4,600 for a family of four) the net cost after tax revenues on the supplement would be substantially less than is now spent on income-maintenance programs. In addition, the gradual increase in tax rates would not be a disincentive to earn more income.

Basic Needs. A full-employment policy coupled with an income-supplement program can provide for the basic needs for all, while maintaining freedom and self-esteem. However, some action on prices of basic goods may be necessary, and a program of housing allowances may be the best way to provide housing.

Since 1973 inflation has been 50 percent more rapid in food, shelter, medical care, and energy than in other sectors of the economy. These four items account for 70 percent of the consumption expenditures of the bottom 80 percent of U.S. income earners. Leslie Nulty and her colleagues at the Exploratory Project for Economic Alternatives have examined these sectors carefully and made a series of recommendations.[25] They recommend solutions to the structural problems of producing each of these products.

In energy, means of conservation — public transit, home weatherization, "lifetime" utility-rate structures — must be developed and additional energy must be produced in ways that fit into an overall national economic plan. Price increases will not reduce energy consumption in the necessities proportionately and thus would actually be inflationary.

In the food sector, farm production costs have to be controlled, the energy intensity of food production reduced, and food distribution made more competitive, increasing the direct links between farmers and consumers.

In health care, a long-term plan for the education of more medical personnel of different types including paramedical personnel is important. A movement away from the present emphasis on high-cost, capital-intensive treatment toward less hospitalization and more outpatient treatment is crucial to contain rising treatment prices. Present insurance schemes have apparently also contributed to rapid price increases, so the *way* health care is paid for must be resolved as part of an overall anti-inflation package. Group practice modeled on the Kaiser Permanente model is one possibility.

In housing, price increases require focusing on local situations, and dealing with their particular housing needs. However, the housing problems of one area (such as inner cities) can drastically influence the problems of another (the suburbs). Also as we saw graphically in 1982, the use of monetary policy to restrict inflation hits housing prices through its effect on mortgage rates. The housing problem and housing prices therefore require a degree of planning that goes far beyond local areas and must be part of a national economic plan.

But one important part of the solution is to ensure consumers the resources needed to get good housing. The best manner for this is a housing allowance program. Because of the high cost of housing relative to a household's annual income, housing problems are not easily solved by merely giving families more income and allowing the market to work. In addition a significant portion of the housing stock in our older cities has been allowed to deteriorate.

CEIs have a ready solution to the housing problems facing many older cities in the Northeast and the Midwest: leave the city alone and it will eventually rehabilitate itself. That is, if urban stress is allowed to continue unabated, over time the price differentials between urban residential sites and suburban residential sites will become so large that investors will find it profitable to redevelop the city.

This process of "market" revitalization has to some extent already begun in some cities, and the process has been accelerated by the impact of inflation on the suburban housing stock. However, we must recognize that if we are to depend solely upon this mechanism to solve our urban housing problems, some neighborhoods must wait ten, twenty, thirty years or more before the price differential will appear attractive to the potential investor. In the meantime sound housing stock is literally thrown on the scrap-heap for lack of maintenance expenditures — a perversion of the idea of stewardship — and more importantly millions of families must suffer the effects of urban neglect as they wait to see whether it will be the wrecking ball or the investor who will displace them.

Thus to the poor who are concentrated in urban places, the market solution is not very appealing. Indeed, for them the market solution is defeatist in nature. It assumes that housing decay will roll like a wave from the urban core toward the suburbs, pushing prices up in front of it and lowering prices in its wake. When prices are low enough, reinvestment will take place. But that is not the end of the process; eventually decay will attack the weakest rehabilitated neighborhood, and start the cycle anew.

This unadulterated market process is unacceptable, but we cannot ignore market influence in our search for equitable solutions to the housing problem. This is particularly true since the electorate seems disinclined to spend from tax revenues the hundreds of billions of dollars necessary to revitalize our cities and their housing stock. Thus at this point we must in large part depend upon private investors for the needed funds.

These funds will be forthcoming if public policy is appropriately designed and implemented. However, in our haste to leverage these funds from the private sector, we cannot neglect our basic goals of providing for human needs, extending freedom, and fostering esteem and fellowship. Unfortunately, these goals have been largely ignored in the past. Public housing, whether in the dehumanizing high-rise, high-density version or in the more recently popular scattered-site version, sacrificed freedom and esteem for the attainment of a minimum standard of housing for the poor. That is, those who are forced to reside in public housing must forfeit their right to choose where they will live and in the process they are branded by their housing unit as a public-housing resident. Thus they are aliens to the larger society.

This need not be the case. A Federal program, the Housing Allowance Program, holds out the promise to the poor of restoring freedom of choice and esteem while at the same time providing for basic housing needs. The program is founded on two basic propositions. First, the poor should not be forced to spend more than 25 percent of their income on housing. Second, the housing subsidy should be the difference between 25 percent of the family's income and the average rental value of a standard home (no code violations) which is of the appropriate size for the family in question. Thus if the income of a family of four is $500 a month and the average rental value of an appropriately sized standard home is $300 a month, this family would receive a subsidy of $175 a month, which could be used to rent or pay the expenses on any home or apartment which is free of code violations.

Thus freedom of choice is maximized for the participant, and self-esteem and fellowship are possible. If the family prefers less ample surroundings, it is free to select such a place of residence as long as it is free of code violations. In our example, the family would still receive the $175-a-month subsidy; however, its contribution would be less than 25 percent of its income. On the other hand, if a family preferred a higher-than-average quality of housing, it would be obliged to supplement the $175-a-month subsidy with a greater share of its income.

A study of a housing allowance experiment showed it to be less costly than present programs and to have a beneficial impact on existing housing stocks.[26]

It is hoped that this freedom of choice also will lead to a heightened sense of esteem and fellowship on the part of the participants. Since the poor are not forced to reside in public housing units, they make the decision as to which community they will join. Some, no doubt, will choose their old neighborhoods where friends remain, the culture is comfortable and acceptance is immediate. Others may prefer to join upwardly mobile neighborhoods. Still others, such as the elderly, may wish to return to high-density housing where companionship, shopping and essential services are not too distant.

So with the housing allowance program and programs to ensure that price increases do not make basic goods inaccessible, basic needs are assured for the poor, freedom of choice is expanded, and esteem and fellowship are encouraged. In the process, the realities of the market have been neither completely ignored nor allowed to work severe hardships on those least able to cope. The jubilee ethic gives very different possibilities from the competitive ethic.

Subsidiarity — Freedom and Equality of Opportunity

Solutions to our economic problems will be found only if citizens are willing to cooperate in the difficult readjustments necessary to revitalize the economy. And that requires that policies be developed and implemented at the lowest feasible levels. This principle we call subsidiarity.

Only 37 percent of the eligible electorate bothered to vote in the last U.S. elections. Yet, there has been an incredible proliferation of neighborhood groups. National institutions have become too large, too uncontrollable, too unresponsive. We must develop smaller institutions more responsive to individual needs.

U.S. society today is characterized by largeness of firms and government institutions. Exxon, GM, and IBM are all mega-institutions. Government agencies such as DOD are even larger. Socialist economies share this same characteristic. Their economic institutions are even larger and more bureaucratized than ours.

The development of the U.S. economy (and most other industrialized economies) has created a fundamental dichotomization of social, political, and economic life. Put most simply, the dichotomy is between the mega-institutions and the private life of the individual. These two divisions of our society are experienced and apprehended by the individual in quite different ways. The GMs, DODs, HEWs, UCLAs, AMAs are "remote, often hard to understand or downright unreal, impersonal, and ipso facto unsatisfactory as sources for individual meaning and identity. . . . By contrast, private life is experienced as the single most important area for the discovery and actualization of meaning and identity."[27]

People could cope with these mega-institutions if the dichotomization process had not so deinstitutionalized the private life of individuals. People have always found their identity through and, in turn, impressed their values on, the mega-institutions through what Berger calls "mediating structures." This is where freedom is nurtured and protected, where the counter to bureaucracy lies, where love can play a role in allocation. However, this interlocking network of mediating institutions — family, church, voluntary association, neighborhood, and subculture — has been severely weakened by the growth of the mega-institutions that have taken over many of the traditional functions of the mediating institutions.

In the face of this dichotomization of modern life the concepts of stewardship and fellowship fall on infertile soil, and people feel their freedom threatened. There are a number of reasons why this is true.

People feel helpless in the face of the mega-institutions. Their sheer size is so alienating that the individual retreats to private life, believing that nothing can be done about *them* out there. However, private life is becoming less of a refuge as mediating institutions continue to decay in the face of the expansion of the mega-institutions. As Berger says, "The situation becomes intolerable . . . when, say, my wife leaves me, my children take on life styles that are strange and unacceptable to me, my church becomes incomprehensible, my neighborhood becomes a place of danger, and so on."[28] The result is a turn to hedonism and me-firstism at the worst, and quietism at the best. And, of course, this further weakens the mediating institutions of private life.

Not only do people feel helpless; but in fact, as individuals, they are unable to make any difference. With the mega-institutions "taking care" of the hungry, the thirsty, the stranger, the naked, the ill, and the prisoner, and with the family, church, voluntary association, neighborhood, and subculture weakened and defensive, the individual finds it difficult if not impossible to exercise effective freedom of choice or to find self-esteem and fellowship.

There is also a direct relation between the problems of fellowship and stewardship and the social limits to growth which are causing difficulties in overcoming scarcity. As noted above, the moral base of the society has progressively been undermined.[29] This collective conscience or moral law has generally operated through the mediating institutions of private life. Because of their remoteness and sheer size, the mega-institutions are "consumers," not "producers" of this type of morality. A general moral code cannot rest on the activities of individuals either. The experiments with "lifestyles" of "consenting adults" are too unstable and unreliable as a basis for the generation and maintenance of a collective conscience. However, without such a moral base, the ethic of stewardship, the possibility of fellowship, and the reality of freedom must languish, even as success in overcoming scarcity wanes.

Our modern political philosophies—liberalism, conservatism, socialism—have failed precisely because they have not understood the importance of mediating institutions. Liberalism has constantly turned to the state for solutions to social problems while conservatism sought the same in the corporate sector. Neither recognized the destructiveness to the social fabric caused by relying on mega-institutions. Socialism suffers from this same myopia. Even though it places its faith in renewed community it fails to see that socialist mega-institutions are just as destructive as capitalist ones.

In terms of our contemporary situation, mediating institutions which may aid in attaining our three goals should be fostered in two ways. The first is through public policy. Berger sums up the guideline in this area quite well in two propositions: "One: *Public policy should protect and foster mediating structures.* Two: *Wherever possible, public policy should utilize the mediating structures as its agents.*"[30]

More importantly, ways must be found to revitalize mediating institutions from the bottom up. A good example is the effort of Germany to bring workers into a direct role in decision-making. We should seriously investigate these possibilities. Indeed, we should be willing to look at new forms of organization such as worker ownership. It was the Federal government which backed worker purchase of South Bend Lathe, a firm which was to be liquidated but whose profits rose 25 percent in the first year of worker ownership and have generally gone up since. We cannot be put off by the failure of efforts such as that of the Youngstown coalition to purchase the closed steel mills. But, of course, such efforts should be urged in newer, more dynamic industries.

An encouraging note in a generally grim picture is the growth of not-for-profit organizations. In many cases—credit unions, ESOPs, neighborhood associations—these have been grassroots responses to the dichotomization of modern life. Thus, an important part of economic policy must be a fostering of not-for-profit organizations. As an example, let us focus on one such not-for-profit mediating institution—the neighborhood association.

Growing numbers of urban residents realize that if their neighborhoods are to remain stable, they must act together and capitalize upon the uniqueness of their "sub-urban" communities. Thus more and more neighborhoods are represented by formal or informal neighborhood associations. In some cities such as Pittsburgh and Birmingham, all neighborhoods within the city have been identified and neighborhood organization has begun. In other cities such as Las Vegas, Wichita, and Madison, Wisconsin, an impressive number of neighborhoods have been identified and organized. All indications point to a growing number of neighborhood associations in the future. They have been quite successful in a number of important areas: (1) they have provided a mechanism for residents to develop real participatory democracy; (2) they have been used extensively to influence local governmental decision-makers; (3) local residents, business concerns, and most importantly the media are beginning to think and act in terms of neighborhoods; and (4) Federal agencies have demonstrated an increasing willingness to recognize neighborhoods for analytical and policy purposes.

Neighborhood associations provide an excellent vehicle to achieve our three economic goals. That is, the development of cohesive neighborhood groups can provide for life-sustenance, extend freedom of choice, and foster esteem and fellowship.

By definition, the collective action of neighborhood residents recognizes that each individual in the community—the rich and the poor alike—is affected by the actions of others in the community. These third-party or spillover effects from individual actions determine the quality of life in a neighborhood. Thus, if a neighborhood association can instill confidence in the future, individual residents will risk new investments in their property, which in turn will raise the value of surrounding property. Or if a neighborhood association can instill pride, there will be a corresponding reduction in vandalism and other criminal behavior. In both cases a successful neighborhood association which induces positive spillover effects improves the quality of life in the neighborhood which in turn helps to guarantee the basic human need for safe adequate housing.

In a like manner, neighborhood associations can protect the freedom of choice of those who reside in urban neighborhoods. Historically, the poor have had limited housing choice, generally restricted to the housing stock that the affluent no longer wanted. Thus, if the affluent wished to return to the inner city, the poor would be simply pushed aside. This no longer needs to be the case. Collective action on the part of neighborhood residents can protect them from the ill effects of "gentrification" and can allow them to share in the benefits of this process.

Lastly and most fundamentally, neighborhood associations foster directly the third goal of esteem and fellowship. Sharing problems, finding solutions, working on projects, all develop a spirit of responsibility not only to the individual but to the neighborhood. It is this cooperative nature of neighborhood associations which ultimately generates the confidence and pride which is essential to neighborhood preservation.

A Summing Up

The road ahead is not easy and the precise directions of change are still ambiguous. One thing is clear: the choices made at the national level cannot be relied upon alone as the most effective manner of working toward revitalization of the U.S. economy. They will create more mega-institutions.

A national planning system will be necessary to ensure full employment, stable prices, and the implementation of social policy — life-sustenance. An economic system in which jobs are guaranteed will require an increased level of democracy in order to function effectively. When workers are freed of the fear of losing their jobs, our system will need democratic cooperation to replace fear as the motive for working. Self-esteem and fellowship will be encouraged.

A careful balance must be maintained between the central economic planning necessary to control the planning sector for the commonweal and the decentralization necessary to make worker self-management, local government, and mediating institutions foster freedom of choice and fellowship.

To be sure, the thrust we suggest will not be accepted immediately and if it were, it would not result in a miraculous attainment of the goals of an economic society. But it is less improbable than the complete transformation of society envisioned by radicals, and it can lead to a more humane society than the existing one, or the one that CEIs hope in vain to return to.

Notes

1. INTRODUCTION

1. As we will see in a number of places, the 1920s provided an earlier example of the phenomenon of the mass consumption society.

2. Richard A. Easterlin, "Does Economic Growth Improve the Human Lot? Some Empirical Evidence," In *Nations and Households in Economic Growth* (New York: Academic Press, 1974).

3. See A. H. Maslow, *Motivation and Personality* (New York: Harper & Row, 1970).

4. The concept of three types of goods, or needs, is from Denis Goulet, *The Cruel Choice: A New Concept in the Theory of Development* (New York: Atheneum, 1971), pp. 241-45.

5. Tibor Scitovsky, *The Joyless Economy: An Inquiry into Human Satisfaction and Consumer Dissatisfaction* (New York: Oxford University Press, 1976).

6. Lawrence Peter and Raymond Hull, *The Peter Principle* (New York: W. Morrow, 1969).

7. U.S., Council of Economic Advisers, *Economic Indicators,* prepared for the Joint Economic Committee (Washington, D.C.: Government Printing Office), monthly reports of 1970-82.

8. Milton Friedman, "Where Has the Hot Summer Gone?" *Newsweek,* 4 August 1975, p. 75.

9. Andrew Levinson, *The Full Employment Alternative* (New York: Coward, McCann & Geoghegan, 1980), p. 25.

10. M. Harvey Brenner, *Mental Illness and the Economy* (Cambridge, Mass.: Harvard University Press, 1973), preface, p. ix.

11. Levinson, p. 28.

12. Allen W. Smith, *Understanding Inflation and Unemployment* (Chicago: Nelson-Hall, 1976), p. 5.

13. Robert J. Gordon, *Macroeconomics* (Boston: Little, Brown, 1978), pp. 278-302.

14. Joseph J. Minarik, "Who Wins, Who Loses From Inflation?" *Challenge,* January/February, 1979, pp. 26-31.

15. See, for example, a COIN pamphlet *There Are Alternatives: A Pro-*

gram for Controlling Inflation in the Necessities of Life (Washington, D.C.: COIN, 1979).

16. *Economic Report of the President* (Washington, D.C.: Government Printing Office, 1979), p. 7.

17. C. Fred Bergsten, *The Dilemmas of the Dollar: The Economics and Politics of United States International Monetary Policy* (New York: New York University Press, 1975), p. 261.

18. Paul A. Samuelson, "Warm Autumn for the West," *Newsweek,* 18 July 1977, p. 80.

19. OECD, *Towards Full Employment and Price Stability,* summary of a report to the OECD by a group of independent experts (OECD, 1977), pp. 16-17.

2. FREE ENTERPRISE AND LAISSEZ FAIRE ECONOMICS

1. Adam Smith, *The Wealth of Nations* (1776; New York: Modern Library, 1947).

2. Thomas Malthus, *On Population* (1798; New York: Modern Library, 1960).

3. See J. R. Poynter, *Society and Pauperism: English Ideas on Poor Relief, 1795-1834* (London: Routledge & Kegan Paul, 1969). Also see Guy Routh, *The Origin of Economic Ideas* (White Plains, N.Y.: International Arts and Sciences Press, 1975).

4. See Poynter.

5. Malthus, p. 33.

6. Ibid., p. 54.

7. Ibid., pp. 8-10.

8. Thomas Malthus, "A Summary View of the Principles of Population," *Three Essays on Population* (New York: Mentor, 1960), pp. 33-34.

9. *Essay,* pp. 69, 75.

10. Ibid., p. 75.

11. Ibid., pp. 591-92.

12. W. Stanley Jevons, "Economic Policy," paper read before Section F of the British Association for the Advancement of Science, September, 1870. Published in R. L. Smith, ed., *Essays in Economic Method* (London: Gerald Duckworth & Co., 1962), pp. 27-28.

13. Alfred Marshall, *Principles of Economics* (1890; London: Macmillan, 1959), p. 149.

14. Ibid., pp. 144-69, 574-77.

15. For a more detailed treatment of this claim see Charles K. Wilber and Jon Wisman, "The Chicago School: Positivism or Ideal Type," *Journal of Economic Issues* 9:4 (December, 1975), pp. 665-79.

16. For a fascinating study of this period see Robert Keller, "Supply-Side Economic Policies during the Coolidge Mellon Era," *Journal of Economic Issues* (forthcoming).

3. THE TRIUMPH OF KEYNESIANISM

1. Gottfried Haberler, *The World Economy, Money, and the Great Depression, 1919-1939,* (Washington, D.C.: American Enterprise Institute for Public Policy Research, 1976), p. 9.

2. Ibid.

3. Goronwy Rees, *The Great Slump* (London: Weidenfeld & Micolson, 1970), p. 85.

4. Indeed, Roosevelt had run on a campaign criticizing Hoover's deficits, saying, "Let us have the courage to stop borrowing to meet continuing deficits. Stop the deficits." Quoted in Robert Lekachman, *The Age of Keynes* (New York: Random House, 1966), p. 43.

5. Mario Einaudi, *The Roosevelt Revolution* (New York: Harcourt, Brace & Co., 1959), pp. 76-97.

6. Lekachman, p. 123.

7. Ibid., p. 220.

8. Ibid.

9. Ibid.

10. Ibid., p. 224.

11. Herbert Stein, "Fiscal Policy: Reflections on the Past Decade," in William Fellner, ed., *Contemporary Economic Problems: 1976,* (Washington, D.C.: American Enterprise Institute for Public Policy Research, 1976), pp. 55-84.

12. Robert Solow and Paul Samuelson, "Analytical Aspects of Anti-Inflation Policy," *American Economic Review* 50 (May, 1960), pp. 177-94.

13. Franco Modigliani, "The Monetarist Controversy or, Should We Forsake Stabilization Policy," *American Economic Review,* 67:2 (March, 1977), pp. 17-18.

14. Paul McCracken, "Reducing the Inflation Rate," *Wall Street Journal,* 15 July 1977, p. 10.

15. Frank E. Morris, "A Fed President Views the Money Supply," *Wall Street Journal,* 23 June 1982, p. 30.

16. Rudiger Dornbusch and Stanley Fischer, *Macroeconomics* (New York: McGraw Hill, 1978), p. 289.

17. Ibid., p. 290.

18. Arnold Weber, *In Pursuit of Price Stability: The Wage Price Freeze of 1970* (Washington, D.C.: Brookings Institution, 1973).

4. THE ASSAULT ON THE KEYNESIANS

1. The books are published as John Kenneth Galbraith, *The Age of Uncertainty* (Boston: Houghton Mifflin, 1977) and Milton and Rose Friedman, *Free To Choose* (New York: Harcourt Brace Jovanovich, 1979).

2. Melvin Reder, "Chicago Economics: Permanence and Change," *Journal of Economic Literature* 20 (March, 1982), pp. 1-38.

3. Milton Friedman and Anna Jacobson Schwartz, *A Monetary History of the United States, 1867-1960* (Princeton, N.J.: Princeton University Press, 1963).

4. Milton Friedman, "National Economic Planning," *Newsweek,* 14 July 1975, p. 71.

5. See George Gilder, *Wealth and Poverty* (New York: Basic Books, 1981).

6. Milton Friedman, "The Role of Monetary Policy," *American Economic Review* 58:1 (March, 1968), p. 11.

7. Beryl Wayne Sprinkel, *Money and Markets: A Monetarist View* (Homewood, Ill.: Richard D. Irwin, 1971), p. 166.

8. See Milton Friedman, *Capitalism and Freedom* (Chicago: University of Chicago Press, 1962).

9. Reder, p. 11.

10. Friedman, "National Economic Planning."

11. Herbert Stein, "Some 'Supply-Side' Propositions," *Wall Street Journal,* 9 March 1980.

12. Ibid.

13. Laissez faire theory is not the only theory characterized by swings from short-run empirical propositions to long-run tautologies when confronted with contradictory evidence. The structure of both Marxism and Rostow's stages-of-growth theory lend themselves to this type of manipulation. See Paul Streeten, "Strength Through Tautology," *New Republic,* 4 September 1971, pp. 27-29.

14. See article by Michael Evans, "The Bankruptcy of Keynesian Econometric Models," *Challenge,* January/February, 1980, pp. 13-19.

15. Harry Anderson and Richard Thomas, "Stockman's Ladder," *Newsweek,* 9 February 1981, p. 66.

16. William Grieder, "The Education of David Stockman," *Atlantic Monthly,* December, 1981, pp. 27-54.

17. Robert Hayes and William Abernathy, "Managing Our Way to Economic Decline," *Harvard Business Review,* July/August, 1980, pp. 67-77.

5. CYCLE THEORIES

1. Nikolai Kondratieff, "The Long Waves in Economic Life," *The Review of Economics and Statistics* 17 (1935), pp. 105-115. Reprinted in *Readings in Business Cycle Theory* (Philadelphia: Blakiston Co., 1944), pp. 20-42.

2. Quoted by George Garvey, "Kondratieff's Theory of Long Cycles," *Review of Economics and Statistics* 25 (November, 1943), p. 204.

3. The exact quotation from J. W. N. Watkins, a follower of Karl Popper, is, "This is a sort of blasphemy." The target of this attack is the idea that a long wave could cause people to do anything. See J. W. N. Watkins, "Ideal Types and Historical Explanation," in *Readings in the*

Philosophy of Science, ed. H. Feigl and M. Brodbeck (New York: Appleton-Century-Crofts, 1953).

4. Geoffrey Barraclough, "The End of an Era," *New York Review,* 27 June 1974.

5. Quoted from Burns and Mitchell by Robert A. Gordon, *Business Fluctuations,* 2d. ed. (New York: 1961), p. 249.

6. The Russian critic is Pervushin, quoted by Garvey, p. 213.

7. Lange is quoted by Ernest Mandel, *Late Capitalism* (London: New Left Books, 1975), p. 140.

8. Maurice Lee, *Macroeconomics: Fluctuations, Growth and Stability,* 5th ed. (Homewood, Ill.: Richard Irwin, 1971), p. 36.

9. There are many sources which treat cycles. One good summary is in R. Gordon.

10. See his criticisms in Garvey, pp. 216-19.

11. Kondratieff, p. 32.

12. Quoted in Mandel, pp. 128-29.

13. Ibid.

14. Kondratieff, p. 35.

15. Ibid.

16. Ibid.

17. Joseph Schumpeter's work can be found in Joseph Schumpeter, *Business Cycles: A Theoretical, Historical, and Statistical Analysis of the Capitalist Process* (New York: McGraw Hill, 1939) and "The Analysis of Economic Change," in *Readings in Business Cycle Theory,* pp. 1-19.

18. The major work by Kuznets was Simon Kuznets, *Secular Movements in Production and Prices* (1930; New York: A. M. Kelley, 1967). Rostow's work appears in "Kondratieff, Schumpeter, and Kuznets: Trend Periods Revisited," *Journals of Economic History* 35 (1975), pp. 719-53, and "Long Swings in the Growth of Population and in Related Economic Variables," *Proceedings of the American Philosophical Society* 102:1 (1958), pp. 25-52.

19. Mandel presents his views in chapter 3 of Mandel, *Late Capitalism.*

20. David M. Gordon, "Up and Down the Long Roller Coaster," in *U.S. Capitalism in Crisis* (New York: Union for Radical Political Economics, 1978), pp. 22-35.

21. Nathaniel J. Mass, *Economic Cycles: An Analysis of Underlying Causes* (Cambridge, Mass.: Wright-Allen, 1975).

6. MARXISM

1. Some examples are Joan Robinson, Martin Bronfenbrenner, J. K. Galbraith, Robert Heilbroner. The *Wall Street Journal* has at the same time decried the influence of Marxism in intellectual circles.

2. David Gordon, "Up and Down the Long Roller Coaster," in *U.S. Capitalism in Crisis* (New York: The Union for Radical Political Economics, 1978), pp. 23-24.

3. See, for example, Robert D. Cherry, *Macroeconomics* (Reading, Mass.: Addison-Wesley, 1980), p. 313.

4. Karl Marx, *A Contribution to the Critique of Political Economy*, trans. N.I. Stone (New York: Charles H. Kerr, 1904), pp. 11-12.

5. Ibid., p 11.

6. Karl Marx, *The Eighteenth Brumaire of Louis Bonaparte* (New York: International Publishers Company, n.d.), p. 13.

7. Marx, *Critique*, pp. 12, 13.

8. Karl Marx and Friedrich Engels, *Manifesto of the Communist Party* (New York: International Publishers Company, 1932), p. 9.

9. Ibid., pp. 9, 12.

10. Ibid., pp. 16, 21.

11. Marx, *Critique*, p. 13.

12. Marx and Engels, *Manifesto*, p. 9.

13. Karl Marx, *Capital* (Moscow: Foreign Language Publishing House, 1961), vol. 1, pp. 170-71.

14. Karl Marx, *Value, Price and Profit* (New York: International Publishers Company, 1935), p. 40.

15. Ibid., p. 41.

16. Marx, *Capital*, vol. 1, p. 235.

17. Ibid., p. 639.

18. Ibid., p. 209.

19. Ibid.

20. Ibid., pp. 152-53.

21. Ibid., p. 595.

22. Ibid., p. 760.

23. Ibid., pp. 762-63.

24. Ibid., vol. 3, p. 241.

25. Paul M. Sweezy, *The Theory of Capitalist Development* (New York: Monthly Review Press, 1956), pp. 191-92.

26. James O'Connor, *Fiscal Crisis of the State* (New York: St. Martins Press, 1973).

27. In a provocative and well-argued book, *Schooling in Capitalist America: Educational Reform and the Contradictions of Economic Life* (New York: Basic Books, 1976), Samuel Bowles and Herbert Gintis point out the conspiratorial side of public education by arguing that in the public schools each class of people is taught according to what will be expected of them later in life. Working class children are taught to respect authority and to carry out tasks given them by obliging teachers. The children of the upper class, on the other hand, are taught to use their creativity and analytical powers, for these will be useful to them when they begin to manage production. In such ways class stratification and often animosity are strengthened and perpetuated.

28. Robert L. Heilbroner, *The Worldly Philosophers*, 4th ed. (New York: Simon & Schuster, 1972), p. 154.

29. Paul A. Baran and Paul M. Sweezy, *Monopoly Capital: An Essay*

on the American Economic and Social Order (New York: Monthly Review Press, 1966).

30. See, for example, Michael Kalecki, *Theory of Economic Dynamics: An Essay on Cyclical and Long Run Changes in Capitalist Economy* (London: Allen & Unwin, 1965).

31. Raford Boddy and James Crotty, "Class Conflict and Macro Policy: The Political Business Cycle," *Review of Radical Political Economics* 7:1 (Spring 1975), pp. 1-19.

32. Ibid., p. 9.

33. See Howard Sherman, *Stagflation: A Radical Theory of Unemployment and Inflation* (New York: Harper & Row, 1976); "Monopoly Power and Stagflation," *Journal of Economic Issues* 11:2 (June, 1977), pp. 269-84; and "Inflation, Unemployment, and Monopoly Capital," *Monthly Review* 27:10 (March, 1976).

34. As evidence for this assertion of perverse pricing behavior, Wachtel and Adelsheim, *The Inflationary Impact of Unemployment: Price Mark-ups During Postwar Recessions, 1947-1970* (Joint Economic Committee, 1976), compare the pricing behavior of firms from 1947 to 1970 and classify the industries into three concentration groups; high, medium, and low. A high concentration industry is defined as one in which four firms produce at least 50 percent of the product; medium concentration is defined as the four largest firms accounting for 25-50 percent of total sales; low concentration industries are characterized by the four largest firms producing less than 25 percent of the total product of the industry. The data show that during recessions over half of the highly concentrated industries employed markup pricing. Medium and low concentrated industries did not engage in markup pricing to any great extent, but since 1948 even these industries have shown an increased proclivity to use markup pricing. Wachtel and Adelsheim conclude by stating first that the more concentrated the industry, the greater the likelihood that price markups would increase during a recession. Second, they claim that economic power has become more prevalent since even low concentrated industries are going more and more to markup pricing practices.

35. Leonard A. Rapping, "The Great Recession of the 1970's: Domestic and International Considerations," in Frank J. Bonello and Thomas R. Swartz, eds., *Alternative Directions in Economic Policy* (Notre Dame, Ind.: University of Notre Dame Press, 1978), pp. 152-79.

36. See Cherry, chap. 16.

37. It is interesting that Arthur Okun, a Keynesian, had a similar notion he termed the "invisible handshake." See "The Invisible Handshake and the Inflationary Process," *Challenge*, January/February, 1980, pp. 5-12.

38. David Mermelstein, ed., *The Economic Crisis Reader* (New York: Vintage Books, 1975), pp. 401-2.

39. Michele I. Naples, "Industrial Conflict and Its Implications for Productivity Growth," *American Economic Review* 71:2 (May, 1981), p. 38.

40. Marx and Engels, *Manifesto,* p. 44.
41. Roger E. Alcaly, "An Introduction to Marxian Crisis Theory," in
U.S. Capitalism in Crisis (New York: Union for Radical Political Economics, 1978), p. 17.
42. David M. Gordon, "Capital-Labor Conflict and the Productivity Slowdown," *American Economic Review* 71:2 (May, 1981), p. 34.

7. TOWARD A NEW POLITICAL ECONOMY

1. I. M. D. Litle, *A Critique of Welfare Economics,* 2d ed. (Oxford: Clarendon Press, 1957); and Milton Friedman, *Essays in Positive Economics* (Chicago: University of Chicago Press, 1953).
2. See Milton Friedman and David Meiselman, "The Relative Stability of Monetary Velocity and the Investment Multiplier in the United States, 1897-1958," in *Stabilization Policies: Commission on Money and Credit* (Englewood Cliffs, N.J.: Prentice-Hall, 1963).
3. Albert Ando and Franco Modigliani, "The Relative Stability of Monetary Velocity and the Investment Multiplier," *American Economic Review* 55 (September, 1965), pp. 693-728; and Michael De Prano and Thomas Mayer, "Tests of the Relative Importance of Autonomous Expenditures and Money," *American Economic Review* 55 (September, 1965), pp. 729-52.
4. Milton Friedman and David Meiselman, "Reply to Ando and Modigliani and to De Prano and Mayer," *American Economic Review* 55 (September, 1965), pp. 753-85.
5. See also Martin Bronfenbrenner, *Macroeconomic Alternatives* (Arlington Heights, Ill.: AHM Publishing Corp., 1979), pp. 185-88; and Peter D. McClelland, *Causal Explanation and Model Building in History, Economics, and the New Economy History* (Ithaca: Cornell University Press, 1975), pp. 132-35.
6. William Poole and Elinda B. F. Kornblith, "The Friedman-Meiselman CMC Paper: New Evidence on an Old Controversy," *American Economic Review* 63 (December, 1973), pp. 908-17.
7. Ibid., p. 916.
8. An interesting example of this was an editorial page piece by Frank E. Morris of the Boston Federal Reserve in which he stated "I have concluded . . . that we can no longer measure the money supply with any precision, the consequences are obviously far reaching." See "A Fed President Views the Money Supply," *Wall Street Journal,* 22 June 1982.
9. Some standard economists have come to the same interpretation but draw different conclusions. See Franco Modigliani, "The Monetarist Controversy or, Should We Forsake Stabilization Policies?" *American Economic Review* 67 (March, 1979), pp. 1-19; and William J. Baumol and Alan S. Blinder, *Economics: Principles and Policy* (New York: Harcourt, Brace, Jovanovich, 1979), pp. 257-71.

10. See Charles K. Wilber and Robert S. Harrison, "The Methodological Basis of Institutional Economics: Pattern Model, Storytelling, and Holism," *Journal of Economic Issues* 12 (March, 1978), pp. 61-89; Paul Diesing, *Patterns of Discovery in the Social Sciences* (Chicago: Aldine Atherton, 1971); and Benjamin Ward, *What's Wrong with Economics?* (New York: Basic Books, 1972).

11. We should recall an earlier distinction. The American followers of Keynes, whom some would call post-Keynesians, took from Keynes the belief that the economy could be fine-tuned with little need for structural change. However, a large segment of British economists and growing numbers in the U.S. find the key to Keynes in his belief that the economy was inherently unstable. It is this branch we find most amenable and they are termed the post-Keynesians. Institutionalist analysis has a long tradition in the U.S. tracing to Thorstein Veblen and John R. Commons in the early twentieth century.

12. K. William Kapp, "The Nature and Significance of Institutional Economics," *Kyklos* 29, fasc. 2 (1976), pp. 209-30.

13. John Kenneth Galbraith, *Economics and the Public Purpose* (Boston: Houghton Mifflin, 1973).

14. Warren J. Samuels, "Interrelations between Legal and Economic Processes," *Journal of Law and Economics* 14 (October, 1971), pp. 435-50, and "The Coase Theorem and the Study of Law and Economics," *Natural Resources Journal* 14 (January, 1974), pp. 1-33.

15. Willard F. Mueller, "Antitrust in a Planned Economy," *Journal of Economic Issues* 9 (June, 1975), pp. 159-80.

16. Charles Craypo, "Collective Bargaining in the Multinational, Conglomerate Corporation: Litton's Shutdown of Royal Typewriter," *Industrial and Labor Relations Review* 29 (October, 1975), pp. 3-25.

17. P. B. Doeringer and M. Piore, *Internal Labor Markets and Manpower Analysis* (New York: Lexington Books, 1971).

18. See the articles in Alfred S. Eichner, ed., *A Guide to Post-Keynesian Economics* (White Plains, N.Y.: M. E. Sharpe, 1978).

19. See many of the works by Thorstein Veblen and Wesley Clair Mitchell.

20. "The hedonistic conception of man is that of a lightning calculator of pleasures and pains, who oscillates like a homogeneous globule of desire of happiness under the impulse of stimuli that shift him about the area, but leave him intact. He has neither antecedent nor consequent. He is an isolated, definitive human datum, in stable equilibrium except for the buffets of the impinging forces that displace him in one direction or another. Self-imposed in elemental space, he spins symmetrically about his own spiritual axis until the parallelogram of forces bears down upon him, whereupon he follows the line of the resultant. When the force of the impact is spent, he comes to rest, a self-contained globule of desire as before." Thorstein Veblen, "Why Is Economics Not an Evolutionary Science?" in *The Place of Science in Modern Civilization* (New York: B. W. Huebsch, 1919; Russell & Russell, 1961), pp. 73-74.

21. See Wilber and Harrison.

22. This is not storytelling in the pejorative sense, but scientific; see Ward, *What's Wrong With Economics?* chapter 12.

23. Cited in Wilber and Harrison, p. 73.

24. Alfred S. Eichner, "A Look Ahead," in *A Guide to Post-Keynesian Economics,* p. 171.

25. Ibid., p. 174.

26. Ibid., p. 171.

27. See Karl Polanyi, *The Great Transformation* (New York: Farrar & Rinehart, 1944).

28. Ibid., pp. 115-16.

29. See Karl Mannheim, *Freedom, Power, and Democratic Planning* (New York: Oxford University Press, 1950), p. 191.

30. Polanyi, pp. 72-73.

31. Ibid., p. 73.

32. Ibid., p. 76.

33. Ibid., p. 134.

34. Ibid., p. 231.

8. STRUCTURE AND OPERATION OF THE U.S. ECONOMY

1. J. K. Galbraith, "The New Conservatism," *New York Review of Books* 27, (22 January 1981), p. 32.

2. There are efforts to coordinate sectors of these firms in demanding particular policies, e.g., the recent stance of the National Association of Realtors in support of a balanced-budget amendment. Given how little such an amendment would affect its members, this is a clear indicator of the relative impotence of such groups. One counterexample is the National Association of Milk Producers, but its power has waned recently.

3. J. K. Galbraith, *Economics and the Public Purpose* (New York: Mentor, 1973), pp. 49-50.

4. Edgar Feige, "How Big Is the Irregular Economy?" *Challenge,* November/December, 1979, p. 10. Another recent study of the illegal components of the sector which finds a large impact is Carl Simon and Ann Witte, *Beating the System: The Underground Economy* (Boston: Auburn House, 1982).

5. John Blair, *Economic Concentration* (New York: Harcourt Brace Jovanovich, 1972).

6. Sometimes newspaper headlines capture this perfectly. For example "Ford Boosts Prices Despite Drop in Sales," *South Bend Tribune,* 3 May 1980.

7. Willard Mueller, "Anti-trust in a Planned Economy," *Journal of Economic Issues* 9:2 (June, 1975).

8. Even the slowing of inflation with the 1981-82 recession owed more to lower farm prices and lower energy prices due to OPEC price cuts than

to price reductions by the oligopolistic firms who were undertaking massive layoffs. Nonetheless, the more recent experience does show that in an extremely severe recession, even oligopolistic prices are affected.

9. In statements made during a speech at a 1977 New York Conference on Corporate Philanthropy, as reported in *Chronicle of Higher Education* 15:10, (7 November 1977), p. 5.

10. D. E. Greer, "Market Power and Wage Inflation: A Further Analysis," *Journal of Economic Issues* 9:1 (January, 1975).

11. Ludwig von Mises, *Socialism,* trans. J. Kanhaus (London: Jonathan Cape, 1936), p. 443.

12. Jerome Rothenberg, "Consumers' Sovereignty Revisited and the Hospitability of Freedom of Choice," *American Economic Review* (May, 1962), p. 274. The experiments of Milgram show how far this can go: a situation can be structured which leads volunteers to administer what they think is a lethal dose of electricity. See Stanley Milgram, "Some Conditions of Obedience and Disobedience to Authority," *Human Relations,* 1965, pp. 57-76.

13. Rothenberg, pp. 274-75.

14. Paul A. Baran, *The Political Economy of Growth* (New York: Monthly Review Press, 1962), pp. xv-xvi (separate printing of new Foreword).

15. Ibid., p. xvi.

16. Maurice Dobb, *Political Economy and Capitalism* (London: Routledge & Kegan Paul, 2d ed., 1940), p. 308.

17. Joan Robinson, *Economics of 1962.* Quoted in *Monthly Review,* October, 1962, p. 300.

18. Tibor Scitovsky, "On the Principle of Consumers' Sovereignty," *American Economic Review,* May, 1962, p. 262. He has dealt with this much more extensively in his book *The Joyless Economy* (New York: Oxford University Press, 1976). It is subtitled "An Inquiry into Human Satisfaction and Consumer Dissatisfaction."

19. Tibor Scitovsky, *Welfare and Competition* (Chicago: Richard D. Irwin, 1951), pp. 68-69.

20. Mark A. Lutz and Kenneth Lux, *The Challenge of Humanistic Economics* (Menlo Park, Calif.: Benjamin/Cummings, 1979), p. 78.

21. See, for example, Sidney Weintraub, "Missing Theory of Money Wages," *Journal of Post Keynesian Economics,* (Winter, 1978-79), p. 59-78. For discussions of dual labor markets see L. C. Thurow, *Generating Inequality* (New York: Basic Books, 1975), P. B. Doeringer and M. Piore, *Internal Labor Markets and Manpower Analysis* (New York: Lexington Books, 1971), and M. Reich, D. Gordon, and R. Edwards, "A Theory of Labor Market Segmentation," *American Economic Review,* May, 1973.

22. Eileen Appelbaum, "The Labor Market," Alfred Eichner, ed., *A Guide to Post-Keynesian Economics* (White Plains, N.Y.: M.E. Sharpe, 1975), p. 111 (henceforth *GPKE*).

23. In the traditional analysis of the supply of labor the concepts of substitution effects and income effects are central. The substitution effect

refers to the idea that as the wage goes up then leisure time is more expensive, so people will tend to want to work more. The income effect works in the opposite way because since the worker has a higher income he or she will be able to "purchase" more leisure than before. Traditional economists spend more of their time analyzing substitution effects. PKIs however, believe such effects are negligible and focus their attention on the income effects. They will also tend to shy away from such a limited framework altogether, since workers do not often have control over their hours.

24. Eileen Appelbaum, "Post-Keynesian Theory: The Labor Market," *Challenge* 21:6 (January/February 1979), pp. 45-46.

25. See J. Tobin, "Liquidity Preference as Behavior Toward Risk," *Review of Economic Studies,* February, 1958; M. J. Baumol, "The Transactions Demand for Cash: An Inventory Theoretic Approach," *Quarterly Journal of Economics,* November, 1952; M. Friedman, "The Quantity Theory of Money—A Restatement," in M. G. Mueller, ed., *Readings in Macroeconomics* (New York: Holt, Rinehart, and Winston, 1966).

26. Basil J. Moore, "A Post-Keynesian Approach to Monetary Theory," *Challenge* 21:4 (September/October, 1978), pp. 44-52.

27. John M. Keynes, *Treatise on Money,* 2 vols., (London: MacMillan: New York: Harcourt, Brace, 1930).

28. John Cornwall, "Macrodynamics," in *GPKE,* p. 20.

29. Ibid., p. 28 (emphasis ours).

30. See Peter Kenyon, "Pricing," in *GPKE,* p. 37-38.

31. Kenyon offers evidence that 75 to 90 percent of gross fixed capital expenditure in manufacturing is financed via retained profits. However, this is a highly disputed finding. For example, see David Kotz, *Bank Control of Large Corporations,* (Berkeley: University of California Press, 1978), p. 61. He quotes a study which claims that non-financial corporations obtained between 40 and 45 percent of their total funds from external sources from 1946 to 1958 and from 1964 to 1974. Unfortunately, much of the evidence is heavily dependent on initial assumptions and definitions.

32. Burton A. Weisbrod, *The Voluntary Nonprofit Sector* (Lexington, Mass.: Lexington Books, D. C. Heath, 1977), p. 21. Also see Barry P. Keating and Maryann O. Keating, *Not-for-Profit* (Glen Ridge, N.J.: Thomas Horton & Daughters, 1980).

33. Milton Friedman, *Capitalism and Freedom* (Chicago: University of Chicago Press, 1962), p. 12.

34. Ibid., p. 9. It is interesting to see what happens when Friedman's views are accepted in other countries such as the military dictatorships of the southern cone of South America. See Kenneth Jameson, "The Market-Military Mix," *Challenge,* September/October, 1982.

35. Ralph Miliband, *The State in Capitalist Society* (New York: Basic Books, 1969), p. 265.

36. James O'Connor, *The Fiscal Crisis of the State* (New York: St. Martin's Press, 1973).

37. Ibid., p. 29.

38. Dwayne Ward, *Toward a Critical Political Economics* (Santa Monica: Goodyear Publishing, 1977), p. 213.

39. Weisbrod, p. 3.

40. Ibid., p. 63.

9. STAGFLATION AND ECONOMIC CRISIS

1. J.K. Galbraith, *Economics and the Public Purpose* (Boston: Houghton Mifflin, 1973).

2. "The Largest U.S. Industrial Corporations," *Fortune,* 3 May 1982, pp. 258-84.

3. Emma Rothschild, "Reagan and the Real America," *New York Review,* 5 February 1981.

4. See Robert H. Hayes and William J. Abernathy, "Managing Our Way to Economic Decline," *Harvard Business Review,* July/August, 1980.

5. A good example is the toothpaste producers: "marketers are pegging their hopes on minor changes in product appearances, packaging, scents or flavors and the companies are spending tens of millions of dollars to advertise those changes." See Bill Abrams, "Warring Toothpaste Makers Spend Millions Luring Buyers to Slightly Altered Products," *Wall Street Journal,* 21 September 1981, p. 27.

6. *Wall Street Journal,* 12 July 1982, p. 1.

7. Lester C. Thurow, "Why Productivity Falls," *Newsweek,* 24 August 1981, p. 63.

8. *Economic Report of the President* (Washington, D.C.: Government Printing Office, 1981), p. 260.

9. We should note parenthetically that the only structural change being undertaken in the administration, aside from the shift to military expenditures, is an apparent relaxation in the enforcement of antitrust laws. This can only reinforce the price insensitivity of the planning sector.

10. See the article by Kenneth Jameson, "Supply-Side Economics: Growth Versus Income Distribution," *Challenge* 23:5 (September/October, 1980), pp. 26-31.

11. See Wassely Leontief, "What Hope for the Economy?" *New York Review,* 12 August 1982.

12. Alfred Eichner, Introduction to Alfred Eichner, ed., *A Guide to Post-Keynesian Economics* (White Plains, N.Y.: M. E. Sharpe, 1978), p. 17.

13. Emma Rothschild sees the mechanization and rationalization of this sector as the only area in which capitalism can move to offset the tendencies we have mentioned. She sees this as problematic, however.

14. Lester Thurow, *The Zero Sum Society* (New York: Basic Books, 1980).

15. See Adam Smith, *Theory of Moral Sentiments* (London: Henry Bohn, 1861) and A. W. Coats, ed., *The Classical Economists and Economic Policy* (London: Methuen, 1971). It is interesting that Milton Friedman,

in his *Essays in Positive Economics* (Chicago: University of Chicago Press, 1966) has a similar starting point when he says, "Differences about policy among disinterested citizens derive predominantly from different predictions about the economic consequences of taking action . . . rather than from fundamental differences in basic values" (p. 5).

16. Peter Berger, "In Praise of Particularity: The Concept of Mediating Structures," *Review of Politics,* July, 1976, p. 134.

17. Fred Hirsch, *Social Limits to Growth* (Cambridge, Mass.: Harvard University Press, 1978), p. 141. We owe him the idea of social limits to growth. Roy Weintraub says the same thing in his new book but doesn't seem to recognize its significance for applied economics. See *Microfoundations: The Compatibility of Microeconomics and Macroeconomics* (New York: Cambridge University Press, 1979).

18. See R. H. Tawney, *Religion and The Rise of Capitalism* (New York: Harcourt, Brace & World, 1926) and Charles K. Wilber, "The New Economic History Re-examined: R. H. Tawney on the Origins of Capitalism," *The American Journal of Economics and Sociology* 33:3 (July, 1974), pp. 249-58.

19. Hirsch, pp. 128-29.

20. This casts new light on the recent attempts to construct theories of justice that are acceptable to all. See John Rawls, *A Theory of Justice* (Cambridge, Mass.: Harvard University Press, 1971) and the literature spawned by that work. The whole endeavor can be seen as an attempt to create a substitute moral law based on rationality rather than religion.

21. Hirsch, pp. 141-42.

22. See Chapter 9 in Richard Barnet and Ronald Mueller, *Global Reach* (New York: Simon & Schuster, 1974) for an earlier treatment of the idea. Also, in the political sphere see Howard Wiarda, "The Latin Americanization of the United States," *The New Scholar* 7:1-2 (1979), pp. 51-85. See also Kenneth P. Jameson, "A New Convergence? The Latin-americanization of the United States," to appear in a volume of papers edited by Jerry Ladman and based on a 1982 conference on the topic.

23. See Leonard Rapping, "The Great Recession of the 1970s: Domestic and International Considerations," *Alternative Directions in Economic Policy,* eds. Frank J. Bonello and Thomas R. Swartz (Notre Dame, Ind.: University of Notre Dame Press, 1978).

24. As Allen Meltzer said, ". . . the then higher expected rate of inflation and the weak dollar that led the Fed to change procedures . . ." in "The Results of the Fed's Failed Experiment," *Wall Street Journal,* 29 July 1982.

25. The slowing of inflation in late 1981 as a result of the major recession is taken to be the exception, one which will be reversed with an economic recovery.

26. One notable new development in this regard was the initiative on the part of the national governors' conference to obtain "foreign aid" in the form of subsidized capital resources from a consortium of Japanese

businesses. They had hoped to obtain $10 billion in this fashion. Such foreign aid would have been a modern-day first for the U.S. (story in *Listín Diario,* Santo Domingo, 20 February 1982). The administrations of both Japan and the U.S. have denied official involvement, and the governors did not pursue the idea further.

10. TOWARD A NEW SOCIAL CONTRACT

1. See Assar Lindbeck, *The Political Economy of the New Left: An Outsider's View* (New York: Harper & Row, 1971).

2. See J. Kornai, "Some Properties of the Eastern European Growth Pattern," in C. K. Wilber and K. P. Jameson, eds., "Socialist Models of Development," *World Development,* September/October, 1981, pp. 965-70.

3. Eugene Genovese, "What's the Most Important Thing You'd Like to See Happen in the United States in the Next Five Years?" *Mother Jones,* September/October, 1976.

4. See a treatment of some Latin American cases in K. P. Jameson, "The Market-Military Mix in South America," *Challenge,* September/October, 1982.

5. See, for example, George Gilder, *Wealth and Poverty* (New York: Basic Books, 1981) or P. T. Bauer, *Equality, the Third World and Economic Delusion* (Cambridge, Mass.: Harvard University Press, 1981).

6. As an earlier quote indicated, CEIs may exclude competition as a model of the family, seeing esteem and fellowship as key there. But, as a number of recent suits for "bad parenting" have indicated, there is nothing in logic that can differentiate the family from other economic units of society.

7. Arne Ruth, "The End of the Swedish Model?" *Social Change in Sweden,* No. 16 (n.d.), p. 56.

8. André Gorz, quoted in Ruth, ibid.

9. See, for example, Michael Reich, *Racial Inequality* (Princeton: Princeton University Press, 1981) or William Wilson, *The Declining Significance of Race* (Chicago: University of Chicago Press, 1981).

10. For a number of treatments of aspects of stewardship see M. E. Jegen and C. K. Wilber, *The Earth is the Lord's: Essays in Stewardship* (New York: Paulist Press, 1977).

11. See the following works by Gerhard Colm: "The Nation's Economic Budget, A Tool of Full Employment Policy," *Studies in Income and Wealth* (New York: National Bureau of Economic Research, 1947); *Integration of National Planning and Budgeting* (Washington, D.C.: National Planning Association, 1968); "Is Economic Planning Compatible with Democracy?" in his *Essays in Public Finance and Fiscal Policy* (New York: Oxford University Press, 1955). For a summary of Colm's work see Allan G. Gruchy, *Contemporary Economic Thought* (Clifton, N.J.: Augustus M. Kelley, 1972), pp. 237-85.

12. See John Kenneth Galbraith, *Economics and the Public Purpose* (Boston: Houghton Mifflin, 1973).

13. For a brief treatment see Allan G. Gruchy, *Comparative Economic Systems* (Boston: Houghton Mifflin, 1966). A recent piece thinking through the need and possibilities for planning is Wassily Leontief, "What Hope for the Economy?" *New York Review,* 12 August 1982.

14. Gerhard Colm, "National Economic Budgets," *Essays in Public Finance and Fiscal Policy,* p. 247.

15. Gruchy, p. 249.

16. See, for example, Sidney Weintraub with Henry Wallich, "A Tax Based Incomes Policy," in Sidney Weintraub, *Keynes and the Monetarists* (New Brunswick, N.J.: Rutgers University Press, 1973); for further discussion of TIP, see Laurence Seidman, "Role of a Tax Based Incomes Policy," *American Economic Review,* May, 1979, pp. 202-6; also Richard Slitor, "Implementation and Design of Tax Based Incomes Policies," *American Economic Review,* May, 1979, pp. 212-15.

17. David Bensman and Luther Carpenter, "Work and Democracy in American Industry" (New York: DSOC Industrial Task Force, n.d.), pp. 5-6.

18. "Pricey Rodeo Drive Finally Begins to Feel Recession's Pinch," *Wall Street Journal,* 5 August 1982.

19. Harvey Brenner, *Mental Illness and the Economy* (Cambridge, Mass.: Harvard University Press, 1973).

20. "Child Abuse Seems to be Increasing in Areas with High Unemployment," *Wall Street Journal,* 6 August 1982.

21. Cited in Don Stillman, "The Devastating Impact of Plant Relocations," *Working Papers for a New Society,* July/August, 1978, pp. 48-49.

22. *Economic Report of the President* (Washington, D.C.: Government Printing Office, 1953).

23. See, for example, Leonard M. Greene, *Free Enterprise Without Poverty* (New York: W. W. Norton & Co., 1981).

24. Ibid., p. 111.

25. See Leslie Ellen Nulty, *Understanding the New Inflation: The Importance of the Basic Necessities* (Washington, D.C.: Exploratory Project for Economic Alternatives, 1977).

26. Ira Lowry, "Experimenting with Housing Allowances," The Rand Corporation (April, 1982).

27. We are indebted to the work of Peter Berger for the following material. See his "In Praise of Particularity: The Concept of Mediating Structures," *Review of Politics,* July, 1976.

28. Ibid., p. 134.

29. The importance of such a moral base has been widely recognized. Gary Wills, "Benevolent Adam Smith," *New York Review,* 9 February 1978 finds a moral system based on cooperation as central to Smith's views. Edward Banfield, *The Moral Basis of a Backward Society* (Glencoe, Ill.: Free Press, 1958) located the moral base in small groups, in this case the family.

James C. Scott, *The Moral Economy of the Peasant: Rebellion and Subsistence in Southeast Asia* (New Haven: Yale University Press, 1976), finds it in a subsistence insurance ethic and shows that its destruction is likely to lead to rebellion.

30. Berger, p. 138.

Index

Appelbaum, Eileen, 184
Arne, Ruth, 235

Baran, Paul, 179
Barraclough, Geoffrey, 96
basic needs, 256-259
Berger, Peter, 220, 260-261
Blair, John, 174
Boddy, Raford, 129-131
Brenner, Harvey, 13, 251
Bretton Woods Agreement, 16, 69,
  134-135; breakdown of, 135, 224
bureaucratic mechanism of allocation:
  and esteem and fellowship,
  235-236; and freedom and equality
  of opportunity, 236-238; and life-
  sustenance, 234-235; problems
  with, 232-233; totaliterian tendencies of, 233
Burns, Arthur, 54

CEIs (Conservative Economic Individualists): their analysis of the
  Phillips curve, 69-74; and the
  crowding-out hypothesis, 74-75;
  debate with Keynesians, 60-61;
  and deregulation, 88-89; falsifying
  their propositions, 85-90; emergence of, 63-68; interpretation of
  the current crisis, 66-69; limited
  role of government, 81-82,
  195-198; on the natural rate
  hypothesis, 72-74; newest version
  of old laissez faire economists,
  51-52; proposals for productive

reform, 81-90; on the rational-
  expectations hypothesis, 75-76; on
  stabilization policies, 67, 82-83;
  and supply-side economics, 65-66,
  83-85; and tax cuts, 84; treatment
  of poverty, 65; and trickle-down
  theory, 88; and uncritical faith in
  the efficiency of private business,
  89-90; underlying philosophy of,
  78-80; views on externalities and
  monopolies, 77-78
Cobb, Sidney, 251
COIN (Consumers Opposed to Inflation in the Necessities), 15
Colm, Gerhard, 241
Condorcet, 27-28
consumer sovereignty, 177-182;
  criticisms of the idea of, 178-182;
  and interdependent preferences,
  178-179; and prevailing socioeconomic order, 179-180
Corn Laws of 1846, 163
Cornwall, John, 154
Council of Economic Advisers:
  coming of age of, 45-49; role in
  Reagan Administration, 87-89
Craypo, Charles, 154
Crotty, James, 129-131
cycle theories, 95-113, 123-133; see
  also economic cycles

democracy: industrial, 244-250;
  foundation, 1
deregulation: of airline industry,

88-89; and CEIs, 88-89
Dobb, Maurice, 180
Dornbusch, Rudiger, 57
DSOC Industrial Democracy Task
    Force: report of the, 246-247
Durkheim, Emile, 220

economic crisis: CEIs' answers to,
    17-18; CEIs' views on, 81-90; how
    can we react to, 17-18; Marxist
    answers to, 139-141; Marxist views
    on, 133-139; structural roots of the
    current, 207-217
economic cycles: Boddy and Crotty
    on, 129-131; concept of, 96-97;
    and engineered recessions, 130;
    Gordon's views on, 108; and in-
    novation, 104-105; Kalecki's views
    on, 128-129; Kondratieff's long
    waves, 100-103; Kuznets and
    Rostow on, 106-107; and labor
    demands, 130-131; Mandel's views
    on, 107-108; Marxism on,
    111-113, 123-133; politically
    motivated, 129; Schumpeter's
    thoughts on, 103-105; *see also* cycle
    theories
economic growth: emphasis on, 2,
    206, 217-223; physical limits to,
    218-219; record of U.S. economy
    on, 11-12; social limits to,
    219-223; and stagflation, 217
economic policy: and basic needs,
    256-259; CEIs' proposals for,
    81-90; and the crowding-out
    hypothesis, 74-75; and difficulties
    in controlling the money supply,
    55; and energy, 256-257; and fiscal
    expenditures, 42-44; full employ-
    ment, 250-255; futility of, 67;
    guaranteed annual income,
    255-256; and health care, 257;
    height of its success, 9; and hous-
    ing, 257-259; and inability to con-
    trol fiscal outlays, 55; incomes

policy, 244; and the international
    economy, 247-250; and invest-
    ment, 190-193; and the labor
    market, 183-187; and mediating
    structures, 260-263; and the
    monetary sector, 187-190; and a
    national employment service, 253;
    and the natural rate of unemploy-
    ment hypothesis, 72-74; and the
    planning sector, 212-214; and
    plant relocations, 254; and pricing
    behaviour of coporations, 191-193;
    and the private economy, 182-193;
    public service jobs, 255; and the
    rational expectations hypothesis,
    75-76; in the Regan Administra-
    tion, 212-214; and time lag, 55-56;
    worker self-management, 244-250
economic theory: as social philosophy,
    32-33; *see also* formal theory
economy: critieria for evaluation of,
    4-5; goals of, 4-7; moral base of,
    220-223; structure and operation of
    the U.S., 167-204; symptoms of
    failure of the U.S., 1-4; *see also* in-
    ternational economy, informal
    economy, private economy, public
    economy
Eichner, Alfred, 154, 156, 214
Eisenhower, Dwight, 43
Employment Act of 1946, 46
employment policy, *see* economic
    policy
English Parliamentary Reform Act of
    1867, 164
English Poor Laws, 26, 163
equity: and freedom, 236-238; and
    subsidiarity, 259-263; what it
    means, 7
esteem and fellowship, 6, 235-236;
    under attack, 10; CEIs' views on,
    80; and impersonal relationships,
    235; and jubilee, 250-259; and the
    welfare state, 236
ethics: *see* social morality
externalities: CEIs' views on, 78; and

collective goods, 202; free market theory did not account for, 34

fiscal expenditures, 42-44; inability to control, 55
fiscal policy: *see* economic policy
Fisher, Stanley, 57
foreign investments: protection of, 2-3
formal theory, 146-151; and basis for theory selection, 150-151; and the Monetarist-Keynesian controversy, 147-150; and predictability, 146-147; testing, 147-151
freedom, 7; CEIs' emphasis on, 79; components of, 7-8; and equality of opportunity, 236-238 and subsidiarity, 259-263
free enterprise economics: *see* laissez-faire economics, neoclassical economics
Friedman, Milton, 62-70, 79-80
Full Employment and Balanced Growth Act of 1978 (Humphrey-Hawkins), 73, 252

Galbraith, John Kenneth, 64, 168-169, 241
Genovese, Eugene, 233
goods: collective-consumption, 202; positional, 219; public and private, 180; types, 5
Gordon, David, 108
Gordon, Robert, 14
Gorz, Andre, 236
Goulet, Denis, 5
Great Depression, 8
Great Society, 9-11, 44
Greene, Leonard, 256
Gruchy, Allan, 242

high-mass consumption, 2, 9
Humphrey, George, 43

incomes policy, 240, 244
inequality: and esteem and fellowship, 235-236; free market theory did

not account for, 34; and freedom, 236-238
inflation: and balance of payments, 227-228; distributional effects of, 14-15; and expectations, 57-59; how harmful, 13-14; loss of U.S. hegemony over the international economy, 225; need to fight, 15; and the planning sector, 207-214; and wage and price controls, 58-59
informal economy, 167; as shock absorber, 215; growth prospects, 215
innovation: and economic cycles, 104-105, 108
international economy: changes in, 16-17; and commodity stabilization, 249; and credit markets, 16-17; and inflation in the U.S., 225; and international economic policy, 240, 247-250; and internationally-induced domestic policy, 224; and Latinamericanization, 223; lessons from Latin America, 228; loss of U.S. hegemony, 206-207, 223-225; and the NIEO, 249; and unemployment, 226; and U.S. balance of payments problems, 226-228; U.S. position in, 134
investment: determines savings, 189, 191; instability of, 39-40, 191, 234; and Kondratieff's cycles, 102; and life-sustenance, 234; PKI's views on, 190-193; and the planning sector, 211

Jevons, Stanley, 29-30
Johnson, Lyndon, 9, 44-45
jubilee, 239; and self-esteem and fellowship, 250-259

Kalecki, Michael, 128-129
Kasl, Stanislav, 251
Kemp, Jack, 1, 67

Kennedy, John F., 43, 45
Keynes, John Maynard, 8, 36, 39-42
Keynesian economics: assault on,
  62-66; debate with CEIs, 60-61;
  the end of orthodoxy, 50-59;
  failure to correct flaws of the
  market economy, 59-60; and fine-
  tuning, 44; and fiscal deficits,
  42-44; and full employment, 40;
  and governmental fiscal intervention, 40-42; and the Great Depression, 8, 32; and inability to control
  fiscal outlays, 55; on the inherent
  instability of the economy, 39; on
  investment, 39-40; major omissions
  of, 49-50; on misguided policies of
  the 70s, 54-57; and New Deal
  politics, 1-2; and the Phillips
  curve, 49-50; on the role of wage
  reductions, 40; on the state,
  195-198; the General Theory,
  39-42; triumph of, 36-49; and
  World War II, 42
Kitchin, Joseph, 98
Kondratieff, Nikolai, 95-103
Kornblith, Elinda, 149
Kregel, J. A., 154
Kuznets, Simon, 98, 106-107

labor market: and big business, 184;
  and collective bargaining, 186-187;
  determinants of, 185; dual,
  183-187, 237; and equality of opportunity, 237; and screening
  devices, 186
labor unions: and the dual labor
  market, 183-187; and stagflation,
  175-176
laissez faire economics, 23-35; the
  decline of (in the 1980s), 33-35; latent pessimism, 25-26; and the
  Malthusian population theory, 28;
  origins of, 23-32; and the doctrine
  of perfectibility of man, 27-28; on
  poverty, 27, 32-33; propositions

held by, 31-32, 163; regulated by
  competition, 24; as a social
  philosophy, 32-33; *see also*
  neoclassical economics
Lange, Oskar, 97
Leviston, Andrew, 13
life-sustenance, 5; under attack, 10;
  CEIs' view on, 79; and stewardship, 239-250; towards, 234-235
Locke, John, 239-240
love (allocation mechanism), 231-233;
  and freedom and esteem, 238; and
  life-sustenance, 233, 238; practical
  problems with, 233-234

Malthus, Thomas, 25-26
Mandel, Ernest, 107-108
market: *see* self-regulating market
market sector, 168; and current
  stabilization efforts, 215; inflationary pressures do not originate
  in, 214-215; *see also* self-regulating
  market
markup pricing: components of,
  192; how established, 192; and
  monopolies, 132; and planned investment, 192; and the planning
  sector, 174
Marshall, Alfred, 30-31
Marx, Karl, 111-142
Marxism: on accumulation, 120-121;
  answers to current crisis, 139-141;
  on the business cycle, 111-113,
  123-133; on class struggle,
  115-117; on the concept of the
  mode of production, 114-115;
  elements of classical, 113-123; explanations of the current crisis,
  133-139; and labor power, 117;
  modern revisions of its theory of
  cycles, 128-133; on the organic
  composition of capital, 123-125; on
  the reserve army of labor, 118,
  127-128; on the role of the state,
  122, 198-200; on the sources of in-

herent capitalist instability,
123-128; on surplus value, 117; on
underconsumption, 125-127; on
the U.S. position in the international economy, 134-136
Maslow, Abraham, 5
mass-consumption: *see* high
mass-consumption
Meiselman, David, 147-149
methodology: and formal theory,
146-151; and pattern model, 155;
and PKI, 151-157; and the systems
approach, 157; and theory-testing,
146-151, 156
Mill, John Stuart, 23
Minarik, Joseph, 14
Mises, Ludwig von, 177
modern corporations: *see* planning
sector
Modigliani, Franco, 51, 54
monetarists: *see* CEIs
monetary policy: and the crowding-
out hypothesis, 74-75; effect on the
planning sector, 213; *see also*
economic policy, monetary sector,
money supply
monetary sector, 187-189; endogeneity
of the money supply, 188-189; and
historical time, 187-188; and the
role and behavior of the Fed,
188-189; *see also* monetary policy
money supply: difficult to control, 55;
see also monetary policy, monetary
sector
monopoly: CEIs' views on, 78; free
market theory did not account for,
34; functions of, 131-132; and
market failure, 234; and markup
pricing, 132; and stagflation, 132
moral base: *see* social morality
Mueller, Willard, 154

national economic planning, 240-244;
components of an economic plan,
243; democratic, 240; indicative,

240; and a national economic
budget, 242; and national
economic councils, 242
natural rate hypothesis, 71-74
needs: hierarchy of, 5
neoclassical economics: concern with
efficiency, 30; and the idea of
equilibrium, 30-31; and marginal
analysis, 30; origins of, 29-30; propositions held by, 31-32; *see also*
laissez-faire economics
NIEO (New International Economic
Order), 249
Nixon, Richard, 16, 58, 224
not-for-profit sector, 202-204; and
mediating structures, 260-263;
reasons for the growth of, 203

O'Connor, James, 122, 199-200
Okun, Arthur, 45
OPEC (Organization of Petroleum
Exporting Countries), 16, 53, 225
OSHA (Occupational Safety and
Health Administration), 11

Peel's Bank Act of 1844, 163
Phillips, A. W., 49-50
Phillips curve, 49-50
Piore, Michael, 154
PKI (Post Keynesian Institutionalism): on consumer sovereignty, 177-182; on economic "laws,"
153; on historical time, 156-157;
on investment and price dynamics,
190-193; on the market system,
157-166; and methodology,
151-157; on nonrational behavior,
155; on the oligopolistic firm,
170-177; on pattern model, 155;
on the planning sector, 168-170;
on policy and the labor market,
183-186; on policy and the
monetary sector, 187-189; on
power and conflict, 154; on the

structure and operation of the U.S. economy, 167-203

planning: *see* national economic planning

planning sector, 169; and bureaucratized large corporations, 210; and conglomerate firms, 172-173; and consumer sovereignty, 177-182; and economic concentration, 173; and fiscal and monetary policies, 212; inflationary bias of the, 208-209; and investment, 211; and labor unions, 175-176; and management practices, 209-210; and the oligopolistic firm, 170-177; pricing behavior, 174-175; and the roots of stagflation, 207-214; and transnational corporations, 176

Polanyi, Karl, 158-163

Poole, William, 149

Poor Laws: *see* English Poor Laws

private economy, 167; and policy, 182-193; and the roots of stagflation, 207-215; structure, 168-182

public economy: the government sector, 194-202; the not-for-profit sector, 202-204

Quesnay, Francois, 158

Reagan, Ronald, 62

Ricardo, David, 29

Rivlin, Alice, 46

Robinson, Joan, 154, 180

Roosevelt, Franklin Delano, 38

Rostow, W. W., 106-107

Rothenberg, Jerome, 178

Say, J. B., 31

Samuels, Warren, 154

Samuelson, Paul, 18, 50

Schultze, Charles, 45-46

Schumpeter, Joseph, 103-105

Scitovsky, Tibor, 6, 180-181

self-esteem: *see* esteem and fellowship

self-regulating market: characteristics and ingredients of, 159-161; and commodity fiction, 161-163; emergence of, 158-159; and equality of opportunity, 237-238; and esteem and fellowship, 235-236; and freedom, 236-238; and interventionism, 163-164; and life-sustenance, 234; problems with the, 232; and protectionist legislation, 164; as resource allocation mechanism, 231-232; and the revitalization of the cities, 257-258; revolt against excesses, 164; as self-destructive mechanism, 162-163; as sole director of human fate, 161-162; underproduces public goods, 202; a utopian vision, 165

Sherman, Howard, 131

Smith, Adam, 23-25, 220

Smith, Allen, 13

social contrast: breakdown, 137; a new, 230-239; and value structures, 239

social morality: erosion of, 221-222; and free competition, 220; and religious heritage, 221; and the role of the state, 222; and social limits to growth, 220-223

Solow, Robert, 50

stagflation: and economic crisis, 205-229; and limits to growth, 218-223; and loss of U.S. hegemony, 223-229; and monopolies, 132; and the planning sector, 207-214

state: the CEI and Keynesian views, 195-198; the Marxist view, 198-200; the PKI view, 200-202

Stein, Herbert, 84

stewardship: differs from the theory of market economy, 239; and life-sustenance, 239-250; and social

contract, 238-239
Stockman, David, 1, 67, 86
subsidiarity, 239; and freedom and
    equality of opportunity, 259-263;
    and mediating structures, 260
supply shocks, 52-53

Thurow, Lester, 216
transfer pricing, 176-177
transnational corporations, 176-177
Trotsky, Leon, 100-103
Truman, Harry, 252

Underground economy: *see* informal
    economy
unemployment: free market theory
    did not account for, 34-35; and
    life-sustenance, 12-13; and
    minimum wage legislation, 74; and
    the natural rate hypothesis, 72-74;
    record of U.S. economy, 12; social

and psychological effects, 12-13,
    251; types, 72-73; who are likely to
    suffer from, 13

Veblen, Thorstein, 155
Volcker, Paul, 54

wage and price controls, 58-59; Marx-
    ist view on, 138
Wagner Act, 39
Wallace, Robert, 25
Walras, Leon, 31
Weidenbaum, Murray, 45
Weintraub, Sidney, 244
Weisbrod, Burton, 194, 202-203
Whitman, Marina von, 45-46
worker self-management, 240,
    244-250; and esteem and
    fellowship, 245; report of the
    DSOC Industrial Democracy Task
    Force on, 246-247